Indiana Wineries
The Ultimate Guide to Wine in Indiana

Todd & Becky Outcalt

Blue River Press
Indianapolis

Indiana Wineries: The Ultimate Guide to Wine in Indiana
Copyright © 2015 by Todd Outcalt & Becky Outcalt

Published by Blue River Press
Indianapolis, Indiana
www.brpressbooks.com

Distributed by Cardinal Publishers Group
2402 N. Shadeland Avenue, Suite A
Indianapolis, IN 46219
317-352-8200 phone
317-352-8202 fax
www.cardinalpub.com

All rights reserved under International and
Pan-American Copyright Conventions.

No part of this book may be reproduced, stored in a database or other retrieval system, or transmitted in any form, by any means, including mechanical, photocopy, recording or otherwise, without the prior written permission of the publisher.

ISBN: 978-1-935628-51-4

Cover Design: Phil Velikan
Illustrated maps by: Nick Jannetides
Cover photo courtesy Oliver Winery
Book Design: Dave Reed

Printed in the United States of America

10 9 8 7 6 5 4 3 2 1

Dedication

To Cathy and Mike

A new friend is as new wine:
when it is old, you will drink it with pleasure.
—Ecclesiasticus 9:10

You have kept the best wine until now.
—John 2:10

Contents

Introduction: Why We Wrote This Book	1
A Brief History of Indiana Wine	3
A Guide to Indiana Wineries	11
Indiana Grapes	275
Wine Trails of Indiana	285
Wine Festivals of Indiana	291
Weekend Wine Trips	295
Helpful Web Sites on Hoosier Wines	303
Wine Shops Around the State	307
Common Questions for Wine Appreciation	310
More Favorite Wine Recipes	323
A Brief Guide to Wine Tasting and Appreciation	325
Glossary of Wine Terminology	333
Acknowledgments	337
Notes	339
Indiana Wine Regions	341
About the Authors	344

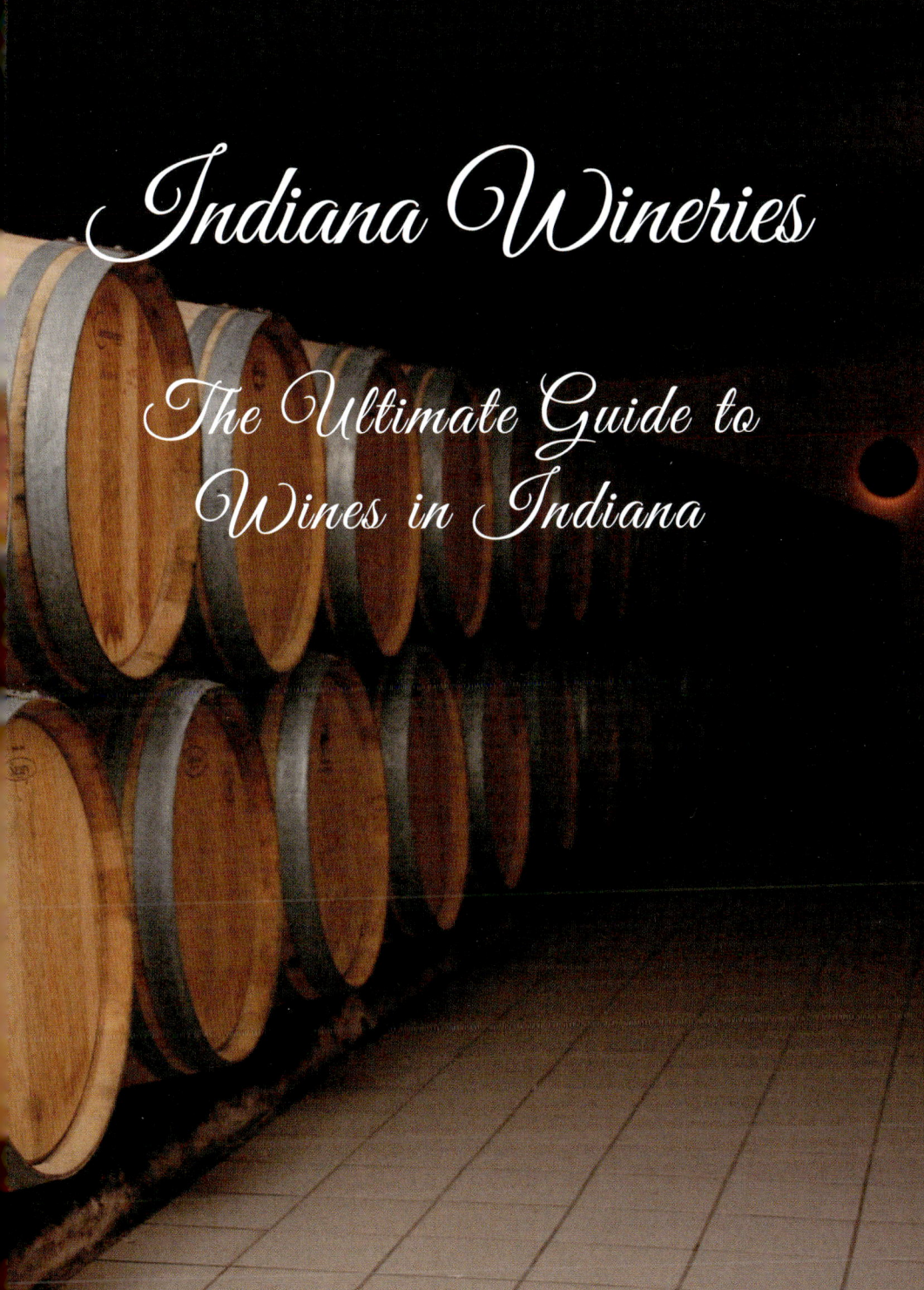

Indiana Wineries

The Ultimate Guide to Wines in Indiana

Introduction: Why We Wrote This Book

A few years ago, as part of a writing assignment, my wife and I completed wine trips to California, Oregon and Washington State. Our visits to wineries in Napa Valley, the Clear Lake region, Sonoma Valley, Amador County (all in California) and the excellent wineries in Oregon and Washington grew our knowledge and appreciation of wines. In many instances, as we toured the wineries of central California, we were offered access to the owners and winemakers and were frequently taken "backstage" to learn more about the winemaking art. These conversations and insights further heightened our appreciation of the craft—and also broadened our understanding of the winemaking journey from vine to bottle.

Upon our return to Indiana we became enamored of our in-state wineries and began planning weekend trips in order to broaden our exposure to the Hoosier labels. Although we were frequent visitors to many of the older wineries in state, we also noted the proliferation of new wineries that were now dotting the landscape north and south.

Eventually, we settled upon the idea that we should write a book about Indiana Wineries. The concept was simple: visit all of the wineries in state, take photographs, conduct interviews, taste the wines, and write a profile of each Indiana Winery. So, that's what we've done here.

This book, as you will discover, is a celebration of Indiana Wineries. We hope that readers and wine lovers will find in these pages the information that is most helpful: a description of the winery facilities, the amenities, the entertainment offered and, of course, a sketch of the wines offered by each, along with our recommendations and ideas for food pairings. We hope that our visits to all of the wineries will also afford readers a glimpse of each, and perhaps grow an interest in making their own wine-tasting excursions. We also hope that the book will offer other meaningful information—history, landscape, tips and resources—that will make this book the most up-to-date guidebook on Indiana Wineries.

Most of all, we hope that our profiles will help readers to plan their own visits to new wineries. Indiana has over seventy wineries now—and the numbers are growing every year. As you read this book, we hope you will discover some new wineries (and wines) that you didn't know existed. Our aim was to help strengthen all of the wineries in state—and to tell the story of Indiana wine. One doesn't have to travel far in-state now to find a winery, and regardless of whether you are a wine expert, a casual critic, or just someone who enjoys a glass now and then, we hope that you will take something away from this book.

We will also be offering our ongoing insights into the growing wine industry in Indiana and we invite you to visit us at www.indianawinery.blogspot.com for an ongoing discussion with Indiana winemakers, winery owners, and Hoosier experts. We desire to keep the interviews and the discussion fresh—and we invite you to learn more about our Indiana Wineries.

We thank you for reading this guide and hope that it is helpful to you as you make your visits. We hope the book will travel with you as you Wander Indiana.

And who knows . . . perhaps we will see *you* at the wineries.

~Todd & Becky Outcalt

A Brief History of Indiana Wine

Many histories of vineyards and winemaking in the United States begin with the Viking explorations at the turn of the millennium, when these explorers discovered a profusion of grapevines along the North Atlantic coast. They called the new land "Vineland"—a reference indicating only the existence of the vine.

Centuries later, as the waves of Europeans began settling the Atlantic Coast, they also discovered these fruits. But they were disappointed in the vines and the wines these grapes produced. These native varietals produced wine that was unfamiliar in taste and quality to the *Vitis vinifera* (the European varietals) that colonists and settlers of the New World preferred.

Because wine was a dependable (safe) and preferable beverage to these early settlers, there were many attempts in these colonial years to plant vinifera vines. Few, however, survived the harsh winters or the diseases that ravaged the fruit. As was the case with the colonists themselves, most of these vineyards did not survive a generation and the colonists grew increasingly dependent upon the all too infrequent shipments of wine.

Early in America's history—pre and post Revolution—winemaking in America had a difficult beginning. In fact, many grew weary of attempting to proliferate vineyards and simply settled on the easier tasks of brewing beer or distilling liquors. For these reasons and others (including taxation and the ever-increasing difficulty of obtaining quality wines from abroad), Americans, unlike their European counterparts, grew more enamored with beers and liquors than with the more difficult to obtain wines. The difficulty of establishing vineyards made the American love of wine all the more precarious.

Thomas Jefferson, noting the absence of a winemaking industry in America, feared that Americans would become dependent upon the more readily available distilled spirits (whiskey and rum). When new legislation of 1791 placed an excise tax on liquor, but exempted American-made wines, he said, "I rejoice as a moralist, at the prospect of a reduction of the duties on wine by our national legislature. It is an error to view a tax on that liquor as merely a tax on the rich . . . No nation is drunken where wine is cheap; and none sober, where the dearness of wine substitutes ardent spirits as the common beverage."

There were, in fact, many early and influential Americans who continued to work toward the establishment of a viable wine industry in the States. William Penn was one, as was Henry Clay and Benjamin Franklin—whose frequent forays in France and his native England served to reawaken his love of wines. Likewise, when Thomas Jefferson was serving as ambassador to France, he would often return to his farm at Monticello with an enthusiasm to plant his own vines, and at various times hired European vintners to establish *vinifera* along his hillsides—work that always and inevitably ended in disease and/or failed crop.

Jefferson's love of wine is legendary—as was his vast collection at Monticello. And yet, prior to the 19th century, a wine industry in America eluded the best efforts along the Atlantic seaboard—where the climate and disease control did not seem suitable to the growing of the vinifera that were so highly prized in Europe.

All of that was to change, however, as people moved westward along the Ohio River. Near the turn of the 19th century, Swiss immigrants began to settle on the north side of the Ohio River (now Switzerland County). These immigrants, like the other European settlers before them, brought along their own love of wine and their wine-making traditions. Like those who had settled along the Atlantic coast, they dreamed of establishing vineyards that would produce wine equal in quality to the ones that they had left behind in Switzerland. And so, along both sides of the Ohio River vineyards began to be planted.

In the late 1700s John James Defour settled on the north side of the

Ohio (present day Vevay, Indiana) and began planting vines. His little experiment was so successful that he wrote to his remaining family in Switzerland and invited them, *en masse*, to join him in this New World and partner in his visionary horticultural experiment. In 1800, Defour's family arrived. They established a settlement and, in a few years, after having established acres of thriving vineyard and producing some of the first wines in America, lived to see the birth of a town around this new industry.

Although there were also successful vineyards by this time in upstate New York and in Ohio, it can be said that the birth of the American winemaking industry, and the first successful winery, was in Indiana—as the wines produced along the Ohio River became known for their quality as well as their value. Being on the river, these wines quickly found a receptive market to the east, and the output of the wine industry in New Switzerland gained notoriety from wine enthusiasts everywhere, including Henry Clay and Thomas Jefferson, who added many of these wines to his collection. The wines in the Indiana region were often compared to the Rhone wines of Europe, and the wine industry along the Ohio River, in these early years, was one of the most productive and respected in the United States.

In the decades that followed this successful Swiss venture in Indiana, other Hoosier towns also became known for their great wines—including New Harmony and Vincennes. Points along the Ohio and the Wabash began shipping their wines up and down rivers and, in no small part, Indiana was a principal wine-producer in the early decades of the 19th century before many of these vineyards perished in harsh winters or to disease. But the stage was set. And southern Indiana was, among other things, known as a wine region.

The wine industry in Indiana (pre-statehood and well into the late 1800s) continued to thrive. Although there were other regions of the United States that eventually outpaced Indiana's vine production, Indiana's smaller region was, nevertheless, an impressive source of both table grape and drinking wine for the growing nation. Larger states such as California, New York, Ohio, Missouri, and Virginia (in that order) laid claim to more production, but Indiana was still a major player at the close of the 19th century.

But the wine industry changed, of course, when the Eighteenth Amendment was ratified on January 29th, 1919—otherwise known as Prohibition. Prohibition not only had a profound impact on the production of beer and distilled liquors such as rum and whiskey, but also made wine production illegal as well. In a matter of months, vineyards which had thrived for generations fell into ruin, and with it, an industry that had employed farmers and families, not to mention winemakers, became but a memory. As the vineyards disappeared, so did the farms and towns that supported them and across the country, including Indiana, vines were plowed under and other crops planted. Families were displaced. And in the matter of a generation, winemaking history and knowledge of the craft was lost.

And, unlike other alcoholic beverages that did not depend upon the cultivation and nurture of fruit (and growth through many years), wine production did not bounce back quickly after Prohibition was repealed. And Indiana, unlike some of the other wine-producing states noted before, continued to lag behind once the ban was lifted. The comeback was not swift.

In fact, there were no wineries in Indiana in 1935 when the Liquor Control Act was passed, a law that further cemented the fate of the in-state wine industry and virtually ensured that Indiana would continue to drag behind those other states that had once again become major players in the wine industry. Although there was interest, and many wanted to once again establish full-production vineyards and wineries, this law essentially prohibited any Hoosier winery from selling directly to the public—a hurdle that all but insured that no winery could exist by selling to wholesalers and distributors only.

It would be nearly another forty years before the Liquor Control Act would be challenged in the Hoosier state.

This work was completed by some enterprising and resourceful people—many of whom are still alive to tell the story. In the late

50s and early 60s several visionaries began to plant vineyards in the hope that this law could be addressed in the near future. Dr. Donald MacDaniel, one of the earliest, planted several of the new French hybrids (another enology development in Europe that was exciting news in America) in his Connersville vineyard. This was 1958. Bill Oliver (of Oliver winery) followed suit in 1966 and planted ten acres of vines near Bloomington. And in 1971, Bill Easley also planted a vineyard at Cape Sandy along the Ohio River.

These men also began working with state legislators to create a new law (Public Law No. 77, passed on April 8, 1971) that would remove the restrictions on wineries and allow them to sell directly to the public. MacDaniel opened his winery (Treaty Line Winery) in Connersville four months after the bill's passage. This was August of 1971. Oliver Winery opened May 1, 1973. More wineries followed, including Easley and Huber—with Gerald Huber being instrumental in helping to see the passage of another law change that allowed wineries to sell on Sunday, a change in 1982 that spawned further growth in the wine industry in Indiana. And in 1989, Jim Butler (Butler Winery) was instrumental in legislation that established the Indiana Wine Grape Council.

Although the new era of Indiana vineyards and wines came late to the party, the Hoosier state is now dotted by wineries. Many of these wineries birthed in the 1970s are mainstays and represent some of the most knowledgeable sources of history, as well as producing some of the most superb, well-rounded, and mature wines one will find anywhere. But there are newer wineries, too. And many of these younger businesses are staffed by expert winemakers who have learned from masters, not only here in Indiana, but from skilled winemakers in Napa Valley and Oregon and Washington State. They are bringing their knowledge to bear upon our Midwest roots.

As you read the profiles of the Indiana wineries you will discover what one wine critic from Sonoma Valley told us: that Indiana wineries are unlike those found in any other part of the country. Our Hoosier wineries are not cookie-cutter in appearance or product—but each winery has its own ambiance in tasting room and facility and each produces wines of particular taste and presentation. Yes, Indiana has its primary varietals to be sure—grapes that thrive in this Midwest climate and condition. But increasingly wineries are finding ways to grow vinifera and hybrids that, up until a few years ago, were deemed an impossibility in Indiana. The gifted and knowledgeable horticulture/enology department at Purdue University is largely responsible for sharing this research and practice—and, in no small way, the University in West Lafayette has deeply impacted the rise and proliferation of vineyards in the Hoosier state.

As this book was going to press there were a number of new wineries readying to open their doors. Indiana now has nearly eighty wineries—and this means that one doesn't have to travel far to find them. There are five wine trails, and more on the way. And festivals and wine competitions continue to emerge every year. Indiana wines are now entered into some of the most prestigious wine competitions in the nation and the world. Many wineries in Indiana can tout their regional and national successes, and there is a kind of camaraderie among the wineries in Indiana that one doesn't always encounter in other parts of the country. There is a sense of family among the Hoosier winemaking community—and if one winery does well, it helps others to be successful, too.

Today, one can still celebrate Indiana's place in the winemaking industry—and the history of winemaking in America—at the Swiss Wine Festival, held in Vevay, Indiana. This southern Indiana festival is a rich source of winemaking history and deftly carves out Indiana's heritage and place in the American winemaking scene. Vintage Indiana, held in Indianapolis each June, is now the premier showcase for Indiana Wineries. These festivities, and many others, continue to recapture our place in the history of winemaking, and serve as a showcase for the great wines still being produced in Indiana today.

Indiana actually has a rich history, and a solid place, in the winemaking industry. We are a small state, but with our agricultural background and our strong work ethic, there is no doubt that Indiana is creating a name, once again, as a wine-producing region worthy of note. *

Bibliography

* For more detailed information on the history of Indiana wine, one should note Jim and John Butler's book: *Indiana Wine: A History,* by James L. Butler and John J. Butler (Indiana University Press, 2001)

Other helpful histories include:

A History of Wine in America, Volume 1: From the Beginnings to Prohibition, by Thomas Pinney (University of California Press, 2nd Revised Edition, 2007)

A History of Wine in America, Volume 2: From Prohibition to the Present, by Thomas Pinney (University of California Press, 2nd Revised Edition, 2007)

American Vintage: The Rise of American Wines, by Paul Lukacs (Houghton Mifflin, 2000)

Inventing Wine: A New History of one of the World's Most Ancient Pleasures, by Paul Lukacs (W.W. Norton, 2013)

The Story of Wine—New Illustrated History, by Hugh Johnson (Mitchell Beazley, London, 2005

The Wild Vine: A Forgotten Grape and the Untold Story of American Wine, by Todd Kilman (Clarkson Potter, 2010)

The World Atlas of Wine, by Hugh Johnson (Mitchell Beazley, London, 2005)

A Guide to Indiana Wineries

As we have made our way across the length and breadth of the Hoosier state we have enjoyed visiting the wineries. Better yet, we have enjoyed talking to winery owners and winemakers, interviewing experts, taking photographs, attending wine festivals, and appreciating a landscape diverse in cornfields and rolling hills, spring and autumn colors, and the unique settings that each winery had to offer. We also enjoyed those times when winemakers invited us "backstage" to the production areas or discussed their winemaking techniques with us. We enjoyed the wines, of course. But most of all, we enjoyed the Hoosier hospitality that is so much a part of the Indiana winery experience.

Writing this guide to Indiana wineries has, indeed, been a labor of love. As you read each of the profiles on the Indiana wineries, we hope that you, the reader, will discover what we already know about these remarkable destinations: namely, that there are some fantastic wines being produced in state, and the winery facilities in Indiana can go head-to-head with some of the best in the world. In fact, as we visited these wineries we often depart with the question: "Why don't more people know about this winery?"

Although Indiana has a solid place in the early history of winemaking (in the United States), it is also true that, in many respects, we are still catching up to other parts of the country when it comes to wine production and appreciation. But that is rapidly changing.

As most Indiana wineries will readily admit, the Hoosier taste leans more heavily toward those sweet and fruit wines produced from the more common Indiana varietals. Nothing wrong with this. In fact, estate wineries are on the rise—and it is far more common now to find a winery established on the backbone of the vineyard on site.

But not all wines are exclusively produced from estate grown grapes—not even the wineries of Napa Valley or upstate New York or Washington state would fill that bill. Rather, there is a mix of winemaking methods at play in Indiana, with some wineries producing only estate grown wines, while others create their wines from grapes (or juices) shipped in from other parts of the country (or the world). Still other wineries produce labels that feature their own, along with other grape varietals, from across the country.

In short, there's no one "type" of Indiana winery—and patrons should be thankful that the wine experience here is both diverse and consistent. No doubt a person will find that Indiana wineries

consistently produce Chambourcin, Foch, or Cayuga, for example . . . but most wineries will also offer some surprises, or their own interpretations of traditional varietals. Those who appreciate the wine experience may discover that it is fun to have a wine tasting at home that features Traminette purchased from around the state. A single varietal such as this has many expressions—and although there is a consistent taste that defines wines produced from this grape—one could do a ladder tasting from several wineries and have a great deal of fun noting the variances in taste, presentation, and region. A Traminette from the northeast will taste a bit different than a Traminette produced along the Ohio River.

Another feature of the Indiana wine experience is proximity. No matter where a person lives in state, there is a now a winery within driving distance—an hour or two by car (and in most regions, far less). In an afternoon, a person can easily visit two or three wineries.

Many Indiana wineries have also made their experiences broad. Some wineries also feature dining—with pizzas, barbecue, and salads the most common. But there are also fine dining experiences to be had in many locations—and in some communities the wineries are *the place* to go for a nice dinner. So a person doesn't have to be a wine connoisseur to appreciate what these Indiana wineries have to offer.

Wineries also provide entertainment, and as you read the profiles of each winery you will note that live music, weekend events, and even fun nights like chili-cookoffs are not uncommon. Again, in some communities, the winery is the place to go for a Friday or Saturday night, an evening out. The amenities that these wineries offer are often as compelling as the labels they offer. And let's not forget that some of the wineries that have spacious grounds can also be appealing for weddings, family and class reunions, and even business parties.

As we visited these wineries we also discovered that, for the most part, there is a relaxing atmosphere. A great many of these Indiana wineries are rural—and getting to them is half the fun. The wine tasting experience can be relaxing, and most of these wineries have quiet corners, nooks and crannies, or back decks where a couple can relax and unwind. Other wineries have such spacious grounds that one can get some exercise walking in the vineyard or even exploring trails. And as you will discover in the wine-tasting tips—one doesn't have to always drink the wine in order to appreciate it. A day dedicated to visiting wineries would be enjoyed all the more by practicing the art of tasting and pouring, and all wineries provide pouring urns expressly for this purpose.

Finally, don't overlook the promise of creating your own collection of Indiana wines. In the writing of this book we collected dozens of Indiana labels, creating our own notes on each one, comparing to others, and often enjoying the bottles themselves and the artwork featured by each winery. We began sharing our Indiana wines with friends, telling the stories behind the wineries, and simply enjoying the company over a nice dinner and a glass. No doubt you will discover some new wineries that will become favorites—places that you will want to return to time and again. Some of these wineries will be close to your home. Others will be destinations.

For those who do prefer a getaway experience, we've also included seven weekend trips that feature regional sites, shopping, and entertainment to go along with three to five wineries. You will find our suggestions and these itineraries in the back of the book and we hope you can use them as we did—for fun, romance, or an opportunity to see another region of this great state.

In many respects, the Indiana wine experience is still in its infancy. Although there are many long-standing wineries (Oliver, Easley, Chateau Thomas, Butler, Huber, etc.) there are a greater number of wineries that have blossomed into being in the past decade. The new wineries have to establish their own identities and reach new constituencies, but that's what makes the Indiana wine experience so exciting. One can never judge a new winery on the basis of its youth, as some of the upstarts actually employ expert winemakers who have honed their skills in other regions of the country or who have, essentially, apprenticed with masters elsewhere.

And don't forget, wineries are always expanding their lists, too. The wines that one may find on the list one year may be very different the next. And as seasons change, and singular grape vines are exposed in different manner to sun, rain, cold and heat, it's a given that a wine that is committed to the bottle one year may have a different taste the next. That's why wine collectors might look for a particular year over another—though the wine came from the same vineyard. Exposure makes a difference. Or, as one winemaker told us: "If you begin with good fruit, there's a very good chance you can make great wine. But if you start with bad fruit, it's difficult to produce something special."

The Indiana Guide is in alphabetical order, but a person can easily gain an overview of the regions by visiting www.indianawinery.blogspot.com. The state map shown here is easy to use, and most of the winery web sites are just the click of a mouse away (usually with accompanying maps and driving directions).

We hope that you will find this Guide to be useful in your travels or as you take notes following your winery visits. We have found our notes to be helpful and trust that we have done some of the legwork for you so that you can have a fuller and more relaxing time making your way throughout the state.

We hope you will also join us in affirming and celebrating the place that each winery has in the winemaking community, and share with us the joy of wine itself.

Finally, it should be noted that all of our winery profiles are as up-to-date as possible—at the time that this edition went to press. But as with all businesses hours, prices and even ownership may change over the course of months. Be sure to visit the winery websites, or give them a call, before you visit. That way you'll have the most up-to-date information possible.

Cheers!

Indiana Wineries: The Ultimate Guide to Wine in Indiana

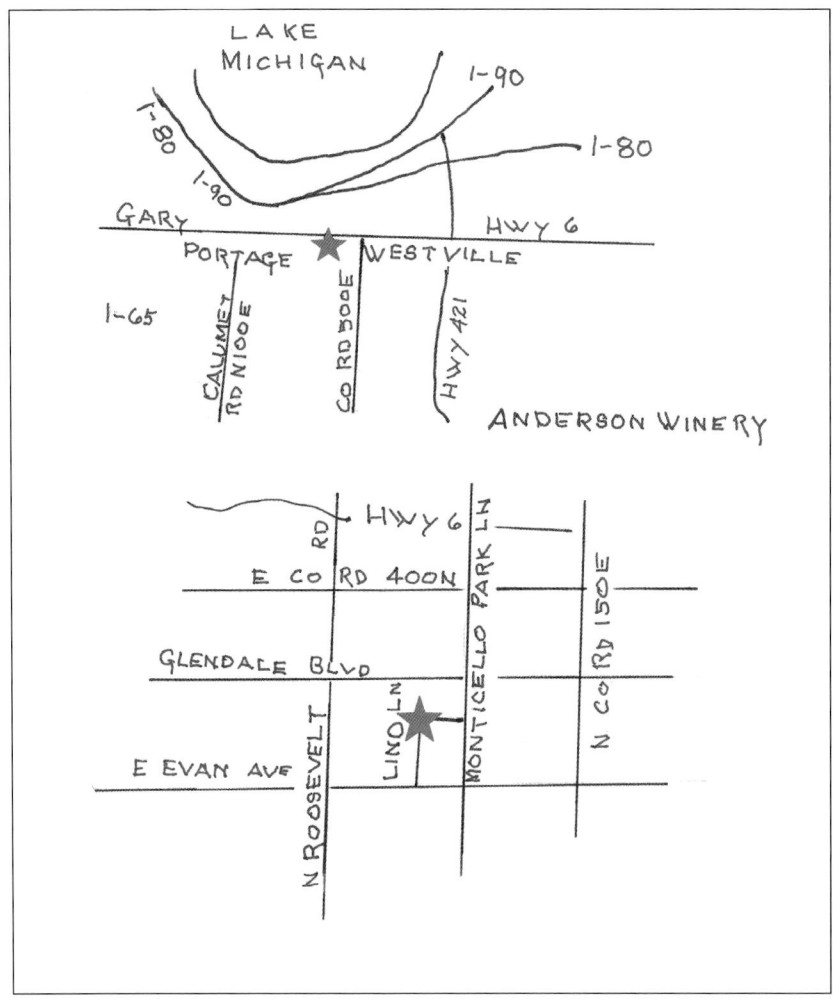

Anderson's Vineyard and Winery

430 E. US 6
Valparaiso, IN 46383
219-464-4936
877-941-WINE
www.andersonswinery.com
wineryandersons@gmail.com

Anderson's has over forty acres of vineyard—and during the fall, especially, visitors will enjoy the wagon ride/tour through these grounds ($8.00). The winery, which is located in a country store theme, has one of the most unique settings in the state—and is located just south of some of the largest sand dunes in the Midwest. Anderson's also provides ample parking and seating, especially in the outdoor gazebo area which can also be used for wedding receptions and large events.

As the country theme implies, most of the wines produced by Anderson are of the apple/fruit variety. However, even if one doesn't enjoy fruit wines, there are options, such as Anderson's award-winning Seyval Blanc. The country market always has fresh baked bread, homemade jams and jellies, pies, cookies, and apple donuts. Fruits and vegetables in season are also available, along with old-fashioned candies. A fudge factory at the back of the store rounds out the experience nicely if one has a sweet tooth—and the blueberry wine that Anderson's bottles pairs very well with these sweeter wonders.

The Anderson's Winery also provides plenty of room for large groups and special events. And they cater food. All in all, Anderson's is one of the broadest and most eclectic wineries in state—and their longevity and history in the winemaking community is a statement in itself.

Those looking for a respite will enjoy the country store ambiance and laid-back atmosphere and rural charm of this older business—the first estate winery established north of Indianapolis.

Information By the Glass

Owner: Bill Anderson

Hours:
January 1 - March 21
Tuesday - Saturday 10 a.m. - 5 p.m.
Sunday 11 a.m. – 4 p.m.
Closed Mondays

March 21 - December 31
Monday - Saturday 10 a.m. – 6 p.m.
Sunday 11 a.m. – 5 p.m.

Amenities: Country Store, Gift Shop, Homemade candies, Outdoor Seating, Restaurant and Catering

Tastings: Free

Price: $10 - $15

Recommendations:
Marechal Foch—a noveau-style wine, light, crisp, and hearty if paired with Italian cuisine

Activities: Hayrides, Tours, Live Music, Special Events

Nearby Attractions: Valparaiso University, Hiking & Biking Trails, Indiana Dunes

Estate Grapes: Marechal Foch, Concord, Chambourcin, Noret, Cabernet Sauvignon, Cabernet Franc, Chardonel, Seyval Blanc, Vidal Blanc.

Old Fashioned Pound Cake

½ cup shortening
1 cup butter
3 cups sugar
5 eggs
3 cups flour

½ teaspoon baking powder
1 cup milk
2 teaspoons vanilla extract
2 teaspoons lemon extract

This is in old-fashioned pound cake recipe like grandmother used to make. Grease a large pan and in another bowl mix together shortening, sugar and butter. Add eggs one by one and slowly add mixture of flour and baking powder along with milk and extracts. Bake for 90 minutes at 365 degrees and cool for 15 minutes before eating. Serve with Andersons apple wine.

Indiana Wineries: The Ultimate Guide to Wine in Indiana

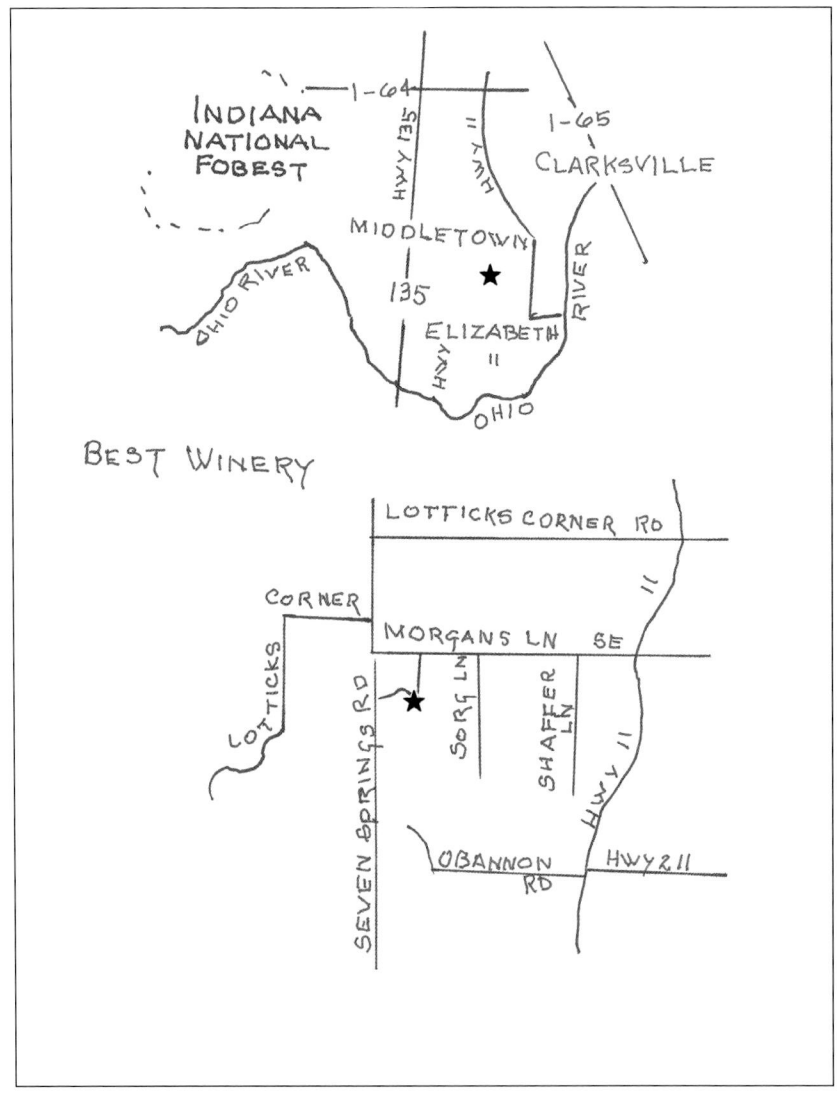

Best Vineyards Winery

8373 Morgans Lane
Elizabeth, IN 47117
812-969-9463
www.bestvineyardswinery.com

The Best Vineyards, with their distinctive green Best label, holds a southern charm and is well-represented at wine showcases and festivals around the state—and across the border into Kentucky. In operation since 2000, the Best family has been producing top-flight wines and entertainment since. In fact, Best Vineyards has enough clout and ambiance to warrant a destination all its own, with homegrown festivals, live music and featured acts through the spring and summer. And chances are, if you attend any of the major wine festivals in Indiana, you are going to find the Best Vineyard in attendance. Look for them.

Best also sports their own line of wine-related stock in their show room and tasting area, including T-shirts. And with their expanding list of wines, they can hold their own across the spectrum of dry to sweet, white to red. Their wines are also found at a number of retailers in state, and so their visibility is greater than many of the other boutique wineries—especially in the southern region.

The Best Chambourcin is wonderfully aromatic and rich with blackberry tones and the Best Plum is remarkable, as is the Mango—a ripe, fruity wine that breathes a tropical paradise and travels well to the beach.

With over a decade of winemaking expertise under their belts, the Best family continues to make strides in the Hoosier market as well as regionally. Upcoming varietals may include Syrah and new expressions of classic fruit wines. So Best is only getting better with age . . . just like their wines.

Plan to visit Best Vineyards on your next southern route—and see how tasty these wines are.

Information by the Glass

Owners: Wilbert, Rachel & Barretta Best

Hours:
Tuesday - Sunday 12 - 7 p.m.

Amenities: Wine Tours, Outdoor Seating

Price: $12 - $19

Tastings: Free

Recommendations:
Catawba—a sweet white grown on estate, with a grassy, green apple flavor with a floral nose that pairs well with summer peaches and homemade ice cream.

County Red—this Best award-winner made from Cabernet Franc has an oaky finish with undertones of ripe currant and dates. Their boldest red supplements a traditional meatloaf and mashed potatoes and gravy fare.

Activities: Concert Series, Festivals

Nearby Attractions: Caving, Falls of the Ohio

Estate Grapes: Chambourcin, Chardonel, Catawba, Concord.

Carmelized Nut Snack

½ pound pecan halves
2 cups brown sugar
¾ cup butter

½ pound walnut halves
1 teaspoon vanilla extract
Water as needed

In a large pan bring brown sugar, extract and butter to a glaze. Add pecans and walnuts. Stir halves gently to allow glaze to settle over nuts. Place on wax paper for drying. Serve with Best Chambourcin.

Blackhawk Winery

28153 Ditch Road
Sheridan, IN 46069
317-771-2814
www.blackhawkwinery.com

The Blackhawk Winery is a family-owned and operated farm that features estate-grown grapes and a countrified atmosphere. Located in the small town of Sheridan, the Blackhawk Winery is just minutes away from northside Indianapolis and visitors here will discover relaxation and some very tasty wines when they drop by.

The estate vineyard here sports some of the most unique grapes one will find in Indiana, including the Sheridan grape (how's that for a hometown wine?). Although Blackhawk winery is still gaining momentum in their own vineyard, they are currently producing wines made from other Indiana-grown varietals.

This quaint country vineyard is a fine place to unwind for an hour or two and as the vineyard takes on maturity, we should expect some nice labels to be forthcoming, especially as Blackhawk works closely with the experts at Purdue University. Thanks to John and Deb for creating another Indiana wine opportunity.

Information by the Glass

Owners: John & Deb Miller

Hours:
Weekend and Holidays 1 - 6 p.m.

Amenities: Tasting Room, Outdoor Seating

Tastings: Free

Price: Check Website

Recommendations:
Chambourcin Rose—a semi-sweet wine with some lasting notes of cherry and apricot.

Activities: Live Music

Nearby Attractions: Town Run Park Mountain Bike Trail

Estate Grapes: Cayuga White, Chambourcin, Traminette, Catawba, Sheridan, Leon Millot.Blue Heron Vineyards & Bed and Breakfast.

Blue Heron Winery
5330 Blue Heron Lake
Cannelton, IN 47520
812-547-7518
www.blueheronvines.com

Gary and Lynn Dauby have created a beautiful winery in Blue Heron—and their vision and artistic gifts can be seen throughout the winery and accompanying grounds. This southern Indiana destination will not disappoint. Along with the beautiful Hoosier landscape overlooking the Ohio River, one will discover here some fantastic wines produced from a small, but vibrant vineyard. A stay in the Blue Heron B & B can also turn this visit into a weekend getaway, perhaps with accompanying visits to Monkey Hollow and Wine Shak wineries—which are not far away. (These three wineries, in fact, are one of the most beautiful winery trifectas one can find anywhere in the state.)

Blue Heron is also available for larger events (weddings and family gatherings) and also reveals the artistic side in the world's largest Celtic Cross—carved in-situ out of an Indiana rock outcropping. Plenty of room to hike, too—and the vistas here are stunning.

As for the wines produced from the three grape varietals found in the vineyard, Blue Heron has nearly a dozen labels. These range from the reds produced from the Chambourcin and Villard Noir grapes to the semi-dry versions produced from the same vines. In other words, there Blue Heron makes the most of their vineyard has a knack for creating varied tastes and textures from single vines.

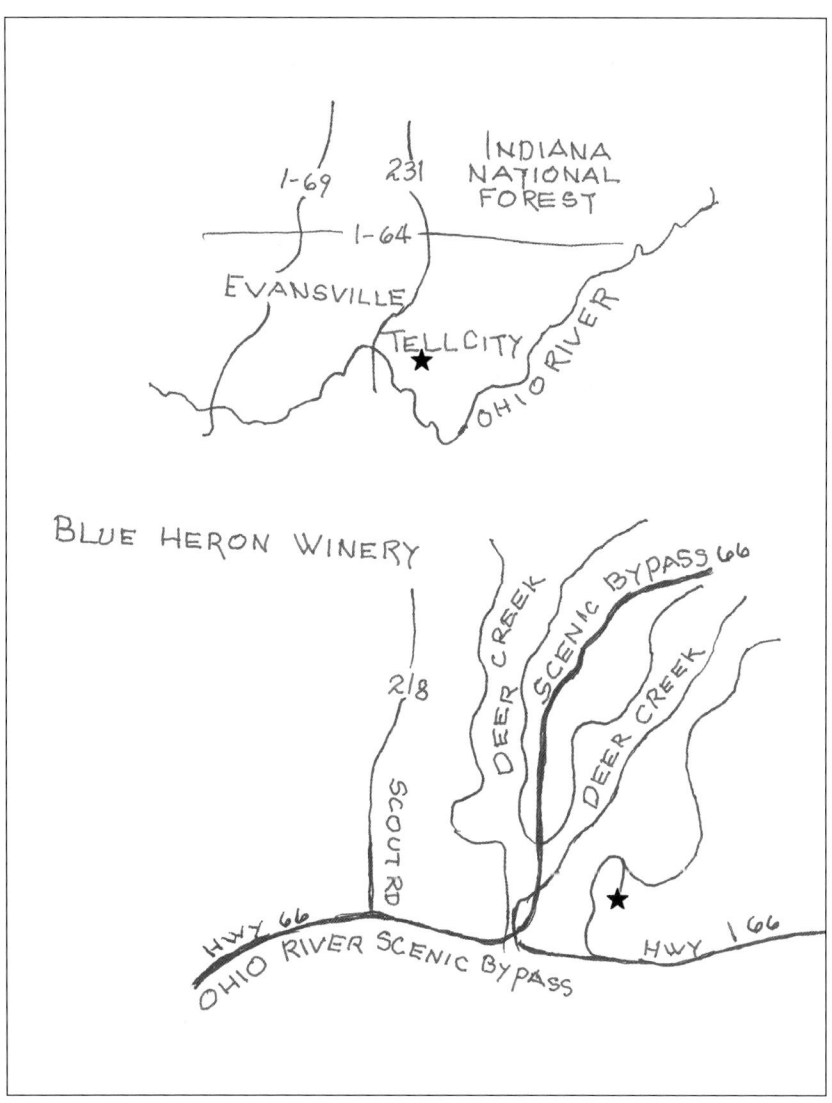

Blue Heron also has sweet wines ranging from reds and whites to blueberry and cherry dessert wines.

This beautiful winery and tasting room also sports some sale art from local artists as well as an eclectic blend of specialty items such as salve, steak sauces, and hand-crafted walking sticks. And again, don't forget the B & B.

Information by the Glass

Owners: Gary & Lynn Dauby

Hours:
Saturday and Sunday, 11 a.m. – 5 p.m.
Other days and hours please call ahead

Amenities: Artwork, Gift Shop, Outdoor Seating, Bed and Breakfast

Tastings: Free

Price: Check Website

Recommendations:
Twin Towers Red (with silver cap)—a barrel-aged Chambourcin that has a spicy finish—hints of cinnamon and sage—along with a deep finish of tannins. Pair this wine with linguine or Asian foods.

Hoosier Red—a semi-dry version of the Twin Towers Red, but without the ageing and a much lighter body. Not too sweet to enjoy with Swiss cheese and garlic crackers.

Activities: Music, Festivals, Art Displays

Nearby Attractions: Lincoln State Park, Cabin Rentals

Estate Grapes: Fredonia, Marechal Foch, Chambourcin.

Swiss Cheese Crisps

1 pound sliced Swiss cheese
Green olives (sliced)

½ pound bacon
Crackers

Fry bacon until crispy, let dry. Slice cheese onto favorite crackers and top with bacon and olive. Serve with Blue Heron Hoosier Red.

Briali Vineyards
102 W. State Road 120
Fremont, IN 46737
260-316-5156
www.brialivineyards.com

Patrons visiting the Briali Vineyards will discover a northern Indiana gem. This winery—one of the newest (youngest) in the state—has a small but distinguished lineup of wines for every taste. Brian and Alicia Moeller, winemaker and manager respectively, have created a winery that is dedicated to the environment and ecologically sound winemaking practices. And the proximity of Briali Vineyards to the Satek Winery—just two miles up the road—offers one of the best one-two punches anywhere in the state.

This winery, located on the Country Meadows Golf Course in Fremont, Indiana, provides a first-blush impression that this winery is devoted to green. Before opening the winery, the Moellers dedicated themselves for eight years to the vineyard using biodynamic techniques—with more than 13 varieties of vines—cultivating fruit that is at the heart of their tasty wines. The winery opened in the fall of 2012 in the basement of the Pro Shop at the Meadows Golf Course and is a small, but quaint, tasting area with a state-of-the-art production facility in the back.

And the wines? Briali's baker's dozen lineup features both the best of Indiana varietals and some unique ones that are difficult to find. For example, the Briali Geez is a crisp white varietal—a hybrid of Chancellor and Riesling—made in the German dry family. Briali also makes a sweeter Riesling and a marvelous Pinot Noir that is spicy with oak and hints of black cherry, currant, and strawberry.

Among the wines that Briali will receive some acclaim for, look to the fruit. This winery is excited about their Bada Bing Cherry wine, a sweet cherry wine that will be available for the first time in winter of 2014. This wine, which Brian Moeller described as a blend of top cherries aged in oak bourbon barrels for that hint of whiskey, is going to be one of the most unique cherry wines that people will have to have for the holidays.

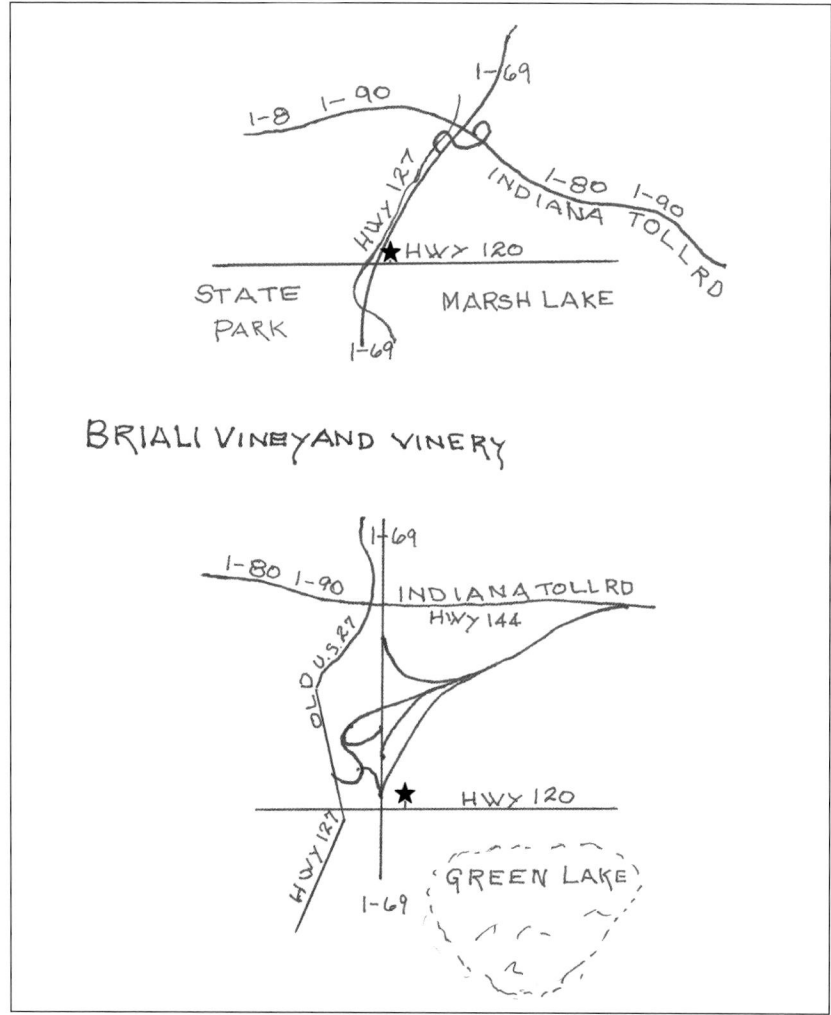

Also, look for the Cabernet Franc and other new varietals that Briali has on their "to-do" list. Exciting times for this new winery.

Round out your experience at Briali with a snack plate or a relaxing departure from the top deck of the club house—where you can enjoy golf shots approaching two greens. And because Briali is located at the juncture of the Indiana Toll Road and I-69, guests here can arrive easily from Michigan, Ohio, or Indiana without feeling that they are making a detour. Enjoy!

Information by the Glass

Owners: Brian and Alicia Moeller

Hours:
Friday - Sunday 10 a.m. - 6 p.m.
Closed Monday through Thursday

Amenities: Gift Shop, Outdoor Seating, Clubhouse Restaurant

Tastings: Free

Price: $12 - $18

Recommendations:
Geez—noted for its bright, crisp floral finish, a unique wine in the family of a dry Riesling that will pair well with fish.

Cabernet Franc—sure to be a hit from the vine

Tart Cherry—A truly unique cherry wine, incredibly tart and dry, that would go well on a cold winter night with dark chocolate or ice cream.

Activities: Live Music, Tours

Nearby Attractions: Pokagen State Park

Estate Grapes: Traminette, Muscat, Chambourcin.

Christmas Fruit Cake

1 ½ cups of raisins
1 ½ cups sugar
1 ½ cups water (boiling)
1 teaspoon baking soda
½ teaspoon salt
½ cup chopped dried apricots

1 ½ cups of chopped dates
3 tablespoons shortening
2 ½ cups flour
2 teaspoons cinnamon
1 cup chopped walnuts

Line a 9 X 5 loaf pan with foil and in a large pan mix raisins, dates, sugar, shortening and hot water. Simmer 10 minutes. Stir in other ingredients, pour into pan, bake at 325 degrees for 1 hour (or until done). Serve with Briali Tart Cherry or Bada Bing.

Brown County Winery
4520 SR 46 East
Nashville, IN 47448
812-988-6144
www.browncountywinery.com

Opening in 1985, the Brown County Winery occupies a solid place in the Hoosier winemaking community and has been producing remarkable wines—and an adaptable and growing list based on Hoosier tastes—for three decades. The winery operates out of two locations—but is principally visible in Nashville, Indiana during the peak autumn colors when foot traffic in the town is heaviest. The winery has been a mainstay in the Chamber of Commerce for many years and is one of the leading wineries in southern Indiana.

The Brown County Winery stamps a distinctive label on every bottle and in more recent years has expanded from fruit wines (and sweeter) to accommodate the growing desire for bolder reds such as Cabernet Sauvignon and Cab Franc. Moreover, the staff at the Brown County Winery is knowledgeable and well-versed in wine-making process and appreciation. In essence, patrons will enjoy a visit to either location and will no doubt walk away with some delectable wines.

The Traminette is a favorite off-dry white, and a Hoosier mainstay, that holds some wonderful floral bouquet and enough sweetness to complement a plate of breads and cheeses. The Chambourcin Rose is another elegant wine that, once chilled, can carry a meal of corn chowder or whitefish. There are also several fruit wines, including peach, cranberry, and plum, that each hold their own in category and possess a delightful opportunity for sipping on the back deck.

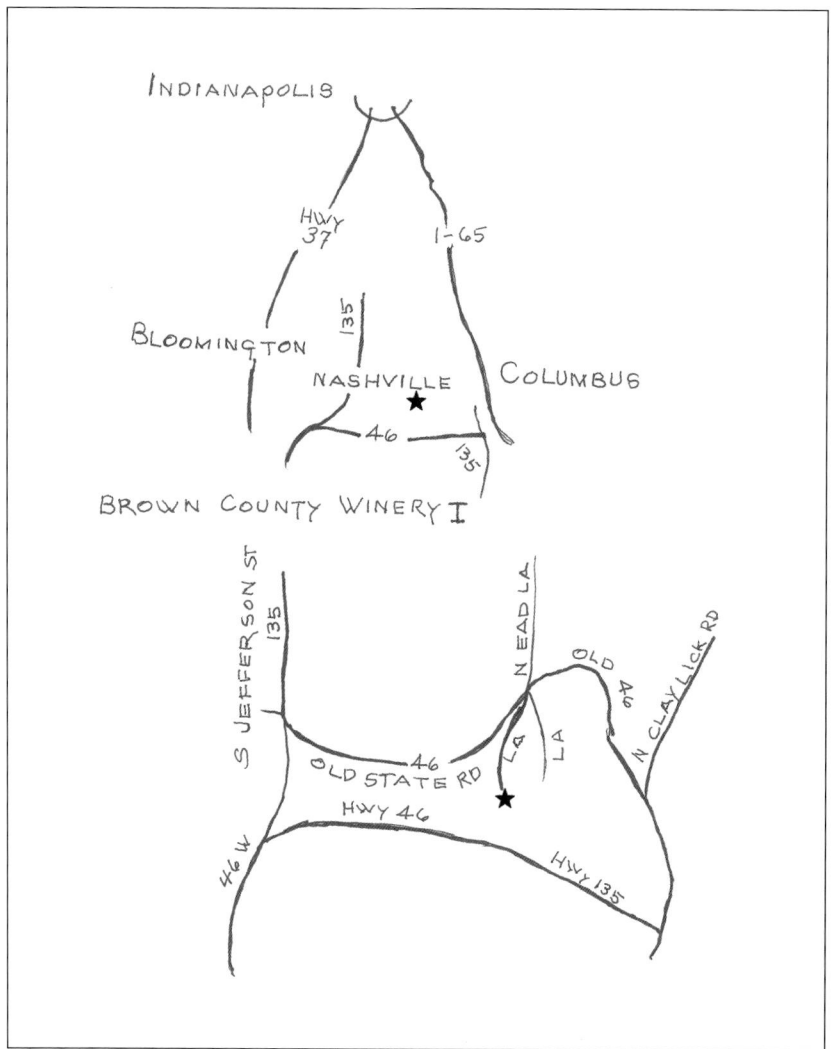

What makes a visit to the Brown County winery doubly special is the ambiance—whether it be fall colors, a summer hike through a state park, or a shopping tour of the town. But any time is a good time for a visit to this winery, especially if one leaves with a bottle or two in tow. Furthermore, watch for Brown County Winery at fairs and showcases around the state—they often have their colors flying . . . and once you've seen the Brown County label, you won't soon forget it.

Information by the Glass

Owners: Dave and Cynthia Schrodt

Downtown Location:
Nashville tasting room
Downtown, corner of Main Street & Old School Way
812-988-8646

Winery in Gnawbone:
4520 State Road 46 East
812-988-6144
888-298-2984

Hours:
Monday - Thursday 10 a.m. - 5 p.m.
Friday & Saturday 10 a.m. - 5:30 p.m.
Sunday 11 a.m. - 5 p.m.

Amenities: Gift Shop, Multiple Locations, Gourmet Cheeses and snacks

Tastings: Free

Price: $10 - $18

Recommendations:
Old Barrel Port—a barrel-aged port (20% alcohol) that does not

overpower or overreach with taste. Touches of cigar and leather make this port a sipping delight, or as an after-dinner dessert wine.

Autumn Red—a Chambourcin expression but with some bolder un-oaked notes makes this red delightfully drinkable with pasta dishes and goat cheese.

Activities: Tasting Tours and Appreciation Classes

Nearby Attractions: Brown County State Park, Nashville shopping

Estate Grapes: Chambourcin, Cab Franc, Traminette, Catawba.

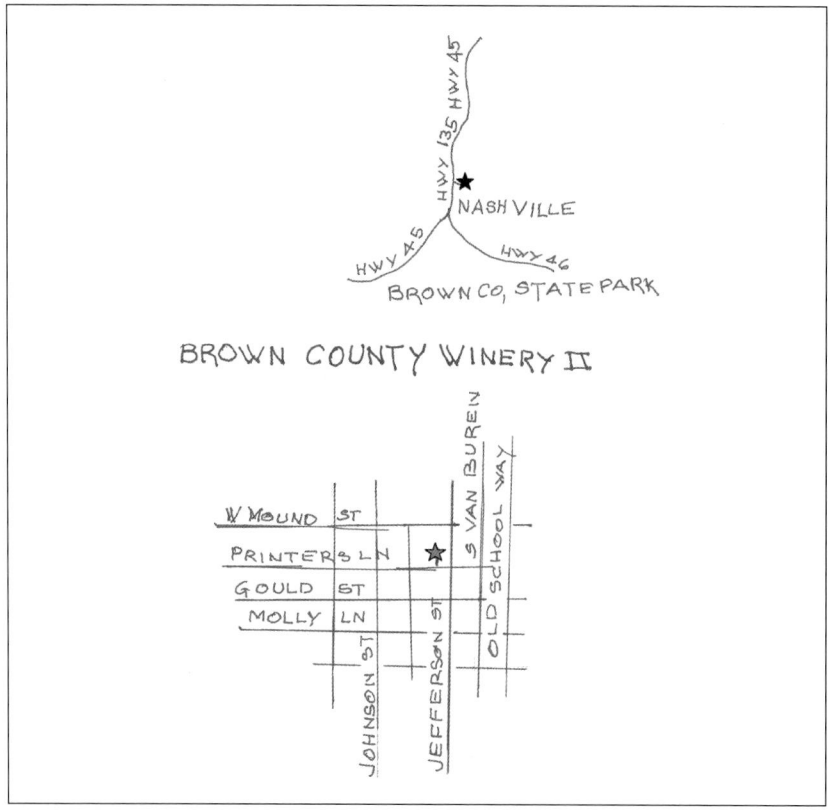

Buck Creek Winery
11747 Indian Creek Road South
Indianapolis, IN 46259
317-862-9463
buckcreekwinery@comcast.net
www.buckcreekwinery.com

Owner, grower and wine-maker Jeff Durm has, in one decade, created one of the premier wineries in Indiana. This, especially, if one is eager to find an expansive wine list populated with stellar tastes. Durm has worked in the Hoosier wine industry for many years, and on his 4 ½ acres grows varietals such as Seyval Blanc, Chambourcin, and Traminette. The William Lloyd Reserve is another vintage singular to Buck Creek—and patrons of the winery will also discover a venue replete with ample parking, easy-accessibility from the interstate (I-74), a nearby playhouse (not related to Buck Creek winery), a quaint bar area and gift shop, and a sprawling yard with shelter house for those quiet summer evenings.

But beyond the amenities, everyone is going to discover a taste—whether sweet or dry, red or white or blush—that will become a favorite. This winery has a broad selection—one of the largest in the state—and the labels range from the inky and oaky (Petite Sirah and Cabernet Sauvignon) to specialty ice wines (Vidal Blanc and Cabernet Franc).

Indeed, there is a taste for everyone at Buck Creek and this winery portrays the most common varietals in tastes that are deep and poignant. For example, among the dry selections one can find Chardonnay, Pinot Grigio, and Sauvignon Banc among the whites along with rich offerings of Zinfandel, Syrah, Merlot, and Pinot Noir. A wide selection of Semi-dry and sweet wines, at least a couple dozen, round out the Buck Creek list.

Buck Creek is one of those wineries that will encourage you to BYOB (Bring Your Own Box). You'll likely want to take home at least three bottles—which will also give you a nice discount.

Visit with some friends and enjoy a country walk, or plan to sit and enjoy a quiet evening. There are plenty of superb wines here and all of it served up with excellence.

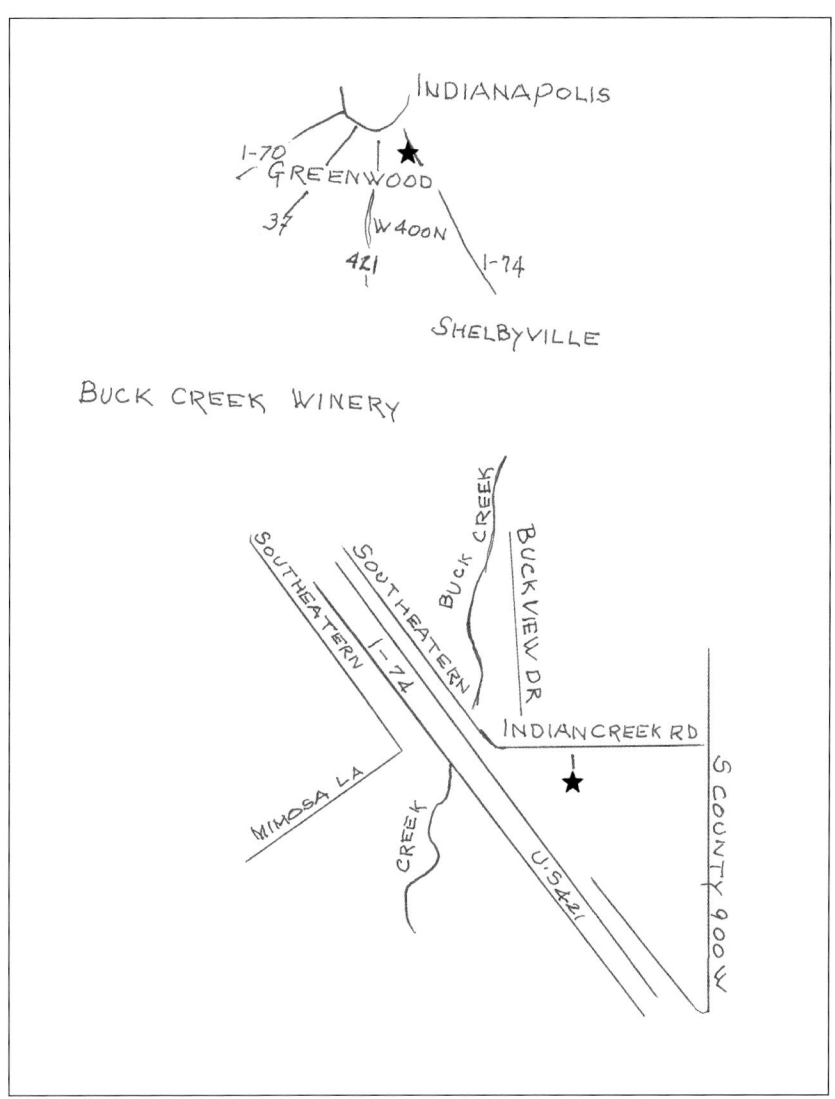

Information By the Glass

Owner, Vintner, Wine-maker: Jeff Durm

Hours:
Monday - Saturday 10 a.m. - 6 p.m.
Sunday 1 p.m. - 6 p.m.

Amenities: Gift Shop, Outdoor Seating

Tastings: Free

Price: $10 - $18

Recommendations:
Zinfandel—a bold, peppery old vine Zin with blackberry and plum flavors.

Seyval Blanc—a medium-bodied wine with layers of floral aroma, grapefruit, and a bit of sweetness from the Cayuga White. A wonderful back-deck, summertime offering.

Trilogy—the only Indiana wine made from a blend of Steuben, Concord and Catawba grapes. Sweet, yes—but a wonderful dessert wine with chocolate.

Activities: Live Music

Nearby Attractions: Indianapolis Restaurants, Circle Center Mall, Monuments

Estate Grapes: Chambourcin, Traminette, Cab Sauvignon, Cab Franc, Catawba, Pinot Gris.

Center Cut Chops in Crème Sauce

Center cut pork chops (boneless) Bacon
2 oz. Half & Half Garlic powder
Rosemary, salt, pepper

Wrap center cut chops with bacon, bake in the over at 350 degrees for 15 minutes. Make crème sauce by stirring Half & Half in a 12 inch sauce pan along with pinches of garlic powder, rosemary and salt/pepper. Remove center cuts and sear in hot iron skillet (with olive oil). Add crème sauce. Serve with rice pilaf and steamed vegetables. Enjoy with Buck Creek Zinfandel.

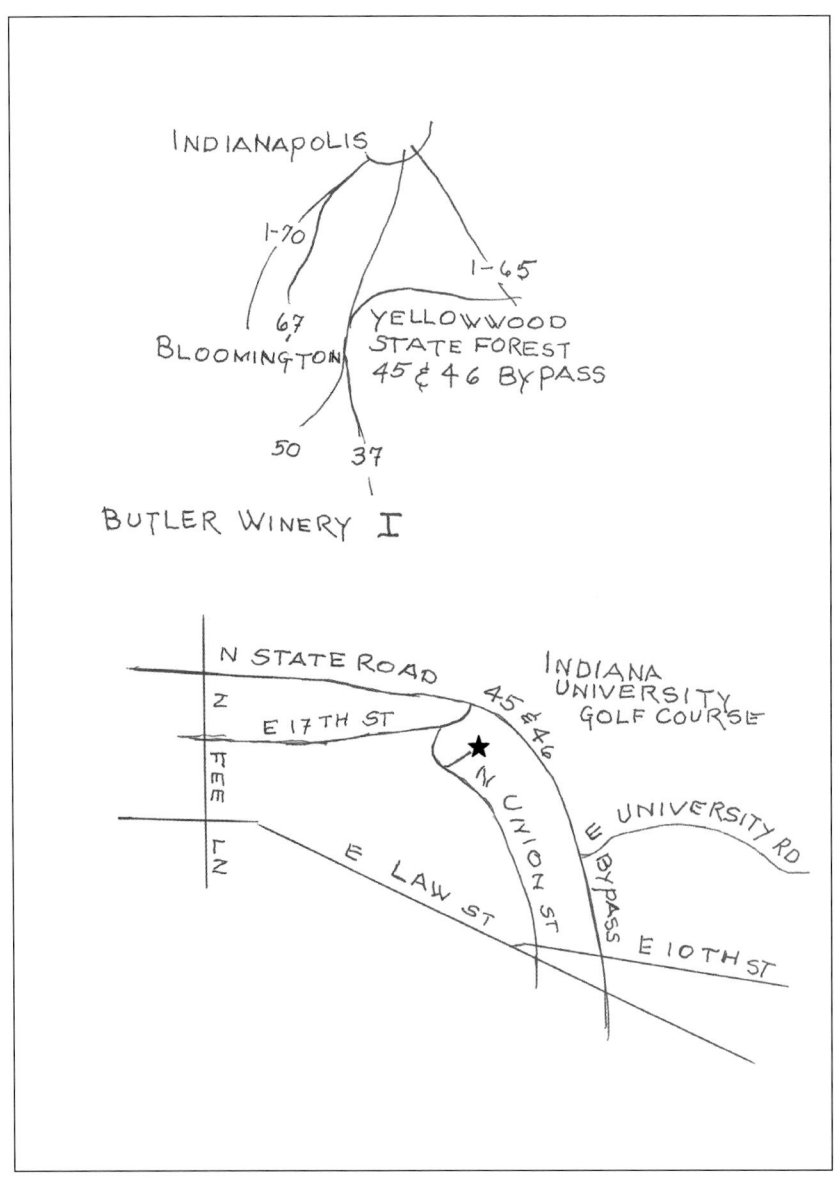

Butler Winery & Vineyards
6200 East Robinson Road
Bloomington, IN 47408
Ph: 812-332-6660
vineyard@butlerwinery.com
www.butlerwinery.com

Visitors to the Butler Winery (Robinson Road location) will be treated to far more than great-tasting wines, especially during the autumn when the iconic Brown County colors are at their zenith. Add a picnic lunch or dinner to a wine purchase and one has all of the ingredients of a perfect day—especially from the vantage point of the spacious back deck, where one can sit at table and appreciate the acres of Chambourcin, Traminette, and Vignoles vines. Butler uses all of these classic Indiana vintages, and more, to create wines of unique texture and flavor, and have been doing so since 1983. All of Butler's wines are estate-grown.

When Jim and Susie Butler began operating their own winery nearly thirty years ago, they were intent on growing their own grapes, varietals that would thrive in the Indiana soil and produce wines of distinct character. And because they are one of the oldest wineries in Indiana, they have been able to utilize the Hoosier climate, topography and sunlight to its fullest advantage in their signature wines. In short, many other upstart wineries around the state have looked to Butler as a model for wine-making, and Butler has been leading the way in the horticulture and tending of the grape varietals that thrive in Indiana's unique landscape.

Although the Butler Winery & Vineyards has three locations (including tasting rooms in Bloomington and Chesterton), the rural Brown County location is a relaxed atmosphere and sports both a large tasting room, plentiful parking, and an array of indoor/outdoor dining nooks where one can bring a picnic basket or purchase cheeses and chilled wines from the display room. A gift area—stocked with a variety of wine products and trinkets—rounds out the ambiance very nicely.

Tastings are free, and at Butler visitors will discover an array of sweet and dry wines that will offer the best of locally-grown vintages. Wine connoisseurs will appreciate the Chambroucin and Traminette expressions, but will also find some of the most unique and flavorful fruit wines in season. The apple, blackberry and blueberry wines are perfect for holiday enjoyment, and Butler is one of the only wineries in the Midwest to produce a Black Currant label.

Mainstays of the Butler Winery include the Indiana White and Indiana Red—blends under $15 that deepen in appreciation if paired with cheese or fruit—and a new Vineyard Rose, under $10, which can be enjoyed on a hot day, chilled. Butler is also represented well around the state in local wine competitions and the Bloomington tasting room location (1022 N. College Avenue) is an easy drive from highway 37 for those who are looking for a taste of southern Indiana wine-making or who need a supplier for home-brew beer ingredients and instructions. The Bloomington tasting room offers this eclectic blend of information and expertise—and the Bloomington downtown and Indiana University campus is a short drive away. And for those in the northern region of the state, the Chesterton location provides a new and adorable setting for an afternoon get-away.

As the fourth oldest winery in Indiana, Butler has been on the leading edge of the wine industry in the Midwest and continues to produce wines of high quality. And if one is looking to travel the Uplands Wine Trail (Southern Indiana), this is one of the stops to be savored.

One unique feature of the Butler Winery is the website (www.butlerwinery.com). Here you'll find a smart-looking site that contains some of the best information about Indiana wineries—including the various wine trails, councils, educational opportunities, and wine-making experts. This site reflects the expertise of owner Jim Butler, who is one of the grand-masters of Indiana wine-making. So don't overlook this website as a smart way to begin your wine explorations or to set up weekend trip through one of the wine trails.

Information By The Glass

Owners: Jim and Susie Butler

Hours: Monday - Saturday 10 a.m. - 6 p.m.
Sunday Noon - 6 p.m.

Other Locations:
1022 N. College Ave
Bloomington, IN 47404
Ph: 812-339-7233

401 Broadway
Chesterton, IN 46304
Ph: 219-929-1400

Amenities: Gift Shop, Outdoor Seating, Gourmet Cheeses and snacks

Tastings: Free

Price: $10 - $20

Recommendations:
White Select—A Riesling-style dry white with a full fruit flavor and crisp ending

Chambourcin Rose—best chilled with a near-sparkling apple finish

Terra Rosa—delicious after-dinner port-style wine perfect for the winter fireplace

Activities: Music, Tours, Festivals, Special Events

Nearby Attractions: Brown County State Park, Indiana University

Estate Grapes: Cayuga, Chambourcin, Cab Franc, Traminette, Noiret, Concord.

Summer Basic Tomato Slices

Large red summer tomatoes
Fresh Mozzarella cheese loaf for slicing
Fresh basil   Olive oil
Balsamic vinegar   Salt

Thick slice fresh summer tomatoes onto a plate and top with equal slices of fresh Mozzarella cheese. Top with freshly sliced basic, sprinkling of olive oil and vinegar and salt. Serve on the plate with dinner or as an appetizer along with Butler White Select.

Indiana Wineries: The Ultimate Guide to Wine in Indiana

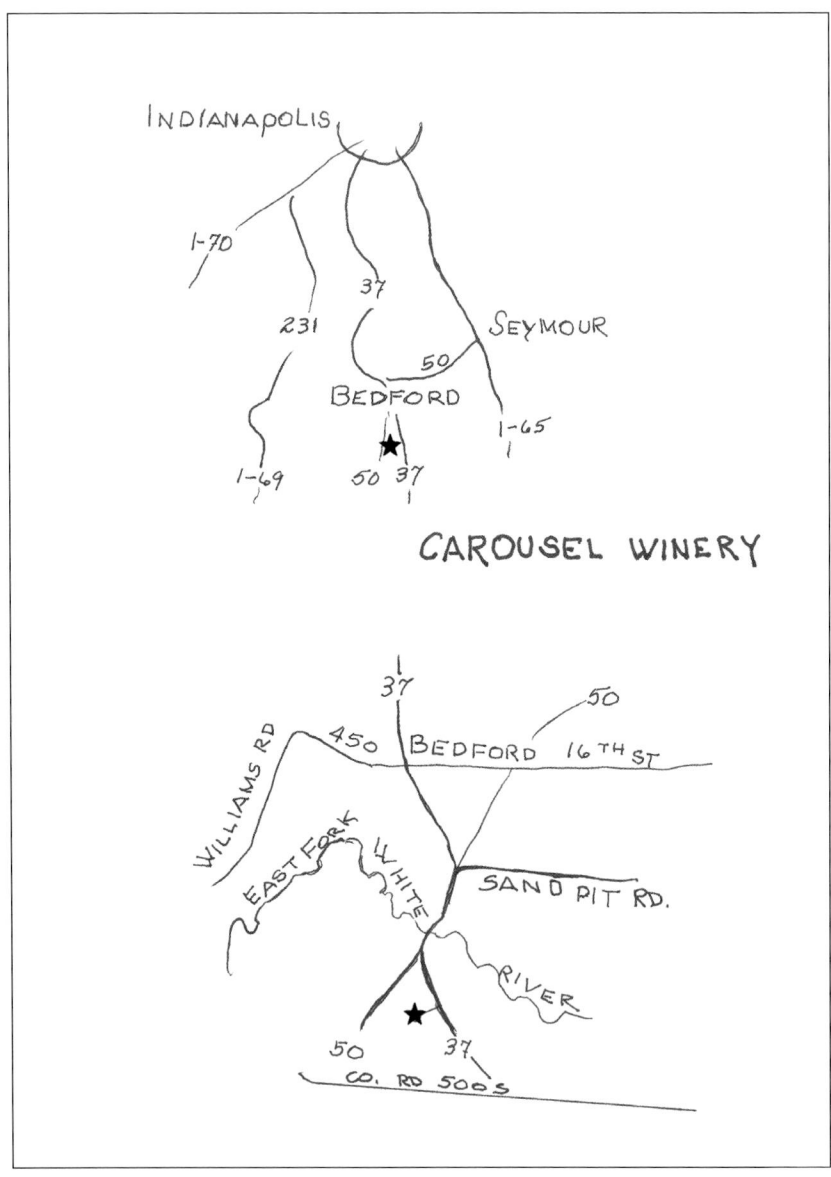

Carousel Winery

6058 Lawrenceport Road
Mitchell, IN 47421
877-A WINE 4 U
812-277-9750
www.carouselwinery.com

This ten-year-old winery, owned and operated by Marion and Sue Wilson, has now been producing award-winning wines for some time, and has emerged as one of the most respected and visible wineries in the state. Carousel can usually be found at wine festivals and wine gatherings—and their knowledgeable and helpful staff will enjoy discussing wine with their patrons. The state-of-the-art production facilities also make Carousel a workhorse in the wine-making community, and they have the labels and awards to show for their hard work and persistence.

Carousel not only appeals to the sweeter side of life with their corpus of fruit wines, including raspberry, cherry and pomegranate—the latter a unique, tart wine loaded with complexity and impact—but also bottles a robust slate of traditional Italian vintages such as Sangiovese, a wine here that, much like a Chianti, pairs well with pasta dishes while also holding its own in the glass.

Likewise, Carousel has always done wonders with Aglianico—a lesser-appreciated Italian grape that uses it plumy and licorice tones to appeal to those offbeat tastes that can't always be described by the Parker scale.

Most of the Carousel wines are also bottled in taller, flowing glass that make this winery's labels stand out on the shelf and in the cellar. And the Carousel theme—found throughout the facility (now in new location)—is reminiscent of the kind of journey one can take with a full slate of tastings. Located near Spring Mill State Park, Carousel also offers an easy access, and visitors will enjoy the décor and awards that are part and parcel of this excellent winery.

For those who enjoy deeper, more complex reds, Carousel has always had a knack with Shiraz and Petite Syrah (the latter of which is currently out of supply). But watch for these vintages as they emerge from production—and don't be surprised by what you might see in future production runs spinning out of the carousel facility. Some of these will age well in the bottle, too—so don't drink them right away. But if you do—no worries. You will appreciate what's in a Carousel bottle.

Information by the Glass

Owners: Marion & Sue Wilson

Satellite Location:
The Village of Winona
1005 E Canal Street
Winona Lake, IN
574-318-1005

Hours:
Monday - Saturday 10 a.m. – 6 p.m., Sunday 12 - 5 p.m.
Closed at times during the winter and on holidays, check for availability during winter

Amenities: Gift Shop, Gourmet Food items, Outdoor Seating

Tastings: Free

Price: $15-$30

Recommendations:
Riesling—this German-style white has a wonderful balance of sweet and dry, tart and fruity, that just creates a marvel in the glass. This one can be paired with Thai foods or can be enjoyed clam chowder or seafood gumbo.

Shadow Dog Port—this old dog is now getting on in years, but if you can find a bottle, it's well worth a taste. You will enjoy a shot glass of Shadow Dog with good friends or perhaps a bowl of Pistachio ice cream.

Activities: Wine Festivals, Jazz

Nearby Attractions: Lake Monroe, Indiana University, Spring Mill State Park

Estate Grapes: Traminette, Cab Franc, Riesling.

Nutty Sherbert

Orange sherbert
Chocolate squares/chopped
Cherries

Chopped pecans
Whipped cream

In sherbert dishes place two dips and top with pecans, chocolate pieces, whipped cream and cherry. Enjoy with Carousel Shadow Dog Port.

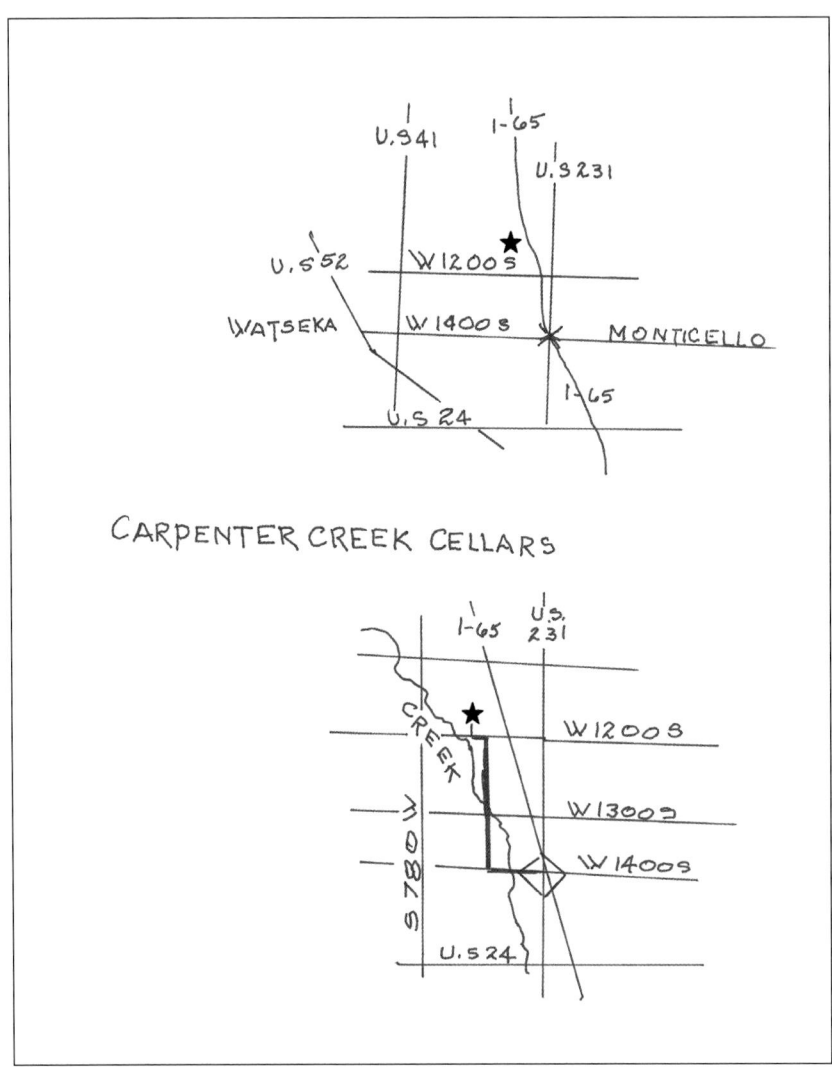

Carpenter Creek Cellars
11144 Jordan Road (780 West)
Remington, IN 47977
219-866-4334
www.carpentercreekcellars.com

This quaint country winery, located on a family farm in Jasper County, has a traditional charm combined with contemporary flair. The half dozen vintages produced here, and served up in a renovated red barn, carry forth the basic spectrum of wines from dry red to white sweet. Labeled in burgundy line drawing on white background, the Carpenter Creek logo features the classic barnyard and hints at the old world tastes produced here (but with new labels on the way).

Opening in March of 2013, Carpenter Creek Cellars is one of the youngest wineries in state, but has continued to bottle tastes both basic and distinctive. Joe McKinney, Ed Courtright, and Randy Rottler have partnered together in the creation of this top-flight winery, each bringing their expertise of the vine and the winemaking art to bear upon the final products that they bottle with pride. Patrons to the CC Cellars will find out how much they know.

As Jasper County's original winery, Carpenter Creek is blazing a trail for sure. Their offerings include Gunny Red and Gunny White—both respective dry blends that have enough complexity and breadth to appeal to both expert and novice connoisseurs. CC Cellars also serves up a nice rose and a Traminette. And the Sunsed Red and Sunset White round out the sweet/dessert wines quite nicely.

Open seven days a week, CC Cellars is a full-service winery with enough pull to bring visitors back, or turn them into regulars. And for those who don't know wines, but are willing to learn, the spacious tasting room in the red barn offers plenty of conversational opportunities with the owners. In addition, the classic picture-postcard charm has its own beauty.

Information by the Glass

Owners: Joe McKinney, Ed Courtright, and Randy Rottler

Hours:
Monday - Saturday 11 a.m. - 6 p.m.
Sunday 12 - 5 p.m.

Amenities: Gift Shop

Tastings: Free

Price: $10-$15

Recommendations:
Gunny Red—a bold, dry blend with a soft tannic backdrop and a hints of raspberry, spice and hickory. Would go quite well with prime rib, filet mignon, or chicken parmesan.

Sunset White—the sweetest of the CC wines, the Sunset has a rich nose and a strong vine taste that would pair well with fresh red pears, dried apricots or aromatic cheeses.

Activities: Special Events and Music

Nearby Attractions: Antique Shopping

Estate Grapes: Chambourcin, Traminette, Cayuga White.

Cedar Creek Winery
3820 Leonard Road
Martinsville, IN 46151
765-342-9000
www.cedarcreekwine.com

If first impressions are indicative of a winery's ambiance and potential, then Cedar Creek in rural Martinsville delivers in style. Opening in October, 2010, Cedar Creek is located among Indiana cornfields, this upscale facility offers a rustic beauty that is rivaled by few wineries in the state. The tasting room, located in a large barn production area, offers a horseshoe bar for guests, with the Cedar Creek wines displayed along the walls. An outdoor seating area provides an additional space for guests to relax with a glass or bottle over a plate of cheese and crackers.

The Cedar Creek wine list includes varietals from dry to sweet, with some intriguing flavors in terms of the way these wines are structured and finished. Cedar Creek wines are built primarily upon old-world varietals such as Merlot, Shiraz, Chardonnay and Savignon Blanc. And Cedar Creek offers an affordable and standard pricing for their varietals (from $11.21 to $13.08 at the time of this printing) that is easy to chart from the moment one looks at the wine list.

Among the finer wines on the Cedar Creek label are the Palamino—a wine made from the Muller-Thurgau grape, which is a semi-dry with the fruitiness of apricot and the tartness of green apple; Serendipity—a marvelous Riesling that could form the centerpiece of a seafood meal; and the Pom-Pourri—a unique blend of Zinfandel and pomegranates that bursting with a rich flavor that sits well on the palate.

Cedar Creek offers free tastings along with ample parking and a large shelter house for parties and gatherings. This is a scenic winery, and can be included in a weekend visit to nearby wineries such as Oliver and Butler (which are just miles south in Bloomington).

Anyone visiting Cedar Creek will enjoy the warmth and ambiance of this place—and the friendly welcome of the helpful and knowledgeable staff.

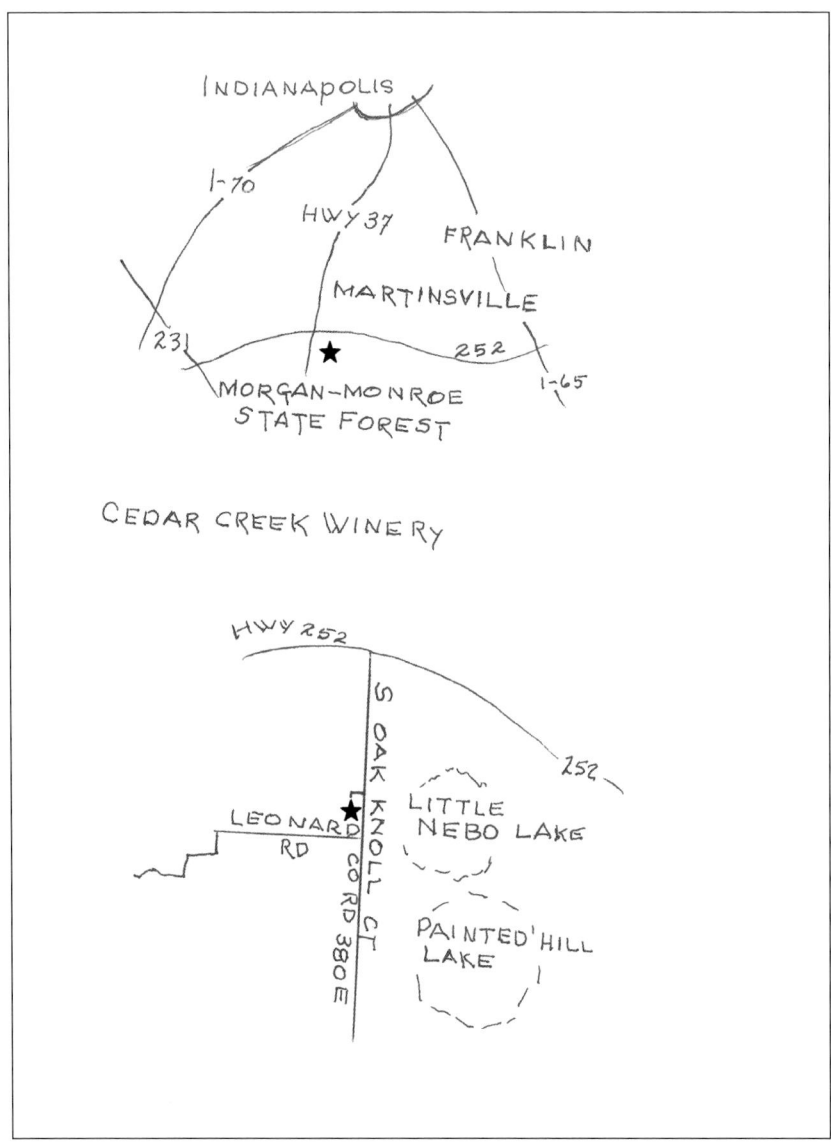

Information by the Glass

Owners: Larry and Donell Elsner

Hours:
Tuesday - Saturday Noon - 7 p.m.
Sunday Noon - 6 p.m.
Closed Mondays

Amenities: Gift Shop, Outdoor Seating, Gazebo, Shelter

Tastings: Free

Price: $12 - $28

Recommendations:
Royal Oak—a Chardonnay with a vanilla oak structure and smooth and appealing finish that would go well with sharp cheeses.

Sweet Sensation—a red port wine rich in orange and chocolate flavors that is perfect for sipping or enjoyed with a bar of dark chocolate or a fruit tray.

Activities: Live Music, Special Events

Nearby Attractions: McCormick Creek State Park

Estate Grapes: Sauvignon Blanc, Muller-Thurgau, Merlot, Malbec.

Grilled King Salmon Garlic-Style

Fresh king salmon fillets
2 pinches garlic powder
Olive oil

2 oz. brown sugar
2 pinches mustard powder

Prepare grill to 350 degrees, line with lightly coated foil (or use birch planks for cooking). Coat each salmon fillet with olive oil, mix other ingredients together and then brush or rub onto the salmon fillets. Grill to personal taste and texture. Serve with fresh tossed salad, fresh organic french fries. Enjoy with Royal Oak Chardonnay.

Chateau de Pique
6361 N CR 760 E
Seymour, IN 47274
812-522-9296
winery@chateaudepique.com
www.chateaudePique.com

Chateau de Pique, located in rural Seymour, Indiana, produces one of the broadest array of labels and varietals in the state. Vintner John McMahan continues to plant the rolling grounds with new varietals that thrive in the unique Midwest climate, and the top labels flowing from this winery are being produced from these on-site vines.

Among Chateau de Pique's better labels include the Cabernet Franc and the Chambourcin—dryer reds with a full-bodied approach that sit well on the tongue and have a heady finish. Likewise, the Traminette and Estate Steuben Rose offer semi-dry options of fruity tones and smoother effect. And for those who prefer sweeter tastes, Chateau de Pique has a broad list of citrusy offerings, including a respectable list of wines that include rhubarb and persimmon (in season).

This winery's parlance into the Hoosier market is also evidenced by the fact that two other tasting rooms are available: one in Clarksville and the other in Indianapolis.

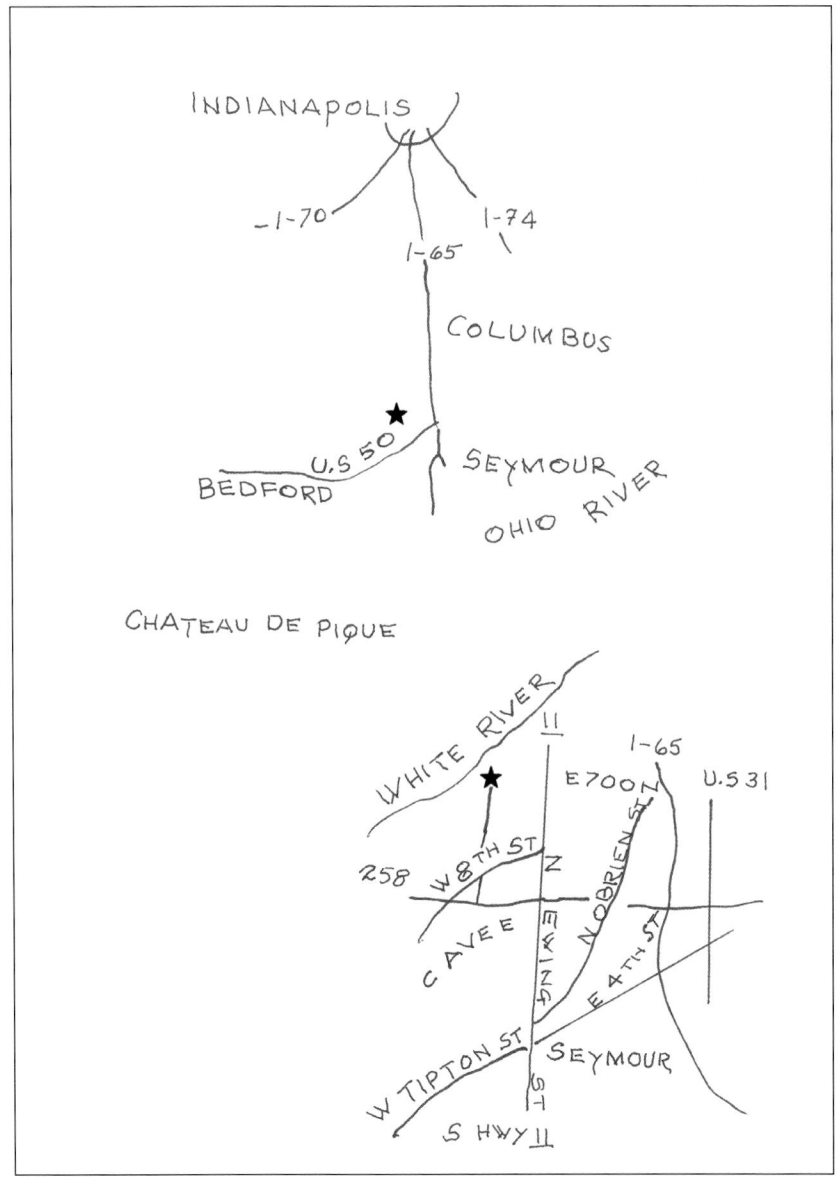

The Seymour location, however, is the place to be. In addition to offering a spacious tasting room—complete with inside table space for nearly 200 people, large screen television, bar and restrooms—the winery is one of the most scenic in the state. A 6000 square foot tent is often erected in the summer months to provide additional space for receptions and gatherings. The grounds are expansive and beautiful, and the Chateau even has an outdoor gathering space and flower gardens that can seat nearly 400 people for outdoor weddings, funerals, and presentations. A tent, available from April through September, can also seat nearly 500 people and be reserved for banquets and larger corporate events. A gazebo in the valley also provides an ample site for family reunions, small group gatherings, and private parties. And the parking at the Chateau? There is no other winery in the state with a more expansive parking lot. One will never feel claustrophobic at the Chateau!

There is no doubt that this winery is still in the early stages of discovery and production and a trip through southern Indiana (the winery is just minutes off of I-65) should include a visit. Brides will find that this location offers one of the best-kept secrets for a wedding site in the greater Seymour area. Businesses and large groups will also find the facilities here to be top-notch.

As this winery matures, both in quality and depth of taste of the labels, the Chateau de Pique will find itself in the upper echelon of Hoosier wineries.

Outdoor Wedding Chapel & Gardens

Information by the Glass

Vintner: John McMahan

Hours: (for Seymour Tasting Room):
Monday - Thursday 11 a.m. - 6 p.m.
Friday & Saturday 11 a.m. - 7 p.m.
Sunday Noon - 6 p.m.

Tasting Rooms:
1305 Veterans Parkway
Clarksville, IN 47129
812-725-7879

6725 E. 82nd Street
Indianapolis, IN 46250
317-578-7413

Amenities: Gift Shop, Banquet Facility, Outdoor Seating, Wedding Chapel

Tastings: Free

Price: $12 - $20

Recommendations:
Dry Riesling—This Riesling is reminiscent of the German tradition and pairs well with white fish and shrimp cocktail.

Chambourcin—a delightful rendition of an Indiana varietal, but here fruity with some tannins. Pair this Chambourcin with spicy rice dishes or Mexican cuisine.

Ice Wine (in season and when available)

Activities: Large Events, Concerts, Corporate Outings, Catering

Estate Grapes: Chardonel, Riesling, Cab Franc, Chambourcin, Merlot, Syrah, Steuben, Vignoles, Traminette.

Summer Shrimp Salad

1 pound shrimp	1 pound corkscrew pasta (cooked weight)
Can of sliced black olives	½ cup freshly diced tomatoes
Olive oil	Balsamic vinegar

In separate pans boil shrimp and pasta to tenderness desired. Add together in large mixing bowl along with olives and tomatoes. Sprinkle with olive oil and vinegar to taste preference. Add salt and freshly ground pepper. Serve with Dry Riesling.

Indiana Wineries: The Ultimate Guide to Wine in Indiana

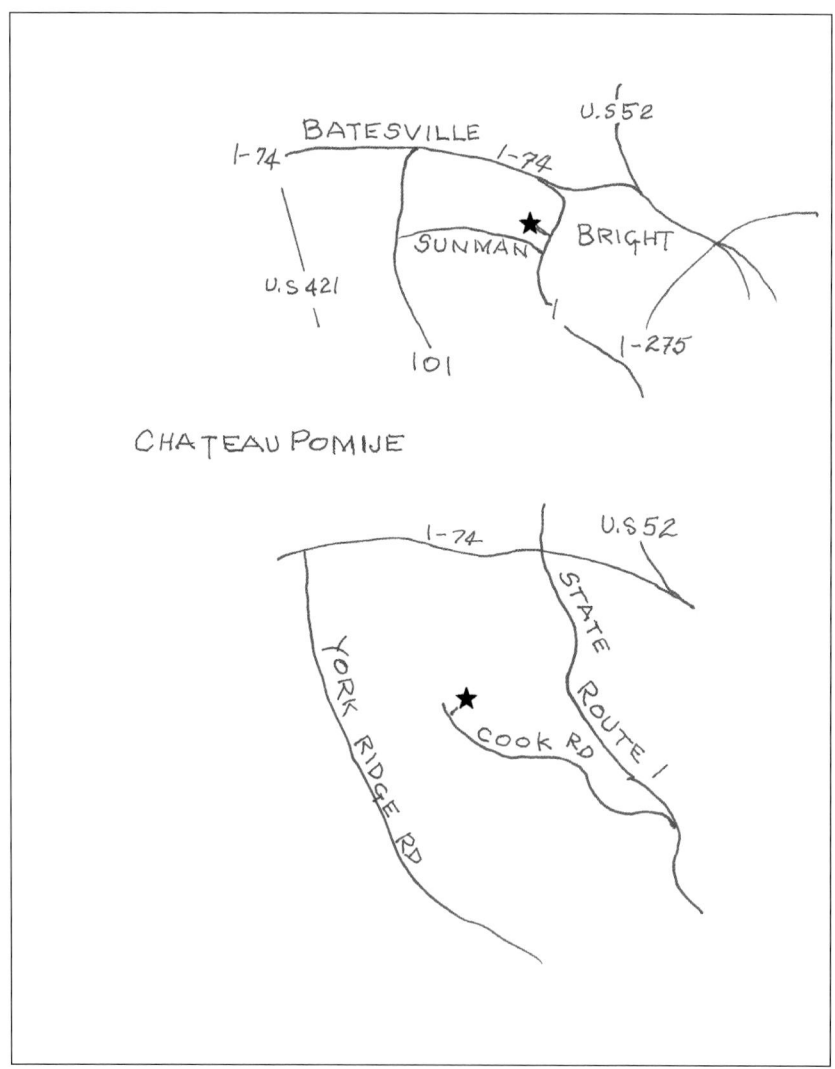

CHATEAU POMIJE

Chateau Pomije Winery
25043 Jacobs Road
Guilford, IN 47022
1-800-791-WINE
812-623-3332
www.cpwinery.com

This south-eastern Indiana winery if one of the best-kept secrets in the Hoosier state. The Chateau, dedicated to a Czechoslovakian family member (and pronounced Pom-ee-aye) features an upscale old-world chateau with banquet facility, multiple dining halls, a back deck that overlooks water and the beautifully crafted vineyards, and one of the most spacious tasting bars you'll find anywhere. The Pomije vineyard is the largest of its kind in the eastern portion of the state—with some forty-seven acres of varietals grown and cultivated for their own production—and over a hundred acres total on the estate. The chateau is a favorite destination for bridal parties, as the winery plays host to over thirty weddings a year—and large events at that!—and because of its proximity to the Ohio border and Cincinnati, this site is also host to many corporate banquets and leadership conferences.

As for the wines—Chateau Pomije is a premier estate winery. But the breadth and depth of the wine experience here is astounding. These Indiana-grown varietals are coupled with several wines imported from a sister Chateau in Macedonia, bottled under a separate label, thus providing one of the most unique wine expressions found in the Midwest.

Chateau Pomije features a full-slate of dry and sweet wines, as well as their signature semi-sweet Steuben and one of the best blueberry wines in the fruit category. Pomije also has ice wine and several signature blends such as the Sunset Crush (blend of Indiana white varietal grapes) and Blush—a sweet blend of Concord, Steuben, and Niagara grapes.

But the Chateau's most promising wines are also some of the most unique among Indiana wine-makers.

Produced in the old world winemaking style, the Vranac (a grape usually not found outside of the Macedonia region), Merlot and Cabernet Sauvignon offer a European presentation in aroma, depth and taste—and hold up very well among the heavier-bodied wines. The Cab grown on the estate—as with all Indiana-grown Cabs—is bold and dry as one would expect, but the shorter growing season doesn't allow the fruit to gain the body and tannins evidenced in a California Cab. The Chateau Pomije Cab is wonderfully rich, with an excellent nose, and offers yet another expression of this King of Wines. Those looking for a fine Indiana-produced Cab will discover one of the best at Chateau Pomije.

From the sweet or semi-sweet varietals, look for the Nectar Kiss or the Late Harvest Ice wine. For semi-dry whites, the Domain Reserve holds promise as a barrel fermented French hybrid that is comparable in taste to some Chardonnays. Likewise, the Riesling has a smooth finish and just a hint of sweetness while maintaining some of the German-cousin depth that will make it a favorite.

For lovers of bold reds, again the Vranac is a must-taste—a grape with an earthy nose and tannin finish that will be unlike anything else in Indiana. And the homegrown Cabernet Sauvignon has hints of chocolate and cherry and a better-than-average oakiness, for those who enjoy a smoky finish. And the Pinot Noir is a superb table wine that is going to go well with a pasta dish or red meat.

As noted earlier, the Chateau is a destination—a place where visitors can spend time in an upscale environment, relax, and even enjoy good food. A rundown of the full Pomije menu is not possible here, but patrons can rest assured that they will come away with a fine dining experience and can certainly find something from among the large salads, and entrees such as Ribeye steaks and Surf-n-Turf, to make their trip worthwhile. Prices range from $15 to $25 for the entrees and, paired with a favorite CP wine, an evening on the Chateau isn't soon forgotten.

Likewise, bridal parties, corporate events, reunions, and family outings can all be accommodated in this spacious villa-like setting, and anyone who enjoys hiking or exploration will not be disappointed in the options available both on and off grounds.

Plan to visit to Chateau Pomije.

Chateau Thomas Winery
6291 Cambridge Way
Plainfield, IN 46168
317-837-9436
800-761-WINE
www.chateauthomas.com

The Chateau Thomas Winery is one of the premier Indiana wineries—and also a leader in the Hoosier wine-making community. Dr. Thomas—founder and wine producer—has been well-known throughout the state for his expertise, leadership and his excellent wines for over twenty-five years. Likewise, the Chateau Thomas tasting room in Plainfield sports a large banquet facility, frequent concerts, and an eclectic and beautiful array of popular wines. Other tasting rooms (such as the one in Fishers) gives CTW a broader presence and their wines have consistently won state and international competitions.

As far as the wines go, Chateau Thomas offers everything from dry whites such as Chardonnay and Sauvignon Blanc to dry reds such as Merlot and Syrah to nearly a dozen sweet wines, along with port and sherry. So . . . Chateau Thomas will always have a varietal for every taste and one can also find rare vintages such as old vine Carignane in the waiting.

Because of its size, the main Chateau Thomas tasting room is also reminiscent of the top Napa Valley wineries, and there are frequent large crowds that make their way to Plainfield for music, special events, and even cooking classes.

Dr. Thomas is also well-known for his private cellar, and the wine classes offered by Chateau Thomas are going to be some of the premier learning opportunities for wine connoisseurs. Classes and times are listed online, as well as the full wine list.

For the red wine lover, don't overlook the Chateau Thomas Zinfandel or the Petite Syrah—a real treat. And one cannot go wrong with the buttery Chardonnay that Thomas produces or the Vintage Port (for a cold winter evening). And for those who simply need a dessert wine that won't cramp the pocketbook, how about taking home a bottle of Reisling or some late harvest Zinfandel?

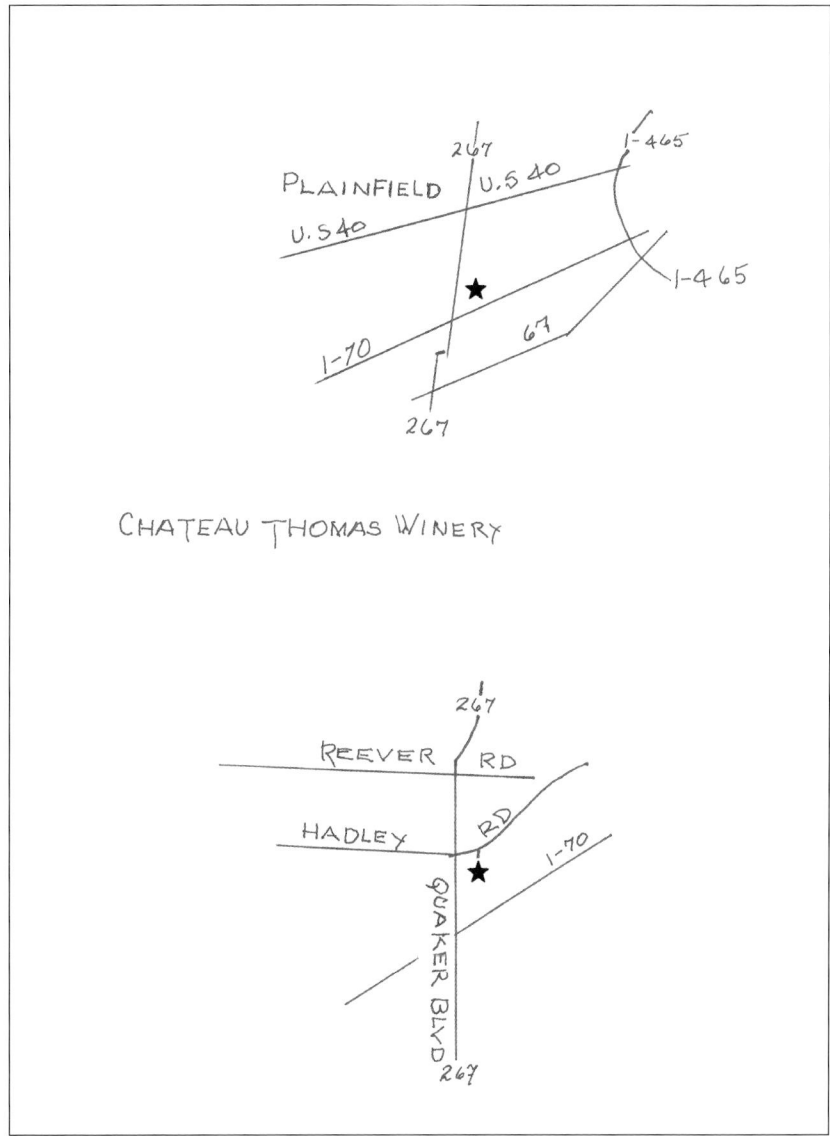

Essentially, Thomas produces vintages of the traditional varietals, but has in recent years also created new niche markets through their "Skinny" line of wines (low-cal, no-sugar options) and their Abe Martin wines (which are bottled in glass jugs and offer several varieties of fruit vintage). The Chateau Thomas winery and production facility in Plainfield is a spacious building that also sports one of the largest wine-related gift shops in the state.

In addition, Chateau Thomas offers private wine tastings, barrel tastings (where the production facility can be toured and vintages can be tasted "in-process" of ageing), and a monthly wine club. The CT website carries the most up-to-date information and, because CT purchases much of their grapes from California, the vintages do change from time to time.

Chateau Thomas is also visible at most of the major wine festivals throughout the state, and their staff is eager to answer your questions about wine. The tasting room in Plainfield is easily accessible from the interstate (I-70) and there are ample restaurants and entertainment in the greater Indianapolis area if one is looking for a day-trip or a full afternoon of sight-seeing.

Information by the Glass

Founder & Owner: Dr. Charles Thomas

Other Locations:
Coachlight Square
225 S. Van Buren Street
Nashville, IN 47448
812-988-8500

Fishers, Indiana show room

Hours:
Monday - Thursday 10 a.m. - 9 p.m.
Friday & Saturday 10 a.m. - 10 p.m.
Sunday Noon - 7 p.m.

Amenities: Gift Shop, Banquet Room

Tastings: Free

Price: $15 - $30

Recommendations:
Chateau Big Red—a signature wine with deep, lasting undertones of blackberry and oak

Sangiovese—an old world Italian wine perfect for pairing with pasta dishes

Zinfandel—always a popular bold vintage with Thomas, peppery but not as full as the Cabernet Sauvignon, and this one goes well with cheese pizza.

Vintage Port—a bottle that will stay with you through winter and warm the heart as well as the tongue

Activities: Tours for large groups, Wine appreciation classes, live music, festivals

Nearby Attractions: Indianapolis Restaurants, Indianapolis Airport, Indianapolis 500 Speedway

Estate Grapes: Cabernet Sauvignon, Merlot, Chambourcin, Syrah.

Big Bend Lemon Pasta Parmesan

1 pound ziti pasta (cooked weight)
1 lemon
Oregano, salt, pepper, basil

Fresh Parmesan cheese
½ cup cream

Cook pasta to taste and then in large mixing bowl add cream sauce that has been prepared in a pan by mixing cream, juice of one lemon, freshly grated parmesan and spices to taste. Pour over pasta and serve with Sangiovese.

Coal Creek Cellars Winery
3573 U.S. Highway 136
Crawfordsville, IN 47933
765-362-3634
www.coalcreek.whg-dev2.com/

When people think of Indiana they frequently picture cornfields, countryside, and brilliant red barns. If this is the picture you have of a Hoosier winery, then you won't be disappointed in Coal Creek Cellars. This winery is one of the most traditional and majestic (in its simplicity) that one is going to encounter anywhere in the state. And as a fairly new winery on the scene, Coal Creek Cellars is all the more impressive.

Driving along U.S. highway 136 outside of Crawfordsville the red barn can't be missed. Ample parking and an inviting back deck and fireplace make this winery a warm place to visit, and patrons will also find the friendliness of the Coal Creek staff all the more warming. The quaint showroom and tasting bar are just perfect for this setting and once the tasting begins, folks will be impressed with the array of offerings that this winery offers.

Coal Creek Cellars currently has fifteen beautiful wines on its list, and these include both typical Indiana grapes such as Chambourcin, Cayuga White, Norton, Traminette, and Vidal Blanc as well as unique labels featuring Vignoles, Merlot and Petite Syrah.

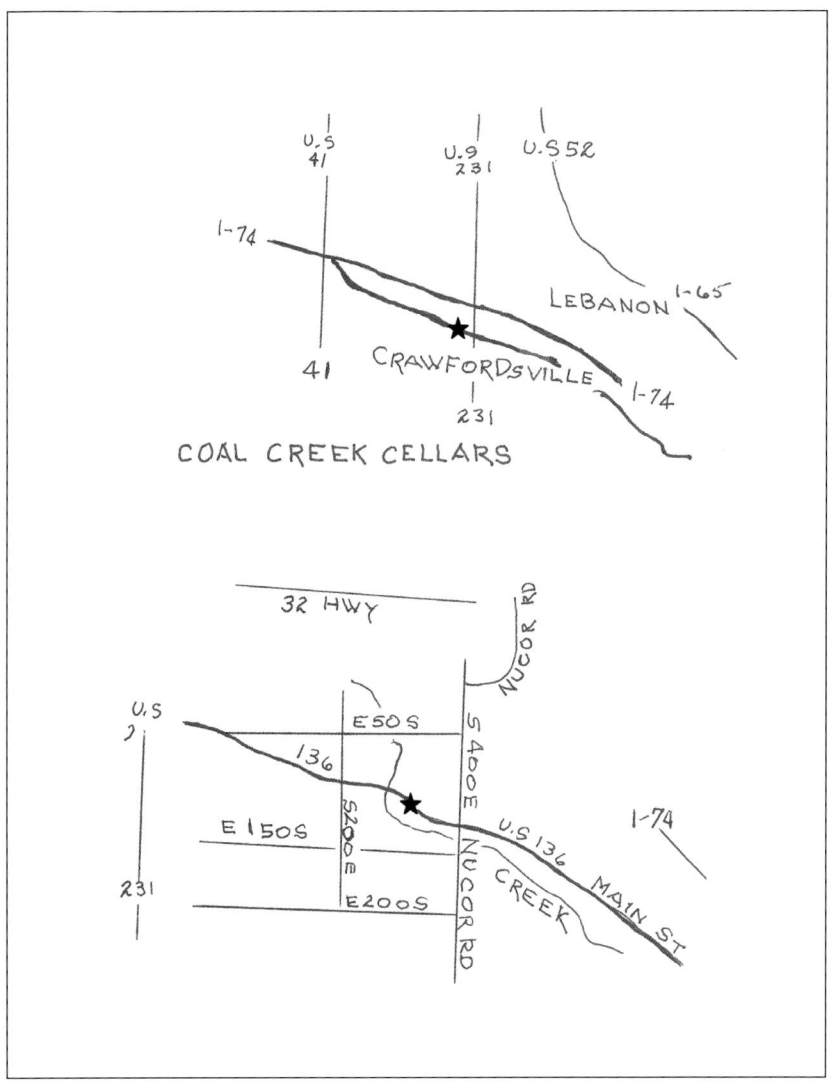

This estate winery is a relaxing destination, and visitors are bound to take away a bottle or two of nice wine. Among the best here one can't go wrong with the Sweet Serenity—a specialty blend that Coal Creek Cellars presents in a fruity, peachy delight. Visitors may also enjoy one of the three red/blush blends that this winery produces.

Driving west on I-74 out of Indianapolis, the winery is not far off of the interstate on 136. But beware, your quick visit may turn into a leisurely stay . . . especially if the sun is bright and the back deck is vacant.

Information by the Glass

Hours: call ahead

Amenities: Parking, back deck, fireplace

Tastings: Free

Price: $12.95 - $14.95

Recommendations:
Petite Syrah—one of the deepest reds, almost inky in color, Coal Creek Cellars offers this one aged in oak barrels and the presentation is peppery with notes of raspberry on the tongue.

Riesling—a traditional German white, here as a semi-dry, semi-sweet presentation with hints of peach and apricot. Pair it with fish or chill and enjoy with a fresh fruit plate.

Country Heritage Winery & Vineyard
0185 CR 68
LaOtto, IN 46763
260-637-2980
www.CountryHeritageWinery.com

Jeremy and Jennifer Lutter, owners of Country Heritage Winery & Vineyards, have created a first-rate estate winery and facility just west of Fort Wayne. With winemaker, Kevin Geeting at the helm and the barrel, this fine winery is already making waves in just its fifth year of full-scale operation. The production facility here is one of the finest anywhere in the state, and the bar area and tasting room can accommodate bus-loads of guests. And guest won't be disappointed.

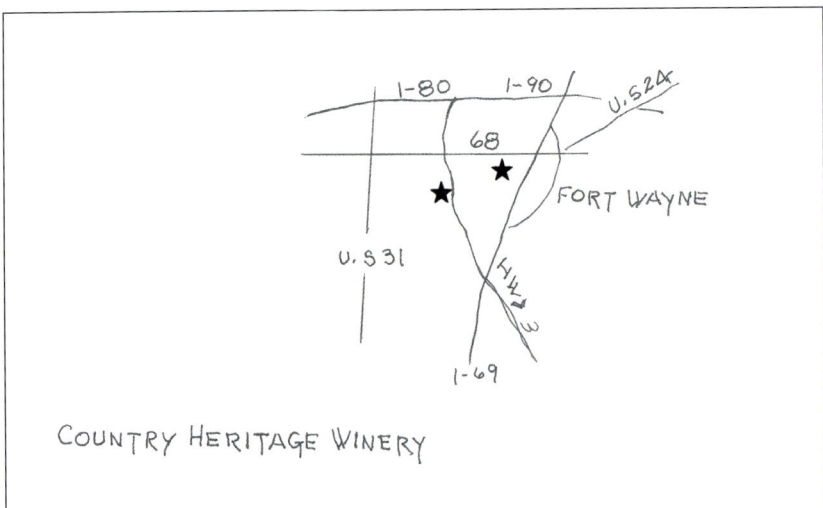

First, driving into the winery, a person will be impressed by the vineyards—and not just their proximity to the tasting room, but the acreage as well. All told, CH has more than 20 acres of Indiana varietals including Cayuga White, Traminette, Vignoles, LaCrescent, Marechal Foch, Marquette, Concord, and Norton. The winery also brings in grapes from California to produce some of their wonderfully balanced and deep reds, including Cabernet, Zinfandel and Shiraz, and among the whites, grapes from Columbia Valley and the Finger Lakes area of New York to produce some nicely textured sweet and dry Chardonnay and Riesling. You won't find any bad wines at Country Heritage—and the staff is superb.

The tasting room also features options for cheese and crackers and some light fare for those guests who want to make a light lunch or just an afternoon get-away. And there is plenty of wide-open space here for hiking or a tour of the grounds. Outdoor patio seating under a large gazebo makes this a fantastic spring and summer destination, too. Watch a sunset.

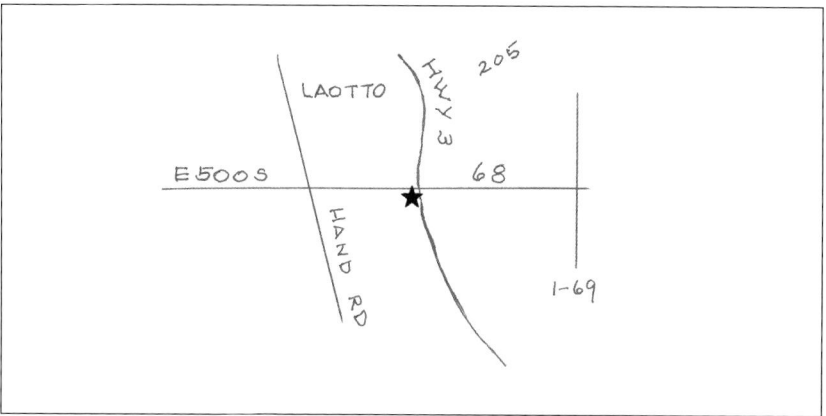

The Country Heritage Vignoles has a citrusy zest that is bold enough to stand up on its own and the Proprietor's Reserve (a blend of Cab and Merlot) is likely CH's top barrel-produced red, a wine that has the depth and balance that a fine wine should have. Also, try the Fall Harvest blend when it is in season—this one a combo of Vignoles, Catawba, and Meade. This one is tasty and complex and has that seasonal flair to it that reminds one of the approaching winter—but in a good way.

For those who like sweet wines—Country Heritage has a full lineup. The Raspberry and Blueberry wines here are excellent, and as Kevin Geeting works his magic, he likes to remind guests that great fruits make great wines—and Country Heritage begins with the best fruits straight from the farm. And when its available, don't overlook the ice wine. This wine, made from the Vidal Blanc grapes, can be over-the-top tasty, and you won't mind the price for the pleasure this one offers.

Again, another Hoosier winery that is easy to find—but more importantly—fun to taste.

Information by the Glass

Owners: Jeremy and Jennifer Lutter

Hours:
Monday - Saturday 11 a.m. - 7 p.m.
Sunday 10 a.m. - 6 p.m.

Amenities: Gift Shop, Outdoor Seating, Hiking Trails

Tastings: Free

Price: $12 - $20

Recommendations:
Cranberry-Riesling—a very unique blend that, chilled, is refreshing and satisfying.

Zinfandel—a peppery and spicy red with medium body that goes well with sauce dishes. Plum aroma gives this one a nice finish also.
Proprietor's Reserve

Honey Mead—one of the few in the state to produce this old-world honey wine.

Activities: Live Music, Restaurant

Nearby Attractions: Chain O'Lakes State Park, Ft. Wayne Restaurants

Estate Grapes: Cayuga White, Traminette, Vignoles, LaCrescent, Marechal Foch, Marquette, Concord, Norton.

Christmas Fudge

2 cups sugar
3 tablespoons cocoa
½ cup corn syrup
Salt

½ cup milnot
1 teaspoon vanilla extract
2 tablespoons butter

Mix ingredients together in large pan over low heat, stirring constantly. Add vanilla and butter, mix again, then allow to cool for 5 minutes. Stir fudge until it browns and then pour into a buttered glass pan. Allow to set until hard or place in the fridge. Serve with Cranberry-Riesling.

Country Moon Winery
16222 Prairie Baptist Road
Noblesville, IN 46060
317-773-7942
www.countrymoonwinery.com

The Country Moon Winery is still a work-in-progress—but what Brian and Becky Harger have done with their property, so far, reads like a storybook. They have worked for the past decade planting a number of varietals on this picturesque landscape and are now producing four sweet wines labeled simply as:

    Apple Spice (apple and cinnamon notes)
    Brambleberry (a sweet semi-red, blush)
    Native Harvest (made from American Concord)
    LaCrescent (their signature wine, semi-sweet made from a
    French hybrid grape)

Country Moon is by appointment only—but the grounds offer plenty of scenery with mature trees, a lush lawn, and a long-view of acres of vineyard in various states of growth. A state-of-the-art production facility may also become a gift shop and restaurant in the near future—so visit the Country Moon web site to catch up on the latest news, developments, and offerings from this up-and-coming winery.

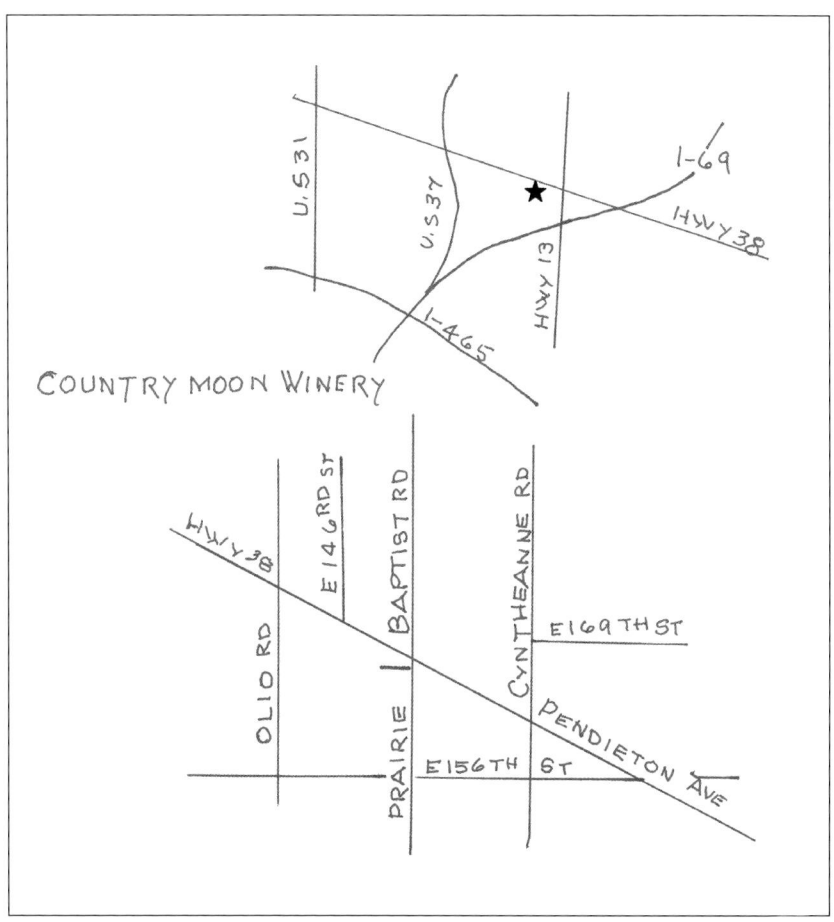

Information by the Glass

Owners: Brian & Rebecca Harger

Hours:
Open by Appointment (call ahead for your own private tour)
Summer Saturday Hours: 1 - 7 p.m.

Amenities: Outdoor Seating

Tastings: Free

Price: $12 - $15

Recommendations:
Concord—The Country Moon Concord wine packs a summer punch, a deft taste of this traditional sweet grape.

Activities: Private wine tastings, campfires, personalized special event packages

Nearby Attractions: Historic Hamilton County Courthouse, Conner Prairie

Estate Grapes: La Crescent, Concord, Prairie Star, Cynthiana, Prairie Red.

Daniel's Vineyard
9061 North 700 West
McCordsville, IN 46055
877-994-7273
www.danielsvineyard.com

At the time of the writing of this book, Daniel's Vineyard—located in McCordsville near the Geist Reservoir—was preparing for their first grape harvest. What makes this harvest so impressive is the time and investment given to the 14,000 vines (80 acres) and 8 varietals of grapes, making Daniel's Vineyard one of the largest in the state.

The eight varietals here in play are Cabernet Franc, Catawba, Chambourcin, Concord, Marquette, Noiret, Traminette, and Vidal Blanc. Check out the Daniel's Vineyard website for job postings and special events. If the Daniel's website is indicative of the quality of the wines they hope to produce . . . well, the Hoosier state is in for a treat.

Let's also anticipate that Daniel's Vineyard will soon become a first-class winery.

Daniel's Vineyard—keep up the good work.

Easley Winery
205 North College Avenue
Indianapolis, IN 46202
317-636-4516
www.easleywinery.com

The Easley Winery, along with select few such as Oliver, Butler, Huber and Thomas, is among the oldest and most influential wineries in the state. Established in 1974, Easley is located in the heart of Indianapolis, but contracts with grape producers around the state and in other regions of the country to create a broad and expansive lineup of wines. This winery, along with six other wineries in the Indianapolis area, is part of the Indy Wine Trail.

Tastings at Easley are seven for $5—and visitors will have no problem enjoying the variety of dry to sweet in the spacious tasting room or outdoor patio/deck. Parking is also located across the street on College Avenue.

Because of Easley's history and expertise, visitors will also discover a wide range of choices. For example, Easley commonly sports two Cabernet Sauvignon options as well as two Chardonnays. These reserve options are usually of a deeper and richer quality—or barrel aged. The Easley Riesling is a marvelous dry wine with a crisp finish with apple blossom aromas and hints of peach. And a sweeter Riesling, made from grapes grown in Michigan, has the quality of a fine summer blush that could be enjoyed with barbeque on the grill.

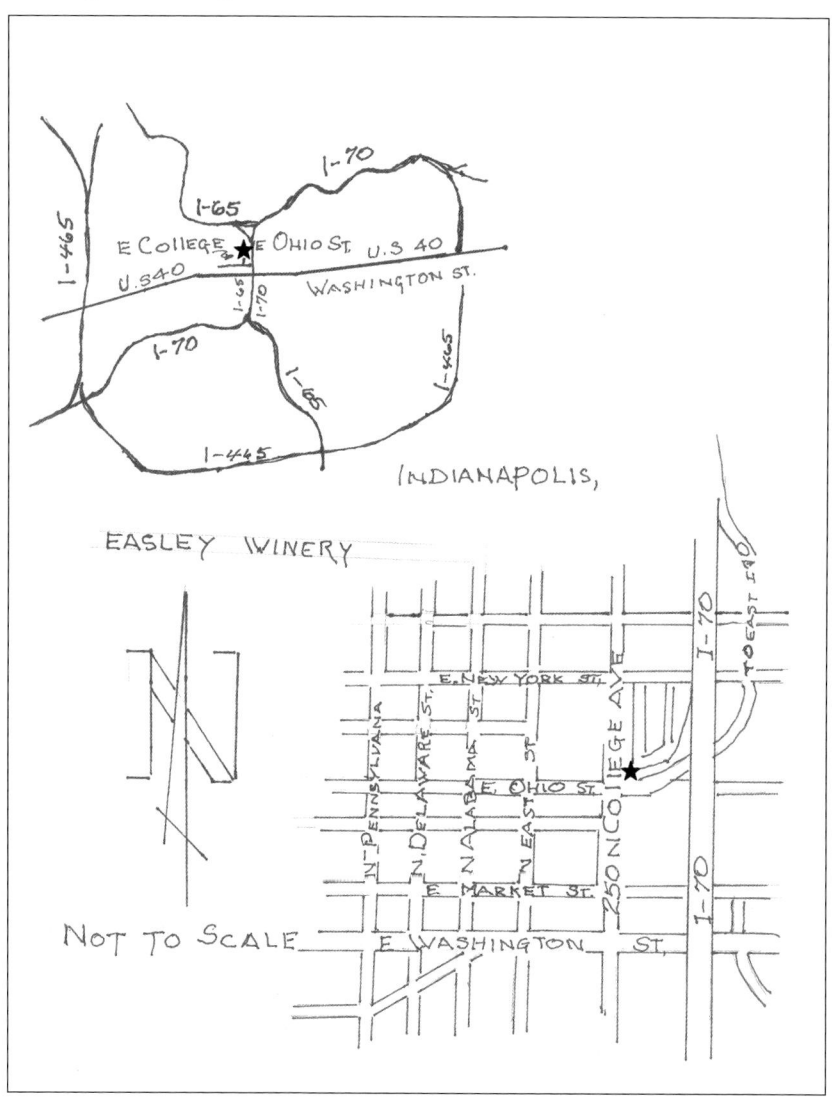

Among the Indiana varietals, the Chambourcin holds up well against the competition, and the Easley Traminette of 2013 was selected as the state's best by the Indy International Wine Competition. This Traminette has a deep floral aroma and has a fruity, honeysuckle flavor. And for sweet wine drinkers, the Sweet Barrel White and the Mulled Wine, with cinnamon and apple flavors, is one to save for a cold winter night.

Easley is also known for the popular Reggae blends: white, blush and red. These award-winning wines are just fun to drink and all three are bursting with fruit flavors. Topping off the Easley lineup are some fantastic sparkling wines, including a non-alcoholic variety.

Anyone visiting the Easley tasting room will also receive expert wine advice—and inside the expansive facility is a spacious party room and one of the largest wine gift shops in the state. This gift shop is an excellent place to find wine accessories, décor, and signage. A back room at the winery also inventories the largest and best-supplied home wine-making products in the state. Anyone who enjoys making wine at home—or enjoys a wine-making class—can't go wrong with the Easley touch. Same holds for home brew products.

Easley wines can be found in many Indy-area restaurants and supermarkets. The Easley label is beautiful and distinctive and whether the taste is red or white, dry or sweet, anyone is certain to discover a varietal that will offer an appreciation for the history and potential this winery has to offer.

Information by the Glass

Owners: The Easley family

Hours: Monday - Friday 11 a.m. - 6 p.m.
Saturday 9 a.m. - 6 p.m.
Sunday 12 p.m. - 4 p.m.

Amenities: Gift Shop, Wine Making Store, Outdoor Seating

Tastings: 7 for $5

Price: $10 - $20

Recommendations:
Cabernet Sauvignon Reserve—white oak aged with a hint of smokiness, pairs well with meat dishes and barbeque

Reggae Blush—an amazing citrus blend that, chilled, pairs well with goat cheese and crackers or cantaloupe.

Indiana Champaign—made from Traminette and Cayuga grapes, this is a smooth blend that would make a perfect wedding reception toast.

Activities: Wine Appreciation Nights, Workshops, Music

Nearby Attractions: Circle Center, Sun King Brewery, Indianapolis Restaurants

Estate Grapes: Traminette, Cayuga, Cabernet Sauvignon, Chardonnay, Chambourcin.

Ranch-Style Burgers

Ground beef   1-2 packages of dry ranch dressing mix
Salt, pepper

Mix ground beef, ranch dressing mix, salt and pepper thoroughly in a large mix bowl. Create beef patties to personal size/preference and grill to taste. Serve on buns with fresh tomatoes, lettuce, and Cabernet Sauvignon.

Ertel Cellars Winery

3794 E County Road 1100 North
Batesville, IN 47006
812-933-1500
www.ertelcellarswinery.com

Certain Indiana wineries have taken on a larger presence at wine fairs, tours, and word-of-mouth, and Ertel is one winery that many people have heard about. No doubt Ertel has produced wines of such reputation, and marketed themselves well, that this winery has a pull far beyond the Batesville area. In fact, there are many people from the Indianapolis area who make the trek east down Interstate 74 in order to have dinner at this Chateau-like restaurant/winery.

Ertel's list is full enough that patrons will discover a bottle for any taste. Reds range from the king Cabernet to Franc to Shiraz and Ertel also offers a number of Indiana varietals that are produced to fine quality.

Among the white varietals, the Vidal Blanc is a keeper—and this one has a remarkable taste of sweet grass and honey that will pair well with whitefish, scallops, or a fresh salad . . . all of which can be had in the gourmet restaurant that is so much a part of the Ertel Winery experience.

Ertel's grounds make the wine tasting experience all the more pleasant, as one can look out over the many acres of rolling vineyard, enjoy the ample blacktop parking upon entry, and then have no problem finding a place at the spacious tasting bar. The restaurant here is an incredible dining experience to boot. And anyone making the drive to Batesville will want to visit for a dinner to make the visit complete.

Indiana Wineries: The Ultimate Guide to Wine in Indiana

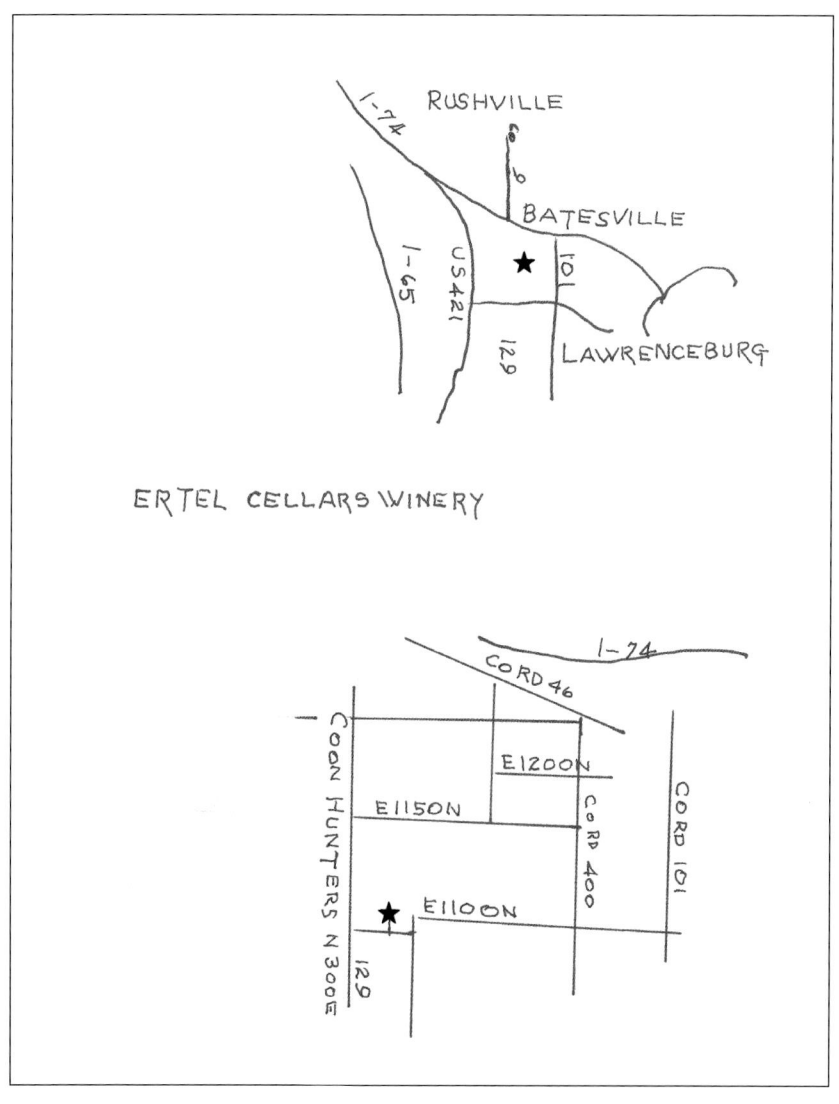

Information by the Glass

Owners: Ertel Family

Hours: (for tasting room only):
Wednesday & Thursday 11 a.m. - 8 p.m.
Friday & Saturday 11 a.m. - 10 p.m.
Sunday 11 a.m. - 8 p.m.

Amenities: Restaurant, Outdoor Seating, Banquet Rooms

Tastings: Free

Price: $14 - $25

Recommendations:
Vidal Blanc—a semi-sweet wine, moderately priced, with grapefruit and pasture-like undertones. Pairs well with fish and salad.

Cabernet Sauvignon—for an Indiana-grown, a decent offering—dry, bold, a hint of oak and smoke.

Activities: Festivals, Live Music, Hayrides

Nearby Attractions: Brookville Lake, Versailles State Park

Estate Grapes: Marechal Foch, Vidal Blanc, Vignoles, Traminette, Steuben, Catawba, Chambourcin.

Cauliflower Toss

Small head of cauliflower
2 sliced scallions
Ranch salad dressing
Salt, pepper, dill

¼ cup sliced radishes
½ pound bacon
¼ cup sour cream

Fry bacon until crispy, place on paper towel to dry. Crumble. Tear cauliflower head into bit sized pieces, add scallions, radishes, sour cream and salad dressing in large mixing bowl. Mix and add salt, pepper, dill to taste. Add bacon bits. Serve with Vidal Blanc.

Fiekert's Homestead Wines
412 South High Street
Rising Sun, IN 47040
812-551-5122
www.risingsunwine.com

Fiekert's Homestead Wines is, indeed, a homestead winery. Located in a 104 year old home in the heart of Rising Sun, this winery has made a name for itself through its superb hospitality (call the Fiekert residence to visit the winery any time), its personalized labels, and the wines. The Fiekert labels are produced from grapes and juices sourced locally and from around the world—which also gives this winery something of an international flair.

But visitors will primarily receive personalized attention, a friendly atmosphere, and of course, a homey touch when they arrive.

Among the Fiekert wine list one can find popular varietals such as Pinot Grigio, Chardonnay, Cabernet Sauvignon, and Merlot. And the winery also makes a fine array of fruit blends accompanying many of these grape varietals. As such, the Fiekert fruit wines are something of an anomaly in state, and here one can find tasty blends such as White Cranberry Pinot Gris, Pomegranate Zinfandel, and Black Raspberry Merlot.

The wine labeling feature at Fiekert's is a popular attraction, too. Here's how it works. Create your own personalized label, purchase a case (of 12), and the labeling is free. Parties and special events are an opportunity to add your own label to the mix—or perhaps serve as a gift idea.

Fiekert's Homestead Wines is the only wine in the state operating out of a living room—and folks who visit will find a warm welcome here. Drop by often.

Indiana Wineries: The Ultimate Guide to Wine in Indiana

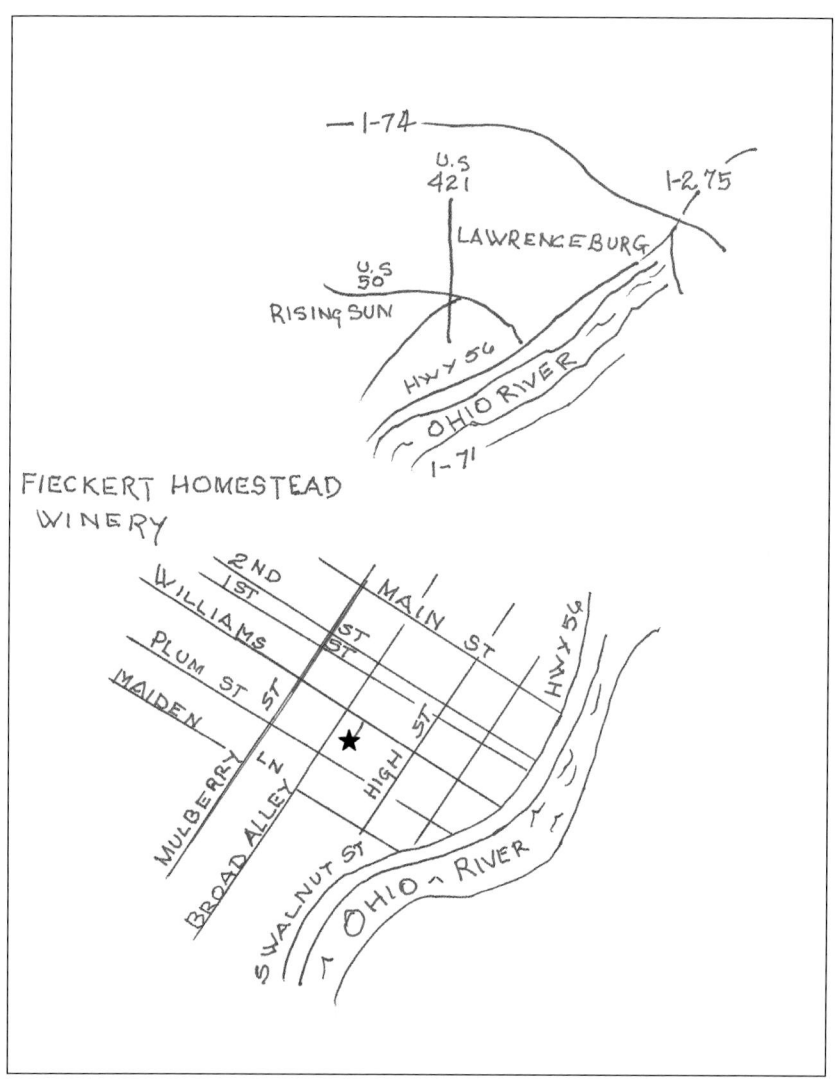

Information by the Glass

Owners: Fiekert Family

Hours: Call ahead for your personalized time

Tastings: Free

Price: $15

Recommendations:
Green Apple Riesling—a tart wine with a semi-sweet expression makes this one perfect for pairing with summer fruit salads or with buttery white fish.

Riesling Ice Style—another great ice wine that doesn't overpower with sweetness.

Activities: Personal tastings

Nearby Attractions: Rising Sun Casino.

French Lick Winery
P.O. Box 169
French Lick, IN 47432
812-936-2293
888-494-6380
www.frenchlickwinery.com

If small town America is a draw for Hoosier travelers, then French Lick is one of those small towns of stand-out quality. Not only will visitors find a rich history in the French Lick Springs Resort, and the nearby West Baden Resort, but they can also treat themselves to some fine wine and cuisine at The French Lick Winery.

This southern Indiana winery—owned and operated by the John & Kim Doty family—is a quality establishment across the board. The winery not only features a restaurant (and spacious parking), but also a fully-staffed tasting bar and a wide array of wines. The French Lick label is one of those that Hoosiers can often find in area supermarkets as well—and with the prominent French Lick moniker and grape cluster on the label, it's one that wine lovers are sure to remember.

One can easily spend a few hours at this winery, which also includes a gift shop complete with unique wine-related accessories—but The French Lick Winery can also be one part of a weekend destination that could include a stay in a resort, a bed and breakfast, or an afternoon of antiquing. But if wine is the reason for this trip south, wine lovers will not be disappointed.

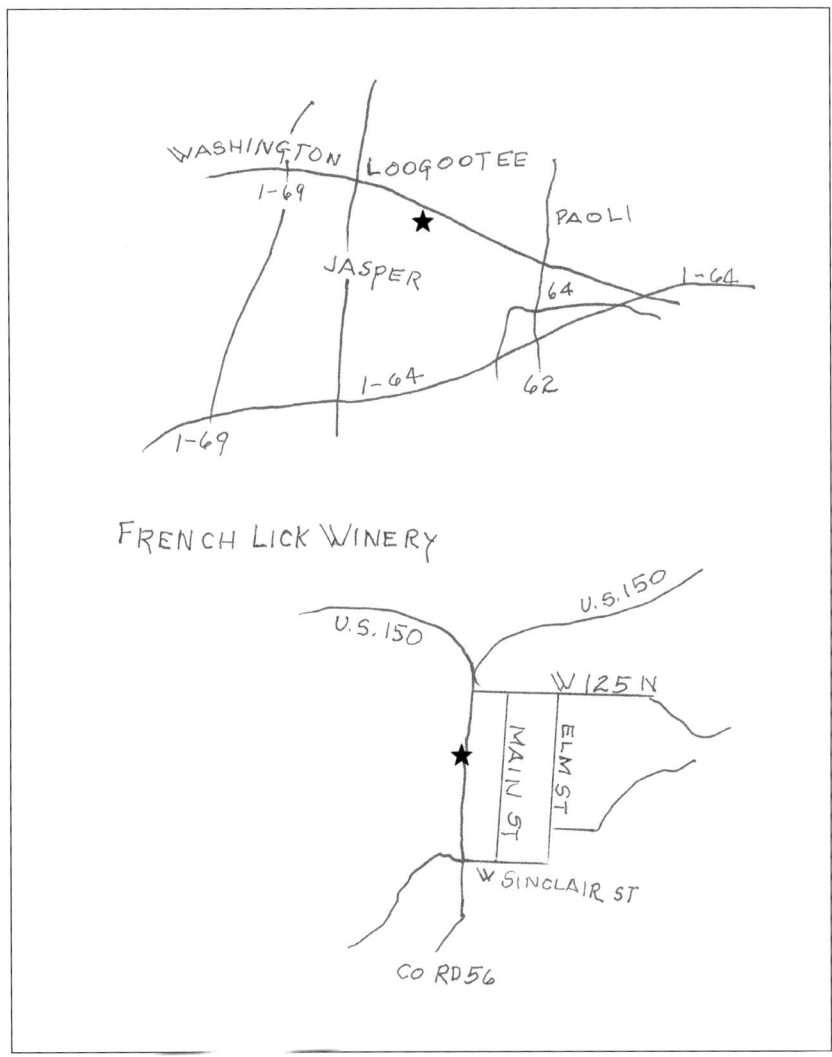

The French Lick Winery offers a full slate of award-winning wines, from dry to sweet. The estate bottled Norton is a keeper, barrel aged, with undercurrents of oak and black cherry. Patrons are likely to find the Norton to be one of the better regionally grown and produced varietals, especially if dry reds are appreciated.

The Pinot Gris, a quality white with beautiful layers of green apple and a fruity flavor, is to be appreciated, as are three of the semi-dry varietals: the Vignoles (with its peach and pear tones), the Steuben (which is always an option for those who appreciate white Zinfandel), and the Foch, (a hearty grape that grows well in Indiana and offers some fine blackberry and cherry flavors). And among the sweet fare, French Lick offers a superb Peach and the French Lick White—their best-selling white which is a blend of the Niagara and Vignoles grapes.

One of the best features of this superb winery is the French Lick hospitality. Visitors will truly experience a southern style welcome and will appreciate the knowledgeable and approachable staff here. And better yet, come for a meal, too. Be prepared to savor some of these wines in the restaurant or, during warmer weather, share a bottle on the patio with good friends.

Check out The French Lick Winery web site for their many upcoming special events—music, chocolate pairings, foods, and an assortment of weekend opportunities. And with the resorts nearby, don't overlook the option of enjoying some of these fine wines in another setting. Everyone is sure to find a favorite here.

Information by the Glass

Owners: John & Kim Doty

Hours:
Tuesday, Wednesday, Thursday & Sunday 11 a.m. - 5 p.m.
Friday & Saturday 11 a.m. - 9 p.m.

Amenities: Gift Shop, Restaurant, Outdoor Seating

Tastings: Free

Price: $12 - $22

Recommendations:
Rose—this semi-dry rose features hints of rhubarb and a full, fruity taste, crisp and refreshing. Enjoy this one with steamed mussels or grilled scallops.

Heaven's View Port—this fortified wine, made of Norton grapes, is one of the sweeter ports found among Indiana wineries, but has a depth of character that should be savored with chocolate and dried fruit.

Cabernet Franc—always in limited supply, this red has a complexity that can either be savored by the glass, or paired with pork chops or lamb.

Activities: Festivals, Wine Club

Nearby Attractions: French Lick Casino & hotels, West Baden Hotel, Antique Shops

Estate Grapes: Pinot Gris, Chardonnay, Norton, Chambourcin, Traminette, Vignoles, Steuben.

Green Apple Bacon Salad

Diced Granny Smith apples   ½ pound bacon
Raisins   Ranch dressing or mayonnaise
¼ cup sour cream

Fry bacon until crispy, place on paper towels for drying. Place apple pieces (peeled), raisins, and crumbled bacon into bowl and add dressing and sour cream. Mix well and serve with Pinot Gris.

Fruit Hills Winery & Orchard
55504 SR 15
Bristol, IN 46507
574-848-9463
www.FruitHillsWinery.com

This northern Indiana winery has a growing list of labels and is producing beautifully-sculpted wines. Owned and operated by David and Michele Muir, the winery first began with apple wines created from the century-old orchard, but has since expanded into other white and red grape varietals. Located in a countrified new tasting room in Bristol, the Fruit Hills experience is drawing an expanding clientele and making a name as one of the premier wineries in northern Indiana.

When you visit Fruit Hills plan to stay for conversation. You will enjoy the countryside drive to and from-but the wine experience itself won't disappoint.

Fruits Hills produces an excellent Noiret—a red varietal that is growing in popularity throughout the state. Here the Noiret has a tannin structure that is reminiscent of a Zinfandel, with strong peppery notes and a deeper structure that would hold up well with a steak or pork chop—and the Two Shades of Red, a Bordeaux-style blend of Merlot and Cab Franc, has plum and blackberry notes and an aromatic nose.

And for those who enjoy sweeter wines, Fruit Hills offers a number of apple and cherry wines along with some of the popular standbys made of the Concord grape. These sweet wines all pair well with desserts, but would offer a nice touch with hot rolls and apple butter, too.

Look for these beautifully-labeled bottles at some of the central Indiana wine festivals or call ahead for a visit.

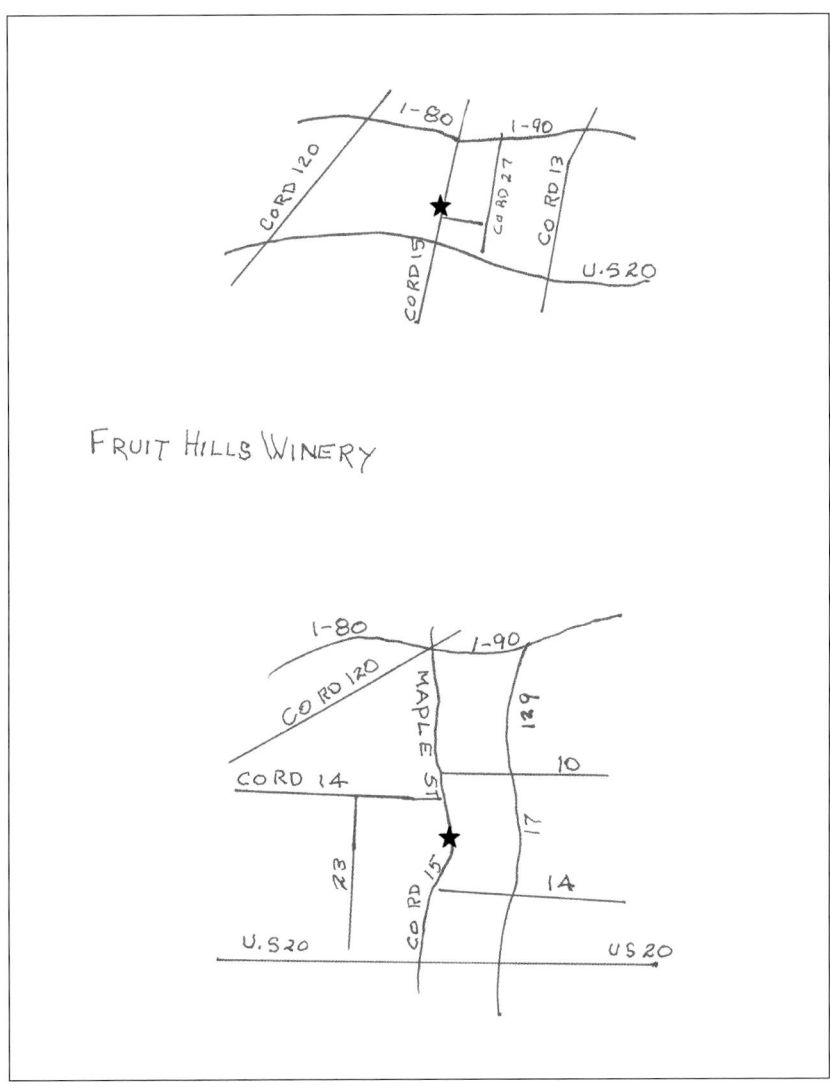

FRUIT HILLS WINERY

Information by the Glass

Owners: David and Michele Muir

Hours:
Spring & Summer, Tuesday - Thursday, 11 a.m. - 5p.m.
Friday & Saturday 11 a.m. - 6 p.m.
Sunday 12 - 4 p.m.
Closed Mondays

Amenities: Gift Shop

Tastings: Free

Price: check website

Recommendations:
Macabla—a dry, red blend of Marquette, Cab Franc, and Seyval Blanc. Complex and rich with both peppery notes and earthiness, this one would make a great partner with red sauces.

Red Sensation—another of the Fruit Hills blends, this sweet wine finishes well with any dessert, especially banana cream pie.

Activities: Special Events

Nearby Attractions: Elkhart & South Bend Restaurants

Estate Grapes: Traminette, Riesling, Cab Franc.

Gateway Cellar Winery

211 South Main Street
Goshen, IN 46526
574-370-4049
Facebook.com/GatewayCellarWinery

Located on Main Street in Goshen, the Gateway Cellar Winery offers a small but eclectic array of wines. Visitors will enjoy the ambiance of this northern Indiana community and Amish way of life. Within walking/driving distance of the winery there are also several beautiful craft shops and an ample number of fine home-style restaurants.

The Gateway Cellar is also a supply house for those looking to make their own wines. The knowledgeable staff here can answer questions and lead wine-making novices in the right direction.

And if new to the area, be sure to take in some of the scenic views of the Elkhart River, the Potato Creek State park, or the Rum Village Pathway Mountain Biking Trail. Great vistas and a laid-back atmosphere.

And enjoy the wine, too.

Information by the Glass

Hours: 4 - 10 p.m.

Amenities: Gift Shop

Tastings: Free

Price: Check website

Indiana Wineries: The Ultimate Guide to Wine in Indiana

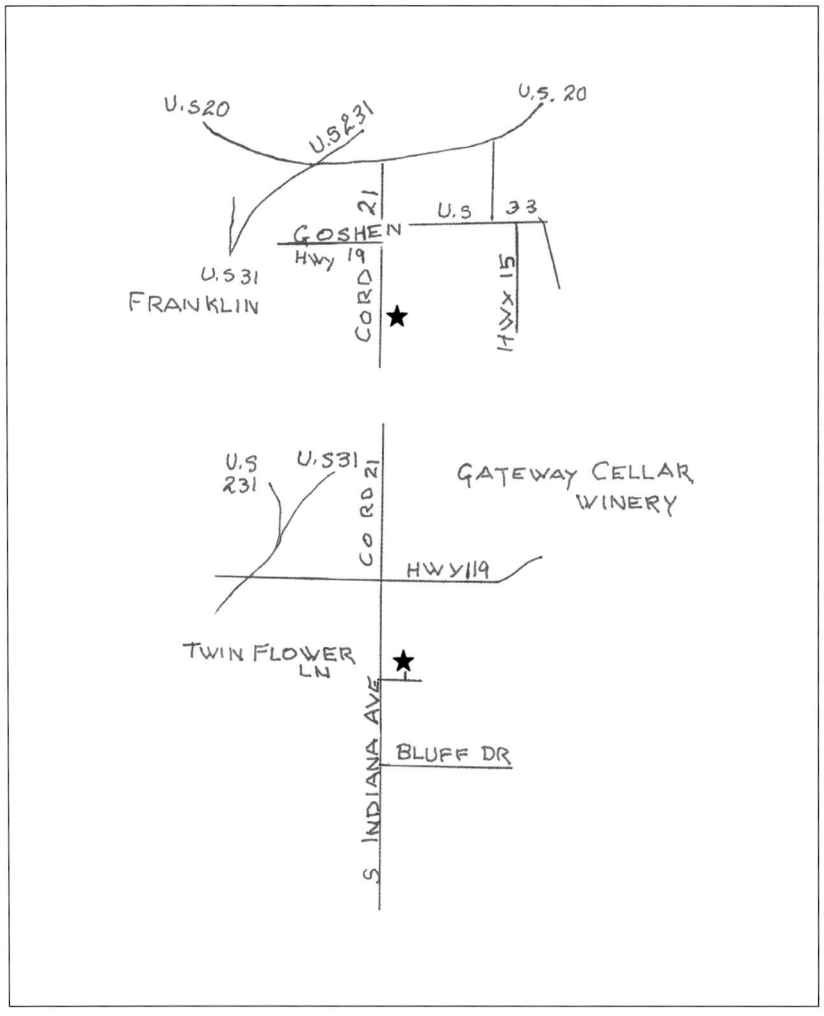

Harmony Winery
7350 Village Square Lane, Suite 200
Fishers, IN 46038
317-585-9463
www.harmonywinery.com

Certain Indiana wine producers have made a name for themselves bottling juices from around the world—and that is what one will discover at Harmony Winery. This one-stop winery offers a remarkable selection from major (and famous) regions—such as Malbec from Chile, Nero D'Avola from Sicily, and Tempranillo from the Rioja region of Spain. Harmony even has old vine Zinfandel from California's famed country regions, and there are also German and Johannesburg Rieslings.

Harmony produces all of these wines from juices shipped in from these well-known regions (and more) and one can't go wrong with the $5-10 wine tasting, an experience that offers nearly a dozen selections from the four corners of the world.

Harmony Winery, located in a small storefront in Fishers, Indiana, is an unassuming shop with a global presence. Better yet, the winery changes out its list every two to three weeks, so a person can discover new sensations from Australia, say, or from Italy or

Argentina. For those wishing to secure a particular vintage or selection from a region, best to contact Harmony to make sure it is still in stock—new wines are being produced all the time.

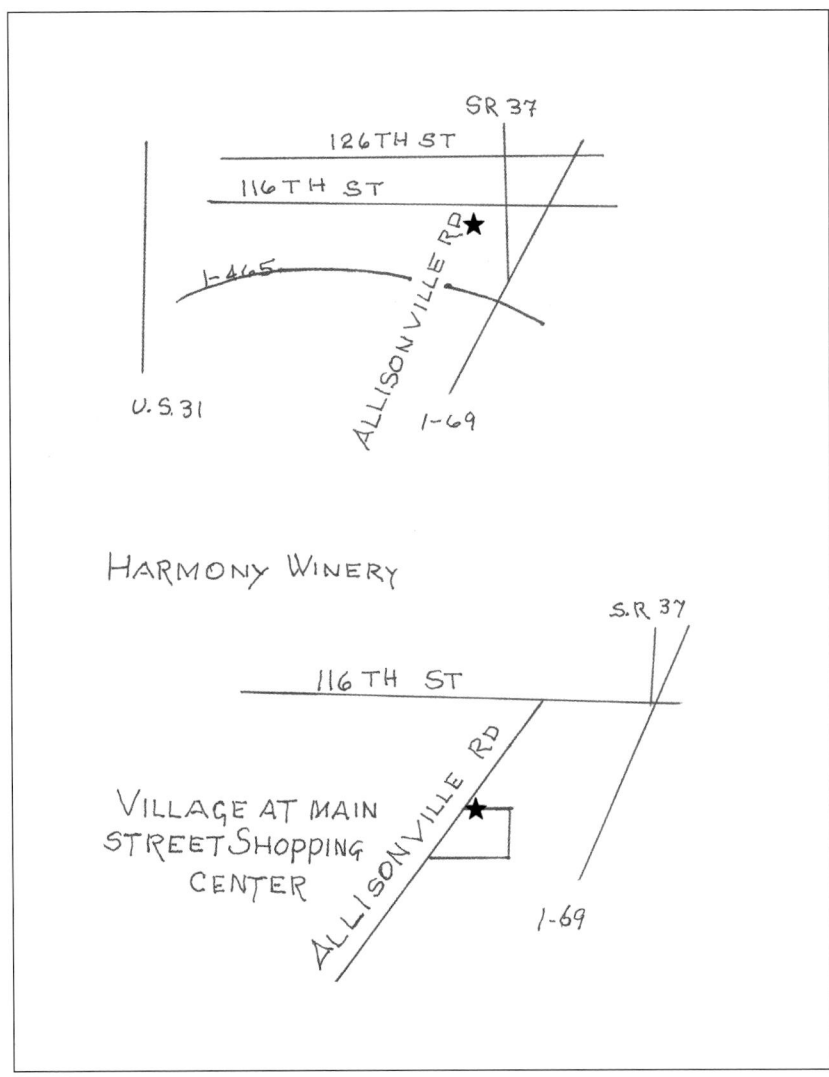

Because of Harmony's unique approach and production facility in house—the various juices offer some of the more travelled and out-of-the-way selections one is likely to find in the Hoosier state. An Italian Armonioso is as likely to be found here as a California

Cab, or a French Sauvignon Blanc just as opportunistic as a wine made from home-grown Granny Smith apples.

Harmony isn't a winery in the traditional sense of vines and grape production, but it has its place—and a unique one—among those in central Indiana. Beautiful labeling and friendly service make the wine-tasting experience, in-house, something to return to. Not much floor space for those wishing to sit and enjoy a bottle, but the bar area is ample enough to accommodate a dozen patrons and in the summer sidewalk tables offer a fresh air option.

If you are looking for selections from other parts of the world, you might try Harmony as a one-stop option.

Harmony also offers a wine-making course as part of a 90-minute wine class designed to assist in food pairing and wine appreciation. A wine club is also available.

Information By the Glass

Owners: Kevin & Tatyana

Hours:
Tuesday - Thursday Noon - 8 p.m.
Friday & Saturday Noon - 9 p.m.
Sunday Noon - 4 p.m.

Amenities: Gift Shop, Lounge

Tastings: Free

Price: $12 - $20

Recommendations:
Since the wine list is always changing and expanding, check out Harmony's web site for their latest offerings, and don't be surprised at what you might find there. Call for more information about upcoming wines they may be producing from juices

around the world.

Activities: Live Music, Wine Appreciation Days, Weddings

Nearby Attractions: Conner Prairie.

Sweet & Sour Beef Chunks

Beef chunks
1 tablespoon corn starch
1/3 cup vinegar
1 green pepper, chopped

1/2 cup brown sugar
1 can pineapple chunks
1 tablespoon soy sauce

Cook beef chunks until tender. Remove from pan. Drain and mix sugar and corn starch in pan, add pineapple and juice, vinegar and soy sauce. Bring to a boil while stirring, and then add beef, cook for 10 minutes. Add green pepper, let simmer for another 10 minutes. Serve over rice and enjoy with Pinot Grigio or Riesling.

Holtkamp Winery
10868 Woliung Road
New Alsance, IN 47041
513-602-5580
www.holtkampwinery.com

This family-owned and operated boutique winery was started by Doug Holtkamp in 2013 with the help of winemaker Jeff McHaan. After planting six varieties of California vines, as well as Hoosier favorites, this winery quickly established a variety of offerings and is now offering a remarkably eclectic list. The distinctive Holtkamp label gives this winery an old-world, nearly regal feel direct from the bottle.

Holtkamp is also making its way around the state and is becoming a staple at wine festivals and special events. Though small, this Dearborn County winery has some beautiful vistas and its quaint presentation and tasting room makes visiting a pleasure. Of course the well-versed and friendly staff also give this winery a promising future.

The Holtkamp wines range from dry reds to sweet whites and include various fruit wines, including plum. In other words there is a taste for everyone.

Look for this winery to continue to expand its offerings and don't forget to locate them at your new wine festival. Ask to try the reserve red—its depth and complexity will surprise you and if you are looking for a sweeter label, try the Holtkamp cherry—a touch of dry combined with some tart sweetness.

On your next drive south consider Holtkamp as one destination on your Hoosier tasting experience.

Information by the Glass

Owner: Doug Holtkamp

Hours: Currently open by appointment only

Amenities: Outdoor seating

Tastings: Free

Price: $12 - $28

Recommendations:
Cabernet Sauvignon (California)—a rich Cab that holds on to the California signature grape and in a Holtkamp bottle has a plumy nose and a blackberry and tannin finish.

Cabernet Sauvignon (Indiana)—compared side-by-side with the California label, this Holtkamp-grown Cab offers a unique opportunity among Hoosier wineries. Here the Indiana Cab makes its statement in a dry, yet not overly-done red that holds some complexity and familiarity in notes of cinnamon and red raspberry.

Activities: Wine Festivals

Nearby Attractions: Hoosier National Forest

Estate Grapes: Cabernet Sauvignon, Chardonnay, Dornfelder, Noiret, Cayuga, Marquette, Seyval Bland, Vidal Blanc, Traminette, Steuben.

Hopwood Cellars Winery

12 E. Cedar Street
Zionsville, IN 46077
317-873-4099
www.hopwoodcellars.com

Hopwood Cellars opened in September of 2012 in historic Zionsville. But winemaker Ron Hopwood had been perfecting his craft for sixteen years before opening this beautiful and expressive establishment in the heart of town. This winery sports a quaint ambiance of old world charm, a spacious horseshoe tasting bar, seating areas, and enough special events and draw to keep people entertained while they are enjoying the Hopwood wines.

A few of the amenities at Hopwood include free Wi-Fi, a small gift shop, outdoor seating in season, and easy access to the downtown antique shops, bookstores, and fine dining. There are also boutique stores and fine art galleries within walking distance. Anyone can make a day in historic Zionsville, and there's plenty of public parking.

But if it's just wine you want—or wines you want to peruse—you shouldn't overlook the Wine Cottage that is located just one block up the road from Hopwood Cellars. The Wine Cottage is one of the best wine stores in Indiana—with selections ranging worldwide and prices to fit any budget or taste. This vast showroom will amaze you and if you enjoy talking about wines, strike up a conversation with some of the staff and they will likely point you to some labels you've never seen.

With Hopwood Cellars just steps away—you can make a day to wine and dine and discuss wine with some experts. When you visit Hopwood you should also be aware of their "crock pot" Saturdays—fare provided by the winery on a first-come, first-served basis—and live music on Fridays. There are also enough special events on the Hopwood calendar to pique the interest.

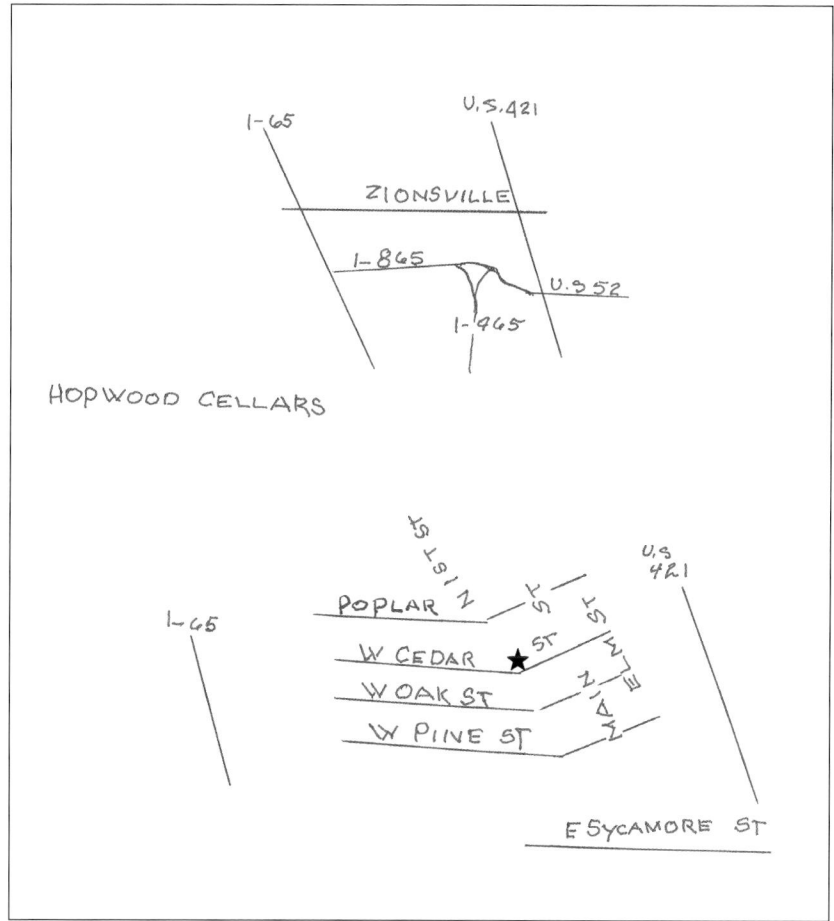

Hopwood offers up a select but growing array of wines—including Hoosier Chambourcin and two other dry reds. The Bekkar is a blend of Chambourcin and Chancellor grapes that offers currant and cherry notes with body. And the Sunbaked Mihr is a Marechal Foch with layers of berry flavor. Hopwood also makes a nice Chardonnay which has apple and pear notes, and two presentations of Riesling, one semi-sweet, the other sweeter and fruitier.

Another half dozen wines, including some fruit labels, round out the Hopwood selections quite nicely. And when you visit, you are certain to fine a wine or two that you can enjoy back home.

Information by the Glass

Owner: Ron Hopwood

Hours: Open seven days a week
Monday - Thursday 12 - 8 p.m.
Friday: 12 - 9 pm.
Saturday: 10 a.m. - 10 p.m.
Sunday: 12 - 5 p.m.

Amenities: Gift Shop, Outdoor Seating

Tastings: Free

Price: $12 - $15

Recommendations:
Dechaunac—a full-bodied red, oaky, with nice tannins. Pair this one with some caviar and crackers or tuna.

Peach—a mighty fine peach wine, supremely fruity, that would pair well with vanilla ice cream topped with berries.

Activities: Cook-offs, Live Music, Special Events

Nearby Attractions: Zionsville Restaurants, Antiques, Raceway Park (Brownsburg).

Caviar Dip

Caviar
Green olives

Black olives
Crackers

Mix small pieces of olives (or crushed) with caviar and serve over crackers. Enjoy with Hopwood DeChaunac.

Huber's Orchard, Winery & Vineyards

19816 Huber Road
Borden, IN 47106
812-923-9463
800-345-WINE
www.huberwinery.com

Huber's Orchard, Winery & Vineyards is, in fact, the largest estate winery in Indiana. It is also one of the oldest and most prestigious. Huber, along with Oliver, Easley and Butler, worked hard to create the winery community as we know it today. And now, these many years later, Huber offers one of the largest and most eclectic lineup of lines to be found in the Hoosier state.

When you visit Huber's Orchard, Winery & Vineyards it will come as no surprise that this is, indeed, a farming operation like no other winery in the state. The orchard, the labeled vineyards, and the easily-accessible entry will make your Huber visit a memorable one. And this complex also sports an ice cream shop and a produce market along with ample parking, walking paths, and several ponds. The full 650 acre farm—and over 80 acres of vineyard—creates a full-fledged winery experience like no other, and save for the Hoosier landscape as opposed to the dry Sierra hills, one might get the impression of Napa or Sonoma Valley. With production of over 400,000 pounds of grapes annually, Huber isn't taking a back seat to too many wineries anywhere.

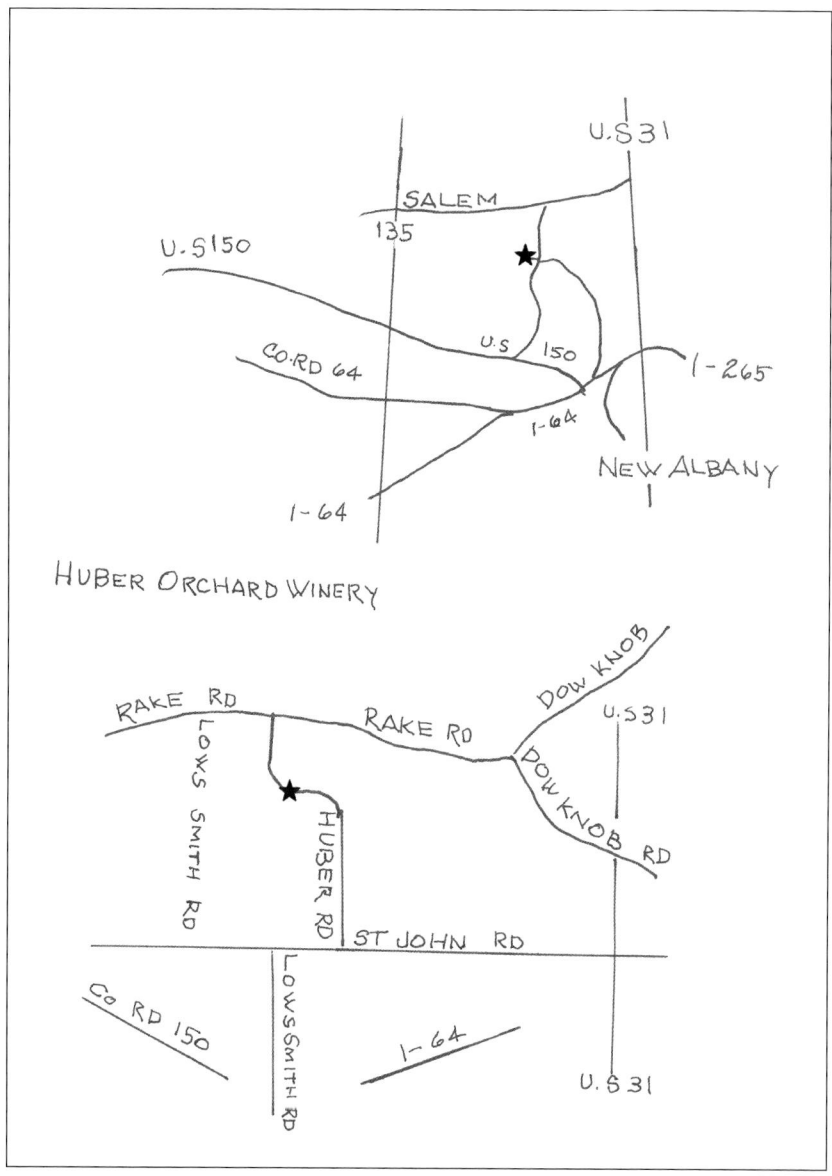

Inside the Huber Winery there is also a restaurant (the Starlight Café) where patrons can enjoy a relaxing afternoon with friends, or perhaps take in a live-music concert on the expansive patio/deck area that could easily seat 200 people. The café features excellent sandwiches and pizzas. In short, this is a large winery that one can enjoy over the course of hours.

Listing the Huber wines here is not possible—but suffice it to say that the Huber winery has over fifty labels and the wines being produced here are gleaning some of the highest honors and awards both in and out of state. Furthermore, the grapes here are being grown on the estate, which makes these tastes and vintages all the more remarkable and points to the expert winemaking skills found inside the production facility.

For those who enjoy bold reds possessing both complexity and depth, one can't go wrong with the Huber Heritage vintages. These—having been produced for nearly a decade—continue to gather strength and value with each passing year, and are an estate blend of three reds aged in oak. Delicious, rich, bold—possessing all of the accolades one would expect form a top Napa wine—the Heritage label holds up as one of the premier estate wines.

Among the whites here, don't overlook the Starlight White (their best selling)—a semi-sweet beauty that can be enjoyed alone or with fish or poultry. The Harvest Rose is a delicious white Zinfandel and the Huber Niagara is bursting with flavor.

Enjoy these tastes and more upstairs in the Huber tasting room—one of the largest bars one is going to find anywhere. The gift room here is also, I would suspect, the largest in state and one is likely to find any wine-related knickknack or sign or accessory on a shelf. One wall of the upstairs also contains the impressive awards garnered by the Huber Winery over the years—too many to count—and the staff here is friendly, gracious and knowledgeable about wines (and not just their own).

The Huber Winery is also expanding, it seems, with new ideas and features year-by-year. In addition to featuring ice wines, fruit wines in season, and some excellent port—a new distillery will soon be creating a stop on the Hoosier bourbon trail. And Huber also produces sherry, brandy and specialty wines of high-quality and value.

Visit the Huber website to get a feel for this working farm and to gander at the long list of wines produced here. No doubt you will find a favorite from this list and can then ask for it when you visit.

Information by the Glass

Owners: The Huber Family

Hours:
Monday - Saturday 10 a.m. - 6 p.m.
Sunday 12 - 6 p.m.

Amenities: Restaurant, Banquet Hall, Indoor/Outdoor Seating, Farmer's Market, Ice Cream Shop, Trails

Tastings: 8 wines for $10 or 4 wines for $5

Price: $12 - $30

Recommendations:
Heritage—this top of the line red blend only gets better with age (ask for the best years) and pairs well with steak, pork, and red sauces. Each Heritage years has a different complexity and full flavor and would make an excellent flight or ladder tasting.

Blaufrankisch—a medium-bodied dry red with hints of crushed black pepper and currant. One of the most unique varietals you will find in-state. Pairs well with lamb and bacon-wrapped appetizers.

Ruby Port—a wonderful port wine that is not overly washed with alcohol. Tasty with jam and flavorful textures of near-rum quality it should only get better with age. Enjoy solo.

Activities: Live Entertainment, Gourmet Foods, Hiking, Hayrides, Wine Club

Nearby Attractions: Charleston State Park, Knobstone Trail

Estate Grapes: Cabernet Sauvignon, Merlot, Chambourcin, Traminette, Syrah, Cayuga, Vidal Blanc, many more.

Beef Burgundy Stew

1 pound lean beef tips
3 sliced carrots
1 medium onion (chopped)
1 yellow bell pepper (chopped)
Salt, pepper, marjoram, thyme, bay leaf
Red wine

2 teaspoons beef boullion
1 stalk celery (chopped)
1 can whole tomatoes

Cook beef tips until tender and then add along with one cup of water all of the ingredients along with ¼ teaspoon marjoram and ¼ teaspoon thyme and a bay leaf. Add ½ cup of red wine. Simmer for 2 hours on low heat, adding more wine or water if needed. Serve with Huber Heritage.

Indian Creek Winery
6491 County Line Road
Georgetown, IN 47112
502-396-6209
www.indiancreekwinery.org

Located between Louisville, Kentucky and Corydon, Indiana in scenic Georgetown, Indian Creek Winery would be typical of the smaller, boutique wineries around the state. This winery, set on 33 acres of rolling hills and vines, offers a small lineup of wines that accompany the free tastings and the eclectic lineup of live music, food and fun that one can discover at this destination.

While the offerings at this point are limited, Indian Creek is always rolling out new wines by the season and as their vines produce. The winery also offers select fruit wines as well.

In order to create a stronger draw, Indian Creek does provide meals for parties and other entertainment. They are also present at many of the wine festivals and fairs—especially in the southern part of the state. Their web site offers a calendar of events, and not all are on the Indian Creek grounds.

The Dry Creek Red or the Sweet Creek Rose are their top offerings, but they also produce a Vidal Blanc which is reminiscent of other Indiana whites. One should be able to drop by Indian Creek on a southern Indiana wine tour, but as the web site indicates, make sure you follow the directions on the site rather than a GPS.

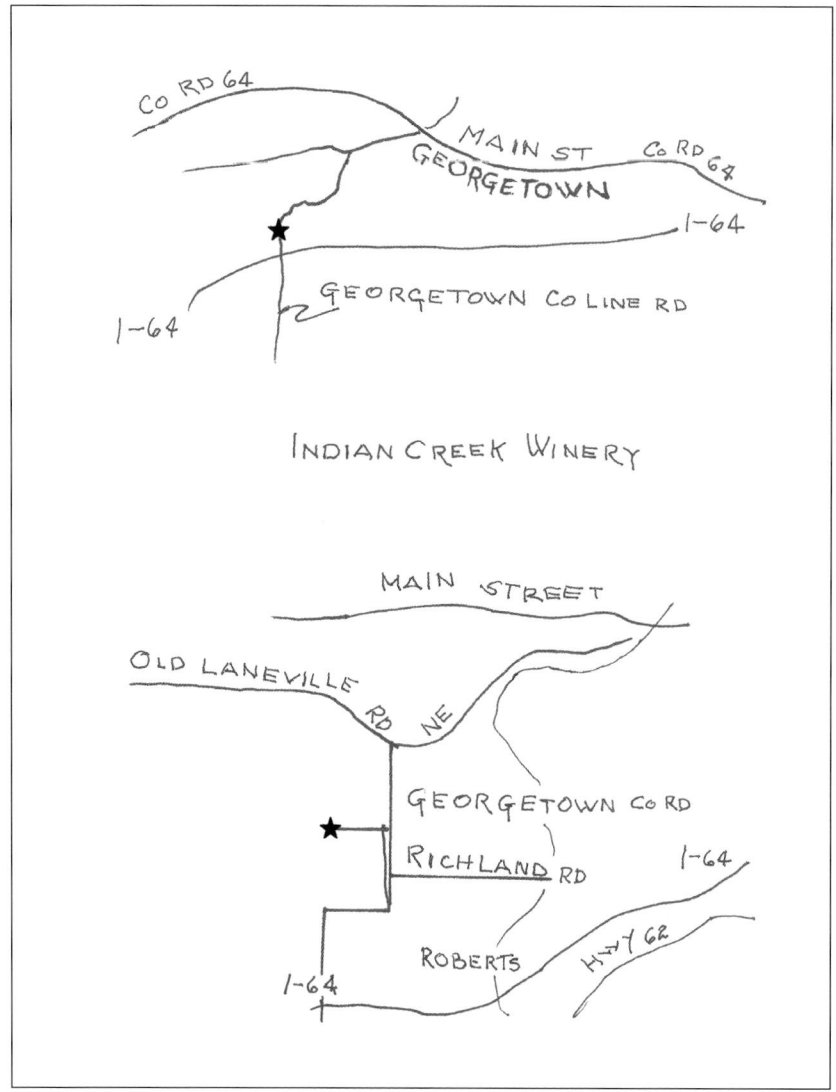

Information by the Glass

Owner: Mark Kendell

Hours:
12 - 6 p.m. daily

Amenities: Banquet Hall, Restaurant, Outdoor Seating, Gift Shop

Tastings: Free

Price: $15

Recommendations:
Dry Creek Red
Cardinal Red

Activities: Live Entertainment, Catering Services

Nearby Attractions: Blue River, Marengo Cave

Estate Grapes: Vidal Blanc, Chambourcin.

Indian Trail Wines
7540 North CR 350 West
Royal Center, IN 46978
574-889-2509
www.indiantrailwines.com

When owners Dan, Phil, and Megan McDonald opened Indian Trail Wines in April, 2010, they wanted to create an estate winery that would be a fun place for friends to gather. Now, years later, their vision has blossomed into a marvelous countrified winery. The tasting room, a ranch-style cabin on the top of a picturesque hill, is situated on several acres of vineyard that features fruit of Steuben, Foch, Traminette, and several other common Hoosier varietals. This winery takes great pride in their product, and the owners—who operate the winery currently as a seasonal business (primarily on weekends)—are knowledgeable and personable. In fact, patrons will make friends here.

Indian Trail offers a dozen or so labels ranging from dry reds to Catawba rose to sweet white and fruit wines. All in all, an impressive array for such a small winery. But don't let the limited lineup fool you.

What you'll discover at Indian Trail are some surprisingly complex and complementary wines. For example, the Homestead Red, is their most popular wine, but this sweet wine has some rich undertones of cherry and pairs very well with chocolate. And as far as unique tastes are concerned, there is the Prairie Sunset Red—a blend that is, at first blush, a sweet wine with an earthy aroma containing hints of licorice and fruit, but as it sits on the tongue, deepens to levels of tobacco and oak. Sipping this one solo, one might confuse the Prairie Sunset Red with a dry port.

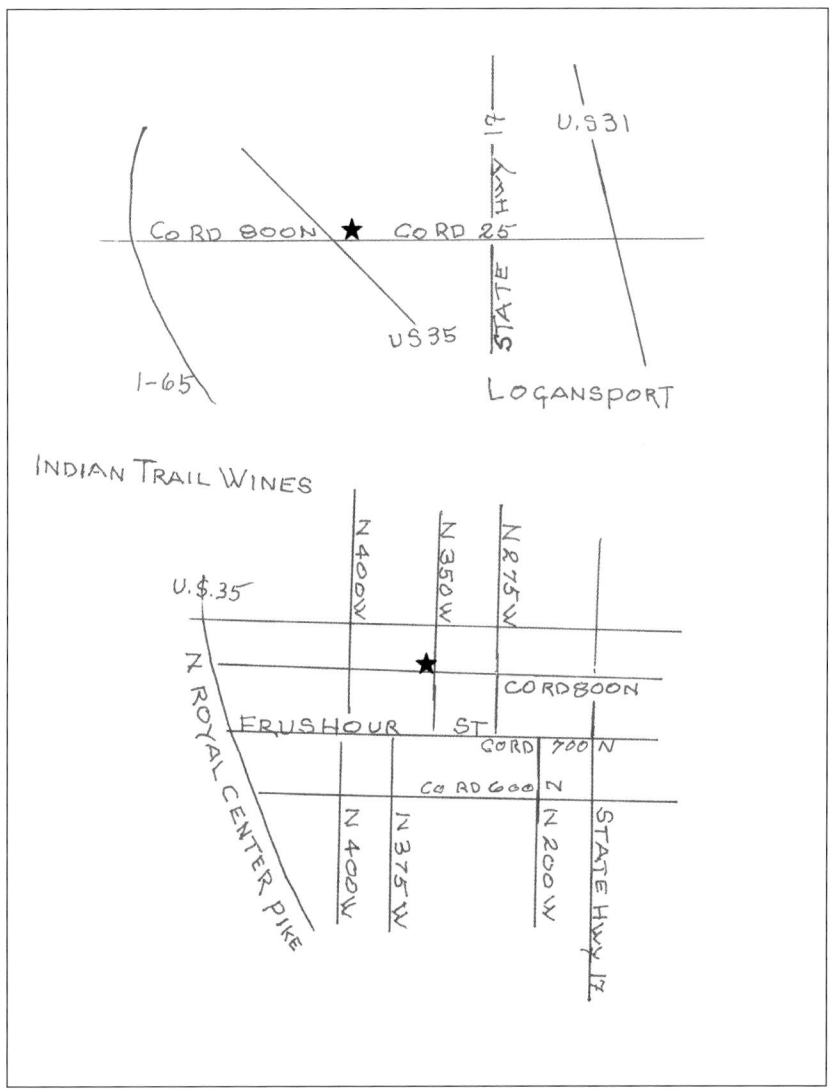

Like many Indiana wineries, Indian Trail does well by its sweeter offerings, too. The Plum Crazy and the Sweet Country White are both to savor, and the latter has the fruity mix of apricot and mint.

In the summer, visit Indian Trail for one of their weekend concerts (live music) in the gazebo. There is plenty of parking—and as the owners explain—this is about enjoying friendship. Bring the family.

There's no doubt that people who visit Indian Trail will enjoy this countrified air and the fine mix of wines. And if the pocketbook is a problem, patrons will discover that this winery offers some of the most affordable wines in the state. Quite the bargain at the trail end of a nice drive.

Information by the Glass

Owners: Dan, Phil, and Megan McDonald

Hours:
Friday 2 - 6 p.m.
Saturday & Sunday 11 a.m. - 6 p.m.

Amenities: Outdoor Seating

Tastings: Free

Price: $15

Recommendations:
Heritage Harvest White—a more serious white with strong notes for a semi-sweet. Let it linger and you'll pick up an abundance of fruits from the bouquet. A nice white that would go well with clam chowder or butternut squash soup.

Prairie Sunset Red—a marvel in the glass on many levels, and something of an experience as the wine aerates in the glass. Swirl it and you can continue to pick up those port notes. Drink this one as a fireside chat or pair with barbeque or a Cheddar stuffed baked potato.

Activities: Special Events and Music

Nearby Attractions: France Park, Tippecanoe River State Park

Estate Grapes: Noirett, Steuben, Chambourcin, Catawba, Frontenac, Traminette, Marechal Foch.

Cheddar Baked Potato

Baking potatoes
Diced black olive
Diced red pepper
Bacon bits
Diced jalapeno
Shredded Cheddar cheese

Bake potatoes to texture, slit tops, place bacon bits, olives, jalapeno and red pepper inside. Top with shredded Cheddar and microwave for 20 seconds. Add sour cream if desired. Serve with Prairie Sunset Red.

J & J Winery
3415 National Road West
Richmond, IN 47374
765-955-9463
www.JJWinery.com

The J & J Winery on old U.S. 41 (Main Street) in Richmond holds the distinction of being the first winery and brewery combo in the state (followed soon after by Simmons Winery & Brew). Located just west of Earlham College, the winery is tucked away behind full-growth trees on a beautiful waterfront panorama and features a production barn, expansive seating decks and frontage tent for bridal parties and gatherings, a wine tasting room and gift shop, and the Gemstone Café—which features their signature wood-fired and hand-tossed pizzas which are prepared on the patio. The entire winery, owned and operated in part by a physician turned wine-maker, is pristine and architecturally crafted for its optimum effect on the grounds. Visitors can not only taste wines here, but can dine-in, stroll the trail along the pond, find a cozy porch swing, or even visit some of the local antique shops or Bed & Breakfasts—which are plentiful in old Richmond and just a few miles east.

Because the J & J Winery is the only option for wine in the area (the closest being Wilson Wines in Modoc), the owners here have sought to produce a full-service establishment ranging from wedding hosting to dining—and, of course, their own brews for those who prefer hops to grapes.

But for those who come to sample the wines—and you should—J & J offers a rather ingenious array of common Indiana varietals alongside others not commonly found in the Hoosier state. Although the winery does not offer free tastings, patrons can get a flight of five wines (2 ounces for glass) for $10, which is a respectable way of sampling as much over a plate of cheese and crackers as for a mere tasting.

Here's where you'll want to go with the flight....

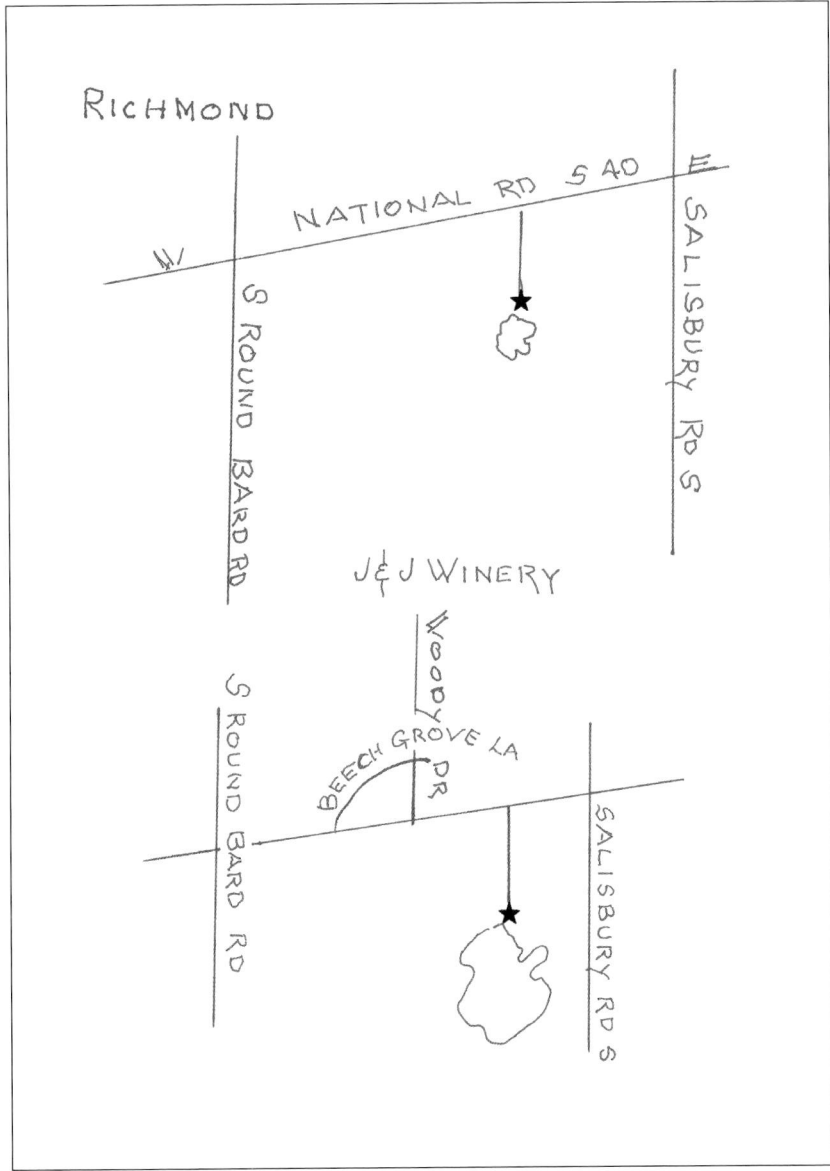

First, if you must, sample one or two of the whites—including one or more of the Chardonnay, the Seyval Blanc, the Pinot Grigio, or the Traminette... all grown in Indiana and spot on for their respective categories of dryness or sweetness. The Chardonnay, in particular, was not overly buttery, so it goes down without the lingering after-taste of some Chardonnays. And the Pinot Grigio can go well with a dinner or just as an dessert or evening wine.

If you work up a red flight, don't over look the Cabernet Sauvignon, made from Lodi California grape with an oaky finish or the Shiraz, another Lodi dry wine that has a soft peppery finish and soft tannins and would go well with red meat. Of more interest, perhaps, would be either the Cabernet Franc, which is grown on the estate and holds with spice and berry on the tongue or the Barbera which, for a traditional Italian varietal, offers a more smoky finish than some but would pair very well with pork or barbeque.

J & J also offers a wide range of sweet reds and whites, including Blackberry, and several blends bottled to the J & J label. The Niagara, for example, is a delicate white wine that has a nice balance of sweetness, but not overpowering.

Another pull for this winery, of course, is its easy accessibility from U.S. 70—or a quick drive up old U.S. 40. For anyone in a hurry, or who simply doesn't enjoy those long treks through the Hoosier cornfields and fall colors, J & J is an option you can explore without any trepidation. And if you are wanting to make Richmond a destination for an overnight stay in a B & B or as an option for antiquing (check out nearby Centerville!), J & J is the type of winery you can visit for a lunch and/or a quick tasting without busting your wallet.

And on a fine day—you'll want to sit and stay awhile.

Information by the Glass

Hours:
Thursday & Friday 3 p.m. - 9 p.m.
Saturday 11 a.m. - 9 p.m.

Amenities: Outdoor Seating, Gift Shop, Brew House, Banquet Facilities, Restaurant, Gourmet Foods

Tastings: Flight of 5 wines (2 ounces each) for $10

Price: $12 - $22

Recommendations:
Barbera—pairs well with poultry, chops, or barbeque

Reisling—semi-sweet option that pairs well with fish, rice, and steamed vegetables

Activities: Weddings, Banquets

Nearby Attractions: Earlham College, Antique Malls

Estate Grapes: Chardonnay, Seyval Blanc, Pinot Grigio, Traminette.

Chicken Kabobs

Chicken chunks
Onion
Worcestershire sauce
Minced garlic

Large fresh mushrooms
Green pepper
Olive oil

Soak kabob spears in water for four hours, add large chunks of chicken, mushrooms, onion, and pepper to each kabob. Brush with mixture of Worcestershire sauce, minced garlic and olive oil. Grill to taste and texture and serve with glasses of Barbera.

Lanthier Winery
123 Mill Street
Madison, IN 47250
812-273-2409
800-41-WINES
www.lanthierwinery.com

If you've never visited Madison, Indiana before you can expect to find yourself transported to a small river town with old-world charm. Madison is the kind of place where visitors can be swept up in the ambiance of early Hoosier history, but still find plenty of contemporary excitement—including shopping, dining, and an abundance of festivals.

The Lanthier Winery is in the heart of historic Madison (not far, in fact, from the Lanthier Mansion—which is a state historic site). The winery tasting room is located in the cellar of a historic home, with large floor to ceiling racks that hold the Lanthier selections. Before entering the cellar, you might want to stroll through the expansive gardens to the north of the house, where gravel paths are lined with a cornucopia of flowers, herbs, and decorative trees. In fact, Lanthier has created a small but amicable winery where a person can spend time beyond the tasting room. Just a block south from the Lanthier Winery you can also stroll through the Chautauqua riverfront park and enjoy the various overlooks and scenic rest points of the Ohio River.

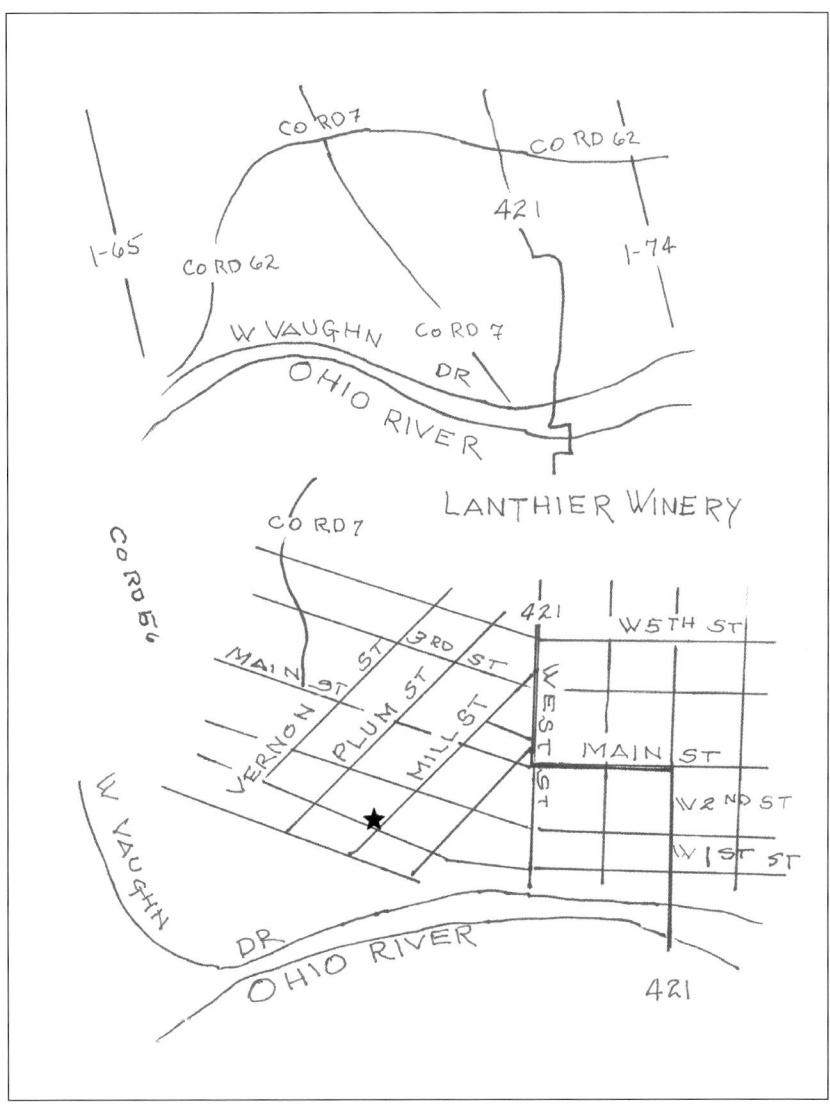

Inside the winery, the cellar tasting room has a historic feel to it—and will likely meet some new friends in the confined space of the split tasting bar. Tastings are free, and although the space is limited, the Lanthier staff will keep you well informed and moving through the tasting experience.

While Lanthier doesn't have a vineyard, they do contract Indiana grapes (and shipments from the Washington-Oregon area as well as California) to create their rather expansive array of wines. Core selections from Lanthier would include their Rivertown White and Rivertown Red—two of their dry wines that were created specifically for pairing with cousine. They also feature semi-dry and sweet wines to meet all tastes.

Many patrons enjoy a glass or a bottle while they peruse the art gallery or the gardens—and with the Ohio River but a few hundred yards away, there is always time for a stroll afterwards as you go in search of a place to dine or some dark chocolate or fudge to complement your bottle of Mill Street Red.

Information By the Glass

Owners: Christ & Tami Lanthier

Hours: Wednesday - Sunday 11 a.m. - 5 p.m.

Amenities: Banquet Facility, Gardens, Outdoor Seating

Tastings: Free

Price: $14 - $20

Recommendations:
Chambourcin—an Indiana-grown grape that, here, has a touch of French Beaujolais'.

Mill Street White—made with Niagara grapes—sweet with a touch of class.

Mill Street Red

Activities: Festivals, Art Shows

Nearby Attractions: Historic Madison, Riverfront Walk, Antiques

Estate Grapes: Chambourcin, Traminette.

Old Fashioned Brownies

1 cup butter
2 cups sugar
4 tablespoons cocoa
4 eggs well beaten

1 ¼ cups flour
1 teaspoon vanilla extract
½ cup chopped pecans

Melt butter and add sugar, cocoa. Mix well and then add other ingredients. Pour into greased 9-inch glass pan, bake for 20 minutes at 325 degrees. Remove, sprinkle with powdered sugar. Serve with Mill Street White.

Madison County Winery
114 West State Street
Pendleton, IN 46064
765-778-1406
www.madisoncountywinery.org

Madison County Winery (tasting room and display) is located in downtown Pendleton amid an array of antique malls, restaurants, and local establishments—and visitors will be reminded of that small town charm. The winery grows many of their own grapes some miles to the east of Pendleton, but the tasting room provides a more visible exposure—and very easy access from the interstate (I-69) if one is in the mind for a country drive or adding an antiquing experience to round out the day.

This winery has a small selection of primarily sweet wines—but also a few more robust tastes, including the Cabernet Franc, which sits deep in the glass and has a fruity taste reminiscent of most Hoosier-grown vintages. The winery also sports a small gift shop filled with wine accessories, knick-knacks, and craft items.

For a small winery—and the only one in the county—Madison produces decent wines of lasting impression and one can't go wrong with a bottle of sweet dessert wine and a cut of apple pie on a summer night.

Visit the Madison County web site for their most recent labels and upcoming offerings.

Information by the Glass

Hours:
Monday 10 a.m. - 3 p.m.
Tuesday - Thursday 10 a.m. - 5 p.m.
Friday - Saturday 10 a.m. - 7 p.m.

Amenities: Gift Shop

Tastings: Free

Price: $12 - $15

Nearby Attractions: Antique Shops

Estate Grapes: Chambourcin, Traminette.

Madison Vineyards & Winery
1456 East 400 North
Madison, IN 47250
812-273-6500
888-473-6500
www.madisonvineyards.com

The Madison Vineyards and Estate Winery is, as the name implies, an expansive estate of rolling hills and acres of vineyard. The vineyards here comprise some of the largest in the state and, since 1995, new vines have continued to be planted and the full vineyard now produces harvests of nearly a dozen varieties of grapes. Guests to the area can also make a weekend in the Madison area by spending a night or two at the Bed and Breakfast on the estate. The B & B is a picturesque hilltop home overlooking the tasting room and vineyards. The B & B has four large guest rooms and a cottage, all with private baths.

Madison Vineyards also has a full-slate of special events that begin in February (an annual Wine Lover's Valentine Dinner) and extends into late fall. A summer music lineup on Sunday afternoons offers an opportunity for visitors to enjoy food and wine while sitting on the hillside overlooking a bandstand, and the wrap-around covered porch on the wine tasting room also provides a relaxing atmosphere.

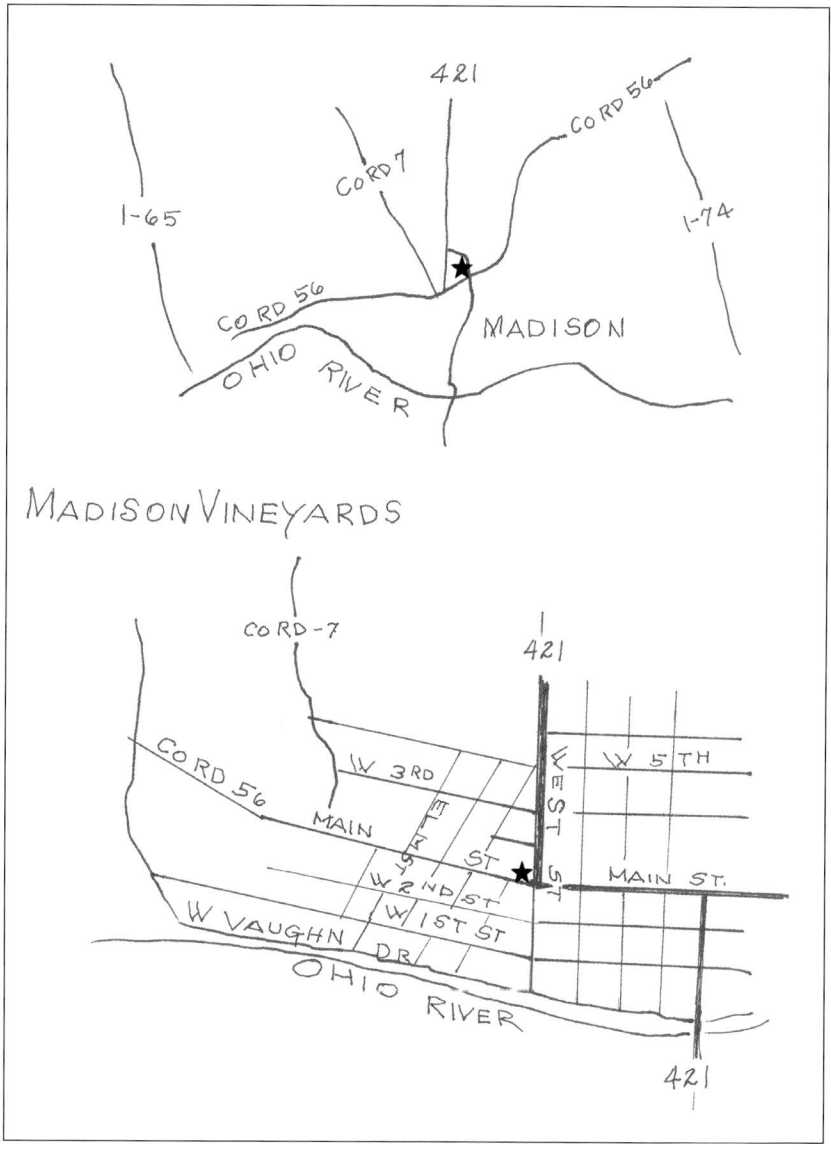

This winery also produces some of the best wines of south-eastern Indiana and has a presence at many of the wine festivals around the state. Madison's Seyval Blanc is a dry, full-bodied white with floral aroma and the Foch Nouveau is a Beaujolais'-style red with a fragrant aroma and hints of cherry and strawberry.

Two old world German style wines—the Kleineweiss, a semi-sweet white with deep fruit flavors and the Edelzwicker, a blend of Vidal, Cayuga and Vignoles, with a unique citrus and butterscotch flavor—provide these Madison labels with a taste of location as well as charm.

The winery also produces a nice Rosato—a blush or rose' wine that would be superb for summer chilling.

Information By the Glass

Owners: Steve & Sandy Palmer

Hours:
Wednesday - Sunday 10 a.m. - 6 p.m.
Closed Monday and Tuesday

Amenities: Gift Shop, Bed & Breakfast, Gourmet Foods, Outdoor Seating, Stage

Tastings: Free

Price: $12 - $20

Recommendations:
Noiret—this Rhone-style red is loaded with flavors of blackberry, raspberry, peppercorn and mint and is one of the most unique southern Indiana wines.

Black Dog—some years back, voted the "Best Sweet Wine in Indiana", this red is produced from hybrid grapes on the estate and has a stark and deep taste that will remind of a young ruby port—but in fact is not. Priced under $15.00 a bottle of Black Dog makes a wonderful gift or, for those cold winter Hoosier nights, the perfect one to break out for a toast by the fire.

Nearby Attractions: Mounds State Park, Biking Trails, Historic Madison

Estate Grapes: Cabernet Sauvignon, Syrah, Cab Franc, Seyval Blanc, Cayuga White, Marechal Foch, Vignoles, Merlot, Petit Verdot.

New Orleans Style Pralines

2 cups brown sugar
1 cup sugar
⅛ teaspoon baking soda
¼ can sweetened condensed milk
½ cup water
12 marshmallows
1 quart pecan halves

Combine all ingredients (except marshmallows) in a large saucepan and cook until soft, stirring to prevent burning. Add marshmallows and continue until these are melted thoroughly. Remove from heat and add pecans. Continue stirring until glassy. Spoon sized portions onto waxed paper and let stand until firm. Enjoy with Black Dog.

Mallow Run
6964 West Whiteland Road
Bargersville, IN 46106
317-422-1556
info@mallowrun.com
www.mallowrun.com

Mallow Run, like many vineyards and wineries in Indiana, started as a family affair. After John Richardson retired following 35 years of teaching, he moved back to the family farm and with the help of his son, Bill, and daughter-in-law, Laura, planted eight acres of vines with the intent of selling the grapes from his 600 acre working farm to other wineries. Those first vines were planted in 2000, but on September 3, 2005, the Richardson's opened this fully-operational winery—now one of the premier wineries in the state.

Among these acres of vines are eight grape varietals: Chardonel, Traminette, Cayuga, Catawba, Vignoles, Chambourcin, Chencellor, and Leon Millot. Mallow Run creates consistently deep and fruity wines from their own vineyard, but also ship in grapes from California, Michigan, and elsewhere in state.

Indiana Wineries: The Ultimate Guide to Wine in Indiana

The tasting room, located inside the renovated barn on the spacious grounds (and ample gravel parking areas) overlooks a scenic valley and forest. Guests will enjoy the amenities and ambiance of the old barn, along with the large inventory of wines which are well-marked and beautifully displayed along the perimeter.

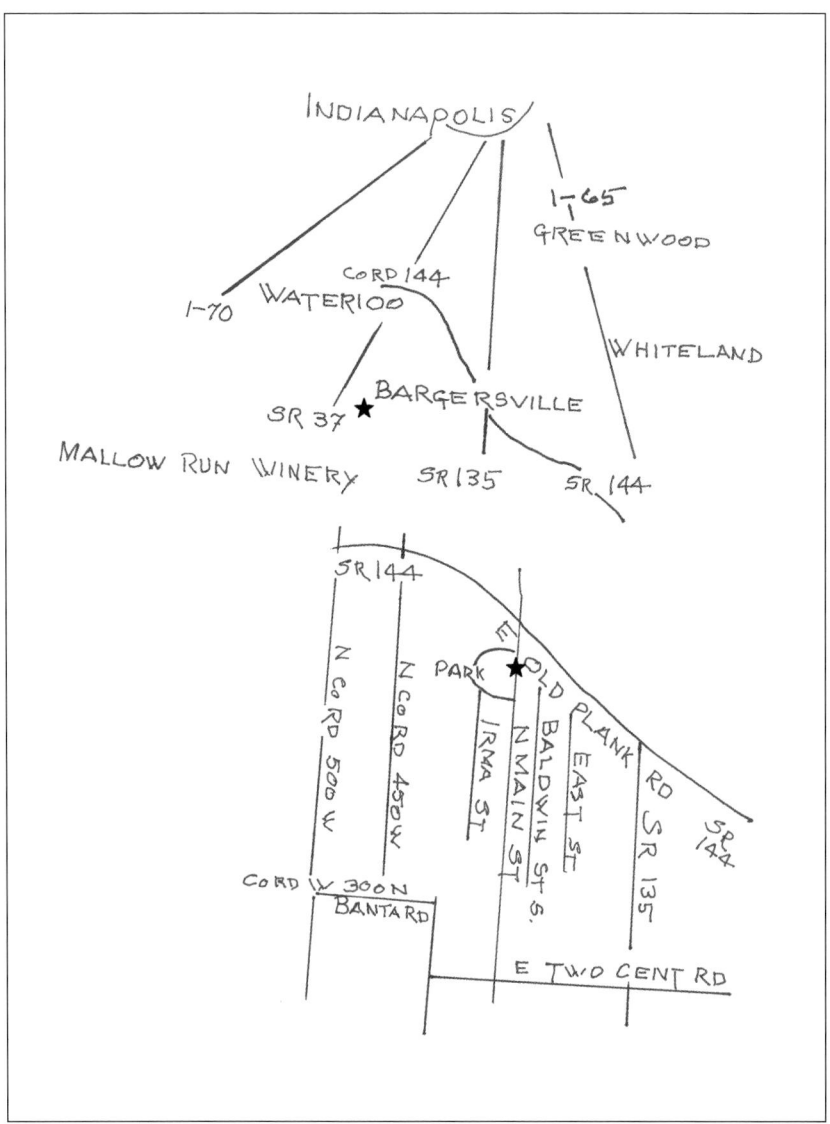

With their expert marketing and friendly and knowledgeable staff, Mallow Run makes a wine-tasting experience both relaxing and fun. Guests will also find exceptional gifts here in the form of pre-arranged wine baskets (some with fruit and cheese), T-shirts, and the frequent free crackers and spreads that can enhance the wine samples.

In the summer and fall, Mallow run sports a full-schedule of entertainment as well. The glass enclosed sun porch and sprawling deck (and picnic areas) serve as seating area for a relaxing evening of music—where Mallow Run serves up a full fare of local bands and single acts. And in the late summer and fall, the farm is turned into a large concert stage with hillside seating, where thousands of people attend concerts and wine-tasting weekends that also feature a carnival of food tents and wine-related booths.

With proximity to Oliver & Butler Wineries (Bloomington), Mallow Run rounds out a triad of excellent wineries that one can visit on a Saturday or Sunday afternoon. Furthermore, be sure to check out the Mallow Run website for their food nights—as they often serve up summer fare as well as excellent winter soups and stews that go very well with a fine red.

But, of course, you'll want to be sure to take advantage of your six selections when you sample the wines. Mallow Run is known for their top-quality Indiana vintages (Chardonel and Traminette in particular), but be sure to sample the Chambourcin Rose, especially on a hot summer evening during a concert. In addition to making some unique wines (Rhubarb) Mallow Run makes excellent sweet wines (Picnic White & Picnic Red), two sparkling varieties, and a number of holiday wines in season, including Winter White and Reindeer Red. Most recently, Mallow Run has taken advantage of its excellent wine-making background to produce some very fine traditional reds . . . including Merlot and Syrah. The Mallow Run Zinfandel is exceedingly dry and bold, with firm tannins that sit on the tongue with a smooth, blackberry finish. And the Cabernet Sauvignon is one of the best if one is looking for a dark, smooth wine that is full-bodied and complex.

To top off the experience, Mallow Run offers some of the best discounts on multi-bottle purchases and is a mere thirty minute drive from Indianapolis or Bloomington. Though a young winery, Mallow Run has all of the amenities and staffing that one would associate with a well-established label, and the winery carries itself well both in its excellent vintages and its personality.

Information by the Glass

Owners: John Richardson; Laura & Bill Richardson

Hours: Daily Noon - 6 p.m.

Amenities: Outdoor Seating, Gift Shop, Gourmet Cheeses

Tastings: Free

Price: $12 - $22

Recommendations:
Chambourcin Rose—an excellent summer wine, chilled, with

strawberry overtones and a beautiful and aromatic mix in the glass.

Zinfandel

Reisling—a traditional sweeter white in the classic German flair with overtones of grapefruit.

Reindeer Red—an excellent table wine for a Hoosier winter, paired with a hearty stew.

Activities: Summer Concerts, Weddings, Fall Harvest Event, Live Music

Nearby Attractions: Greenwood Antiques, University of Indianapolis Observatory

Estate Grapes: Chambourcin, Traminette, Chardonel, Pinot Grigio, Seyval Blanc, Cabernet Sauvignon, Cayuga, Marechel Foch.

McClure's Orchard
5054 N. U.S. 31
Peru, IN 46970
765-985-9000
www.McCluresOrchard.com

If travelling along one of Indiana's most scenic northern highways (31), take time to stop at the McClure's Orchard—just north of Peru. This 100-year-old orchard is well-known in the area for its fall apple festival and fruit productivity, but in recent years has expanded to incorporate a full-fledged country store and diner along with a tasting bar. Now known for their hard ciders and fruit wines, McClure's sports an expanding array of intriguing labels.

As a lunch or dinner destination (The Apple Dumpin' Inn), McClure's offers a tasty menu featuring sandwiches, soups and breads. Most of the entrees feature some presentation of the McClure apples—sauces, butters, stewed—and all are delectable. The country store entryway also shelves an array of organic and natural products, including apple butter, honey, maple syrup, and a cornucopia of jams and jellies. Hand-crafted items, décor, wall hangings, and wine-related items round out the store quite nicely, and in the back one will find a beautiful tasting bar lined with cases of the McClure ciders and wines.

The spacious McClure grounds also feature the colossal apple barn—where one can pick up produce by the bushels—and an animal barn. This is a kid-friendly place with plenty of parking.

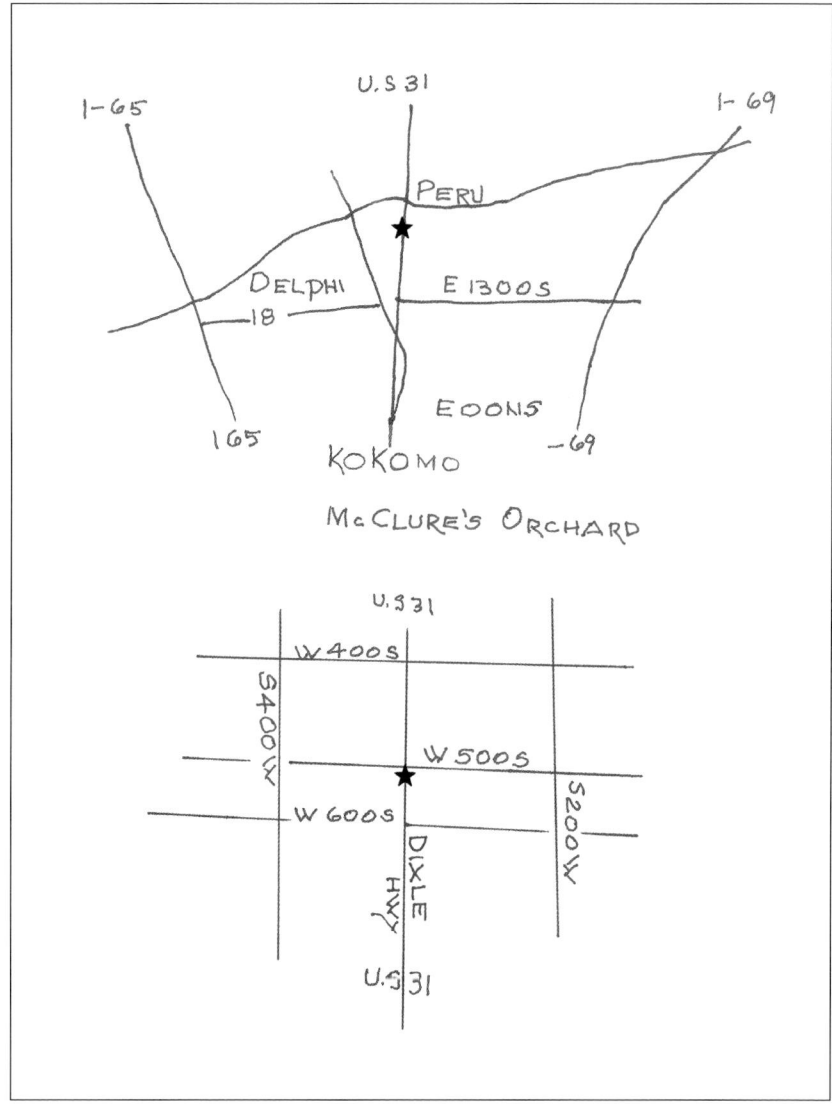

McClure's began producing their ciders and wines in 2009 from their own farm products—not just apples, but also berries and fruits—and has been expanding its list ever since. In addition to the hard ciders—which are bottled in pop-top sizes for easy chilling—McClure's now offers a dozen fruit wines including apple, peach and strawberry. These sweet wines all have a fruit taste indicative of their respective origins, with the apple wines as the backbone of their presentation.

McClure's also has an award-winning ice cider which, sipped judiciously, can compare favorably to some of the best ice wines in the state. And considering the variety of the hard ciders one can find here, it is difficult to imagine any orchard in the Midwest producing such an array of sensations from the apple—including some Bourbon barrel aged ciders and jalepeno flavors.

In season, this orchard/winery is a happening place and is one of the few wineries to be found in north/central region of the state.

Information by the Glass

Owners: McClure Family

Hours:
Daily 9 a.m. - 5 p.m.
Sunday 11 a.m. - 5 p.m.

Amenities: Gift Shop, Gourmet Foods, Apple Barn

Tastings: Free

Price: $12 - $15

Recommendations:
Rhubarb wine: Sweet as cherry pie, this wine has a crisp, slightly bitter taste that reminds of a tart Bing Cherry wine. Would pair well with milk chocolate and almonds.

Coffee Honeywine: Certainly a unique wine—this coffee-flavored mead has both the distinct aroma and flavor of a Columbian coffee layered with honey and apricot notes. This wine would go very well with bread pudding, dates, and rum-raisin ice cream.

Activities: Hayrides, Harvest Events, Music

Nearby Attractions: France Park.

Cinnamon French Toast

Sliced bread
Cinnamon
5 eggs beaten
Powdered sugar

Make an evening meal of French toast—dip bread into egg batter and fry in a pan coated with vegetable oil. While bread is wet, add dashes of powdered cinnamon to each side. On the plate, add a dash of powdered sugar. Serve with Coffee Honeywine.

Monkey Hollow Winery
11534 E. County Road 1740 North
Saint Meinrad, IN 47577
812-357-2272
www.monkeyhollowwinery.com

A ny wine trip to southern Indiana should include the Monkey Hollow Winery—located near Santa Claus, Indiana and Holiday World Theme Park. Monkey Hollow is a small, country-themed winery with a big heart for their eight acre vineyard that features French, American and French hybrid grapes. Their well-rounded list includes dry, semi-sweet, sweet, and specialty small batch wines.

Complete with the country, farm theme one can also pick berries in season—with acres of strawberries, red raspberries and blackberries on the bush. The beauty of the southern Indiana hills is evident from the tasting room, which also displays local arts and crafts for purchase.

Although Monkey Hollow does not have a large lineup—usually less than a dozen wines produced and bottled at any one time—one can find the signature Hoosier Chambourcin here year-round and their unique Pasture Mark, which is a Catawba Rose—pink

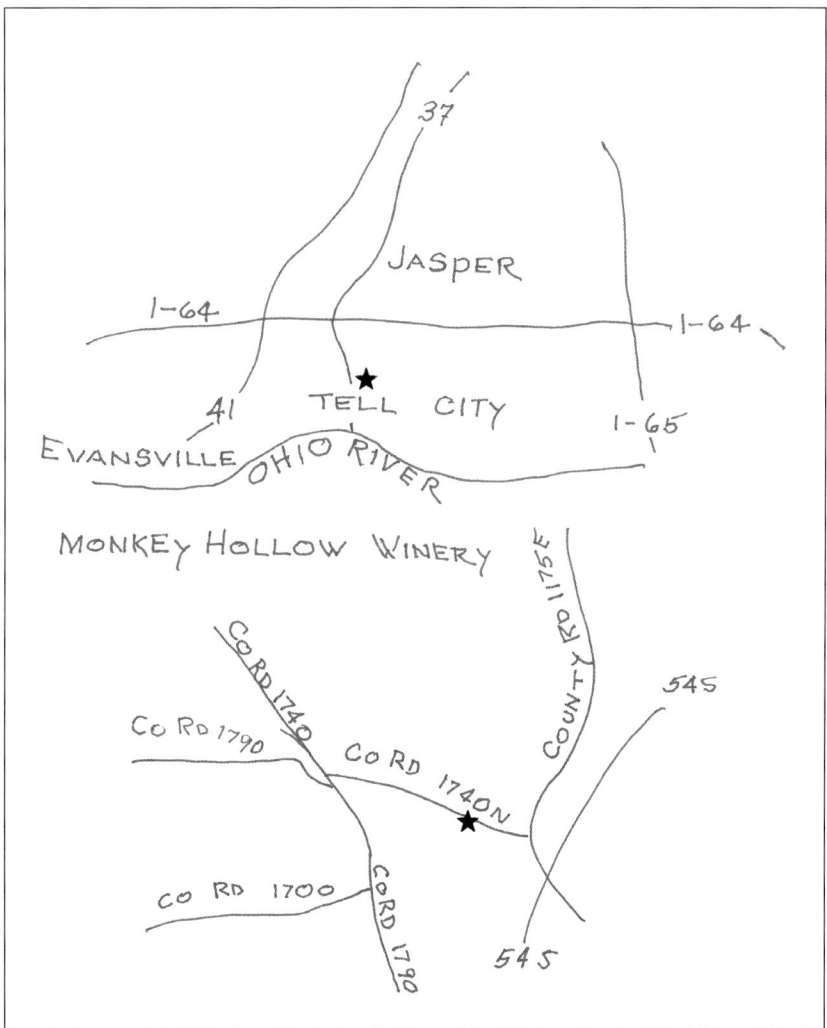

and beautiful in the glass—refreshing and aged in Kentucky barrels for a smooth finish. The Pasture Mark, along with the Pasture Limit 2—a very sweet Concord grape wine with a deep, inky Petite Sirah appearance in the glass—are two of Monkey Hollow's best selling labels.

Don't forget to ask the staff about the history of Monkey Hollow (and the name!) and if you enjoy your trip to the deep south, be sure to take home a Monkey Hollow T-shirt or hat. And make time to amble through the valleys—either toward the Kentucky side or back north—after you have enjoyed these tastes of hand-crafted wines.

Information by the Glass

Hours:
Tuesday - Sunday 11 a.m. - 6 p.m.

Amenities: Gift Shop, Outdoor Seating

Tastings: Free

Price: $15

Recommendations:
Pasture Mark—the Catawba rose has an oaky finish and chilled is best served up with burgers or chicken on the grill.

Late Harvest Vignoles Dessert Wine—very sweet for those who are looking for an after-dinner wine with ice cream or berries.

Spiced Christmas Wine—served in season near the holidays and a favorite to sip by the winter fire.

Activities: Live Music

Nearby Attractions: Hoosier National Forest

Estate Grapes: Various Vinifera and Hybrid.

Sloppy Joe Turkey

1 pound ground turkey
½ celery stalk, chopped
⅓ cup green pepper, chopped
1 tablespoon Worcestershire sauce

1 medium onion, chopped
½ cup catsup
¼ cup water
Salt, pepper

Cook turkey, onion, celery and green pepper until golden and soft. Drain. Stir in catsup and sauces, salt and pepper to taste. Serve on whole wheat or white bread bun. Add jalapeno for a kick and serve with Catawba.

Mystique Winery
13000 Gore Road
Lynnville, IN 47619
812-922-5612
www.mystiquewine.com

Beginning in 2009, when the first vines of Niagara, Steuben, Vignoles and Chambourcin were planted, Mystique began building the dream of producing quality wines. Today, with their small, but growing list of wines, they have certainly arrived as a destination for patrons who would enjoy a southern Indiana experience.

Mystique has one of the most colorful and vibrant tasting rooms found in the state—with pastels abounding—and their spacious patio deck with umbrella tables makes this a superb spring and summertime gathering spot for friends. Moreover, this seating area plays host to one of the most eclectic and energetic music venues one if likely to find in any winery—and patrons of the arts, or those who enjoy painting, should not overlook the opportunities afforded through the Mystique Winery Canvas & Conversation series: a perfect blend of wines and blank canvas in the waiting.

This winery also offers a selection of cheeses and crackers, for those who would like to make their way through a light, but delicious dinner.

The slate of Mystique wines currently features:

- Bacchus—Pinot Noir, light bodied, with medium tannins.
- King Rex—Riesling, in the old world German tradition, but fruity.
- Hoosier Red—Chambourcin, with a peachy-finish and semi-dry.
- Mystical White—sweet Cayuga with a light finish.
- Zulu—a black cherry sweet wine for desert.
- Carnival—Chardonnay, with peach tones, beautiful in the bottle.

Mystique also offers some tasty slushies. Check out the Mystique web site for upcoming events and musical groups.

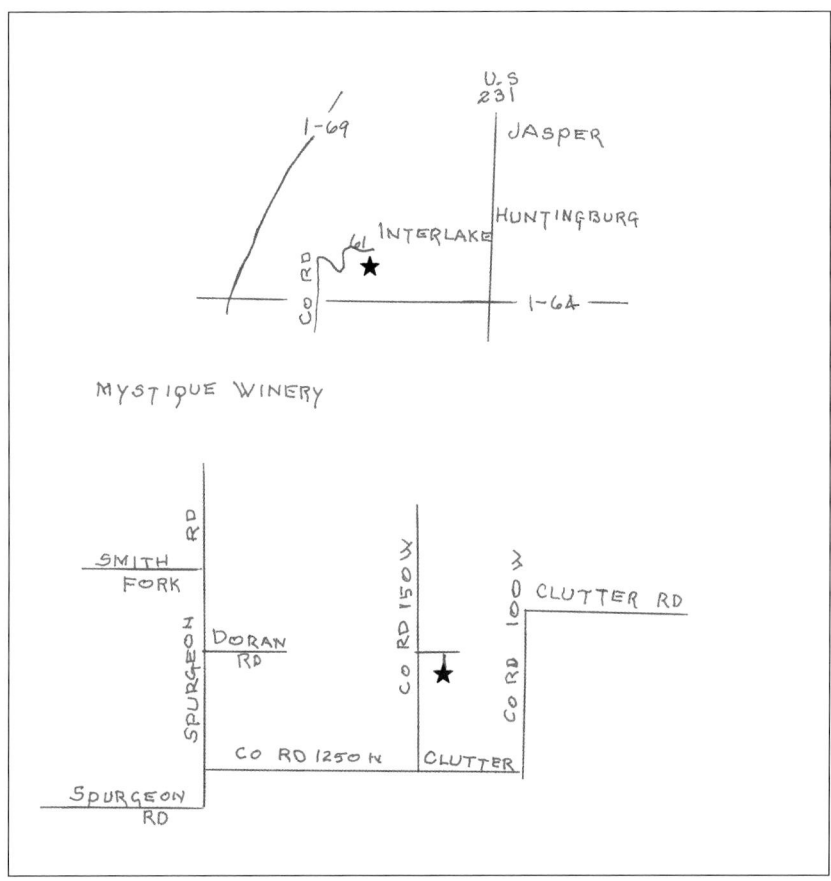

Information by the Glass

Hours:
Wednesday, Thursday, Saturday, Sunday 11 a.m - 6 p.m.
Friday 11 a.m. - 8:30 p.m.
Closed Monday & Tuesday

Amenities: Live Music, Tastings and Tours

Tastings: Free

Price: $12 - $15

Recommendations:
Carnival—pair with Vanilla Bean ice cream and strawberry toppings.

Chambourcin—pair this signature Indiana wine with lasagna or bourbon-glazed pork chops.

Activities: Food Trucks, Vendors, Special Events

Nearby Attractions: Lincoln State Park, Patoka Lake

Estate Grapes: Niagara, Steuben, Vignoles, Chambourcin.

New Day Meadery
1102 Prospect Street
Indianapolis, IN 46203
888-632-3379
www.newdaycraft.com

Perhaps the most unique winery in the state, New Day Meadery offers old-world honey-based wines in refillable growler jugs at a great price. Those who have never tasted mead before will discover that these wines, made from fermented honey and water, provide a sensational taste experience.

The New Day Meadery, located in the revitalized Fountain Square area of Indianapolis, is a charming stop along the Indianapolis Cultural Trail, and is one of the must-see wineries on the Indy Wine Trail. This spacious tasting area inside the Meadery also offers sweet honey delights, cheeses and soft drinks, and a seating area where visitors can gather with friends to play a board game or scout out some of the other Fountain Square area dining options.

The Meads here—which are of several varieties and tastes—proceed from ciders to meads made from fruits such as apple, apricot and cherry, to a semi-dry mead made entirely from fermented honey and water. The best option here is to enjoy the $5 tasting of six generous selections and learning about the migration of mead production as you go. It's a very scintillating and educational. Be sure to ask questions.

The ciders at New Day range from a basic apple cider of 7% alcohol to a hard apple cider that has been sweetened with Indiana sorghum (The Johnny Chapman—aka "Johnny Appleseed). Meads range from the various carbonated wines made from blueberry, strawberry and currant to the semi-dry mead (alcohol at 13%) that, with a taste of honey, brightens to hints of mineral and spice as the mead is warmed in the mouth.

New Day also provides a sizeable range of specialty drinks—which guests can enjoy in the lounge area with friends—and these are served by the glass only, most for $5. The unique growler concept for the New Day wines also provides a renewal resource that patrons can refill at subsequent visits.

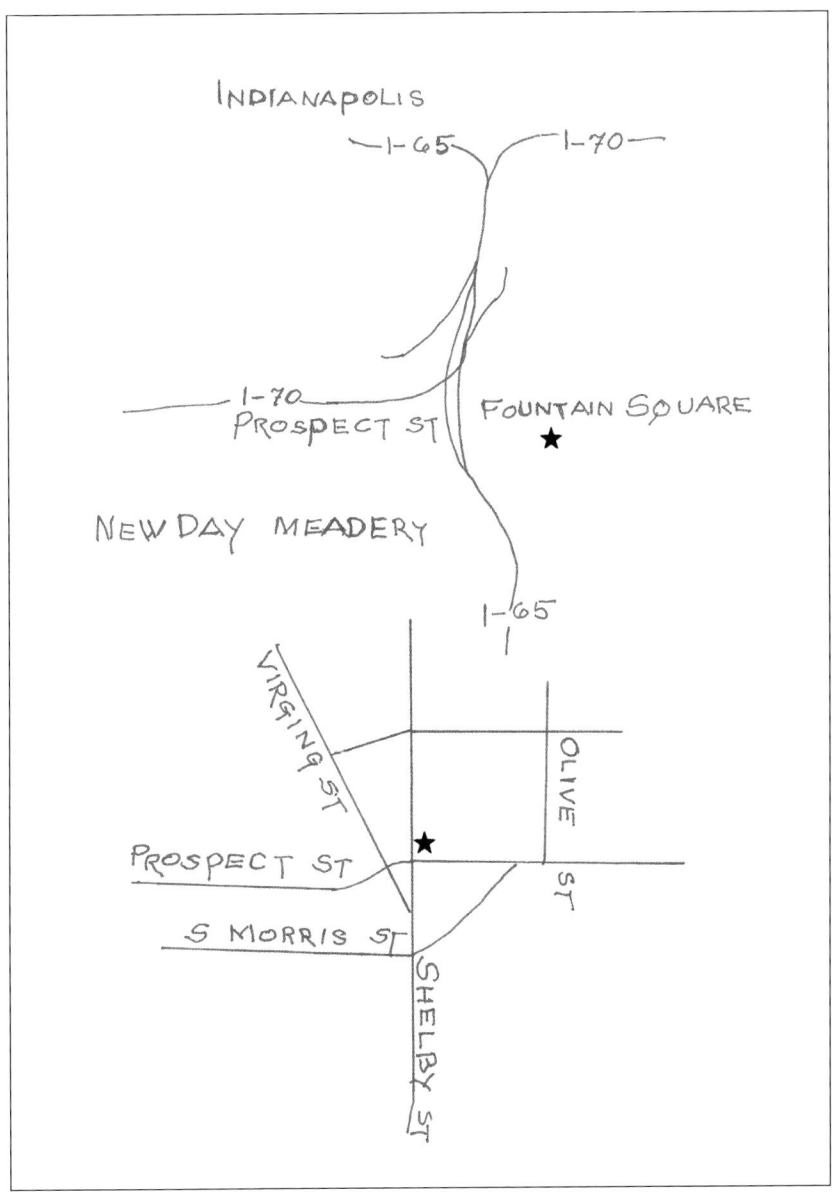

Those visiting New Day for the first time may also want to enjoy an afternoon or an evening in the Fountain Square area—one of the reasons that New Day is opened later than many wineries in the state. Pick up a game of duck-pin bowling across the street, or enjoy a rooftop meal and spectacular view of the Indianapolis skyline. There are also antique shops, specialty stores, Greek fare, and amazing pizzas within walking distance of New Day.

Information by the Glass

Owners: Brett Canaday and Tina Agnew

Hours: Tuesday - Friday, 2 - 9 p.m.
Saturday 12 - 9 p.m.
Sunday 12 - 6 p.m.
Closed Mondays

Amenities: Gift Shop, Gourmet Foods

Tastings: $5 for six selections

Price: $12

Recommendations:
Snap Dragon—a carbonated apricot honey wine fermented with orange peel that does not have an overpowering sweetness, but a delicate tartness that would go well with candied pecans and nuts.

Washington's Folly—a carbonated cherry mead that provides a balance of sweet and tart, would pair well with glazed pork chops or a summer evening with vanilla ice cream.

Semi-dry Mead—this traditional honey mead wine has a smooth mineral finish that would pair well with German foods such as sauerkraut and sausage, roasted red potatoes, and strong cheeses.

Activities: Music, Special Events

Nearby Attractions: Fountain Square Restaurants, Antiques.

Spicy Trail Mix

Salted peanuts
Pistachios
Jalapeno powder

Raisins
M & Ms

Add nuts and M&Ms to mixing bowl and add dashes of jalapeno powder to your taste. Bag in individual zip-locks for hikes and travel. Enjoy the mix with Snap Dragon.

Oak Hill Winery

111 East Marion Street
Converse, IN 46919
765-362-3634
www.oakhillwinery.com

Open weekends in Converse, Indiana—between Kokomo and Marion—Oak Hill serves an impressive lineup of wines from an 1894 Carriage House that is much larger than outward appearances. Inside, up the staircase, one will find a beautiful tasting bar and ample seating. Operating for more than thirteen years, the Oak Hill Winery is one of those northern Indiana treats that weekend travelers should visit. Oak Hill can also play host to private parties.

In addition to their weekend hours, Oak Hill also has a monthly "wine night"—where the establishment stays open until 9 p.m. A wine club also rounds out this winery quite nicely and gives regulars an opportunity to stock up on favorites during the week.

Like many of the boutique wineries in state, Oak Hill acquires their supply from vineyards around the country (and the world) and creates their own special blends and varietals. Among the tops here you should expect to find Red Bridge—a cranberry wine that is one of the best sellers—along with the Wabash Valley Red, a new Malbec that Oak Hill began making in 2014. In addition, there are some carefully crafted whites here, such as the Catawba, which provides an old world taste of Indiana, not too sweet, but balanced with some zest.

Oak Hill also makes a mead wine, which is a rarity in state, and for those who enjoy these decadently sweet wines, it's a must-taste.

Oak Hill has its own clientele and promise and is a winery that has enough variety to please anyone. A small town with a gem of a winery—don't miss it.

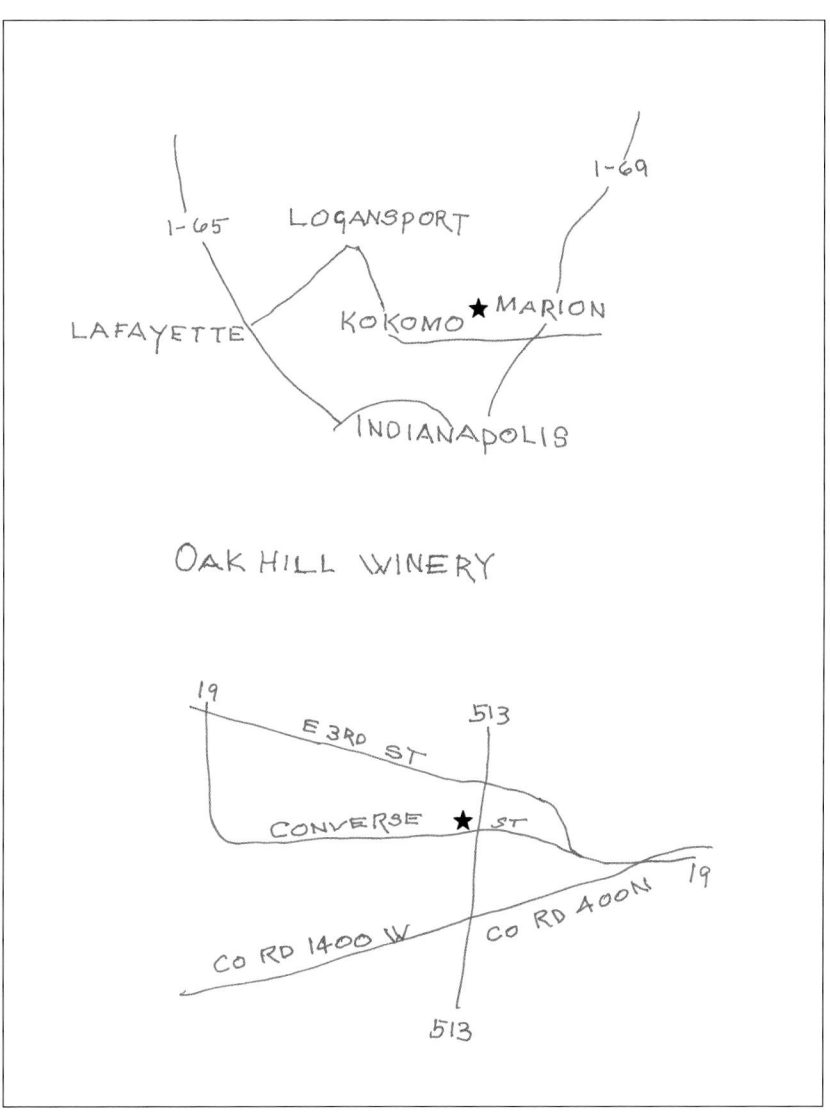

Information by the Glass

Owners: Rick and Betty Jo Moulton

Hours: Saturday & Sunday 1 - 6 p.m.

Amenities: Gift Shop

Tastings: Free

Price: $13

Recommendations:
Van Buren—the Oak Hill Zinfandel which has a balance of pepper-spice but with a lighter body than many Zins, making it perfect for chilling or to pair with beef tips and asparagus on the grill.

Activities: Music

Nearby Attractions: France Park and Huntington Lake

Estate Grapes: Cayuga, Vidal, Sauvignon Blanc, Chardonnay.

Grilled Skirt Steak

2 lbs. Skirt Steak
Fresh black pepper
Coarse salt
Olive oil

Heat grill to high. Pat steaks dry with paper towel. Rub steak on both sides with olive oil. Sprinkle Salt and fresh cracked pepper on both sides of steak. Place steaks on grill. Cover Grill. Cook 4 minutes, then flip and cook 3 minutes for medium rare. Remove steaks to a large cutting board with edges to catch liquid. Loosely cover steak(s) with aluminum foil for 5 minutes. Thinly slice on a diagonal and serve.

Recipe courtesy of Steven Libman.

Oliver Winery
8024 N State Road 37
Bloomington, IN 47404
812-876-5800
www.oliverwinery.com

Oliver is not only one of the oldest and most respected wineries in Indiana—but is among the premier wineries in the U.S. In many respects—in terms of history and production and quality—Oliver Winery stands at the pinnacle of Indiana wineries. Starting in the 1960's as a hobby, winemaker Bill Oliver began planting vines in Bloomington and sharpening his winemaking skills. William Oliver was also instrumental in the legislative process that allowed small wineries to operate in the state. The year was 1971, with Oliver becoming one of the leaders in the winemaking craft and providing the leadership that helped other wineries flourish.

Today, Oliver produces more than 270,000 cases of wine per year—and anyone visiting the Oliver Winery (located on US 37 north of Bloomington) will quickly take note of this winery's place among the premier producers in the country. And the wines are the reason.

The Oliver label (and Creekbend) can be found in many outlets, but in order to get a true taste of the fine wines, and the huge selection offered, one must visit the Oliver estate for a round of glasses. The Oliver lineup is far too lengthy to offer here—but visitors are going to appreciate most of all the insights and expertise of the tasting room staff. Whether an affectionado of dry or semi-dry or sweet, Oliver is going to offer more selections among the individual categories than many wineries offer in total.

Among Oliver's finest, however, the Shiraz and Zinfandel are always winners, with bold and peppery finishes that will remind one of a visit to Napa Valley. As with most of Oliver's finest, the "Reserve" label offers a step-up in quality (and in value) for those who desire more depth from the ageing process.

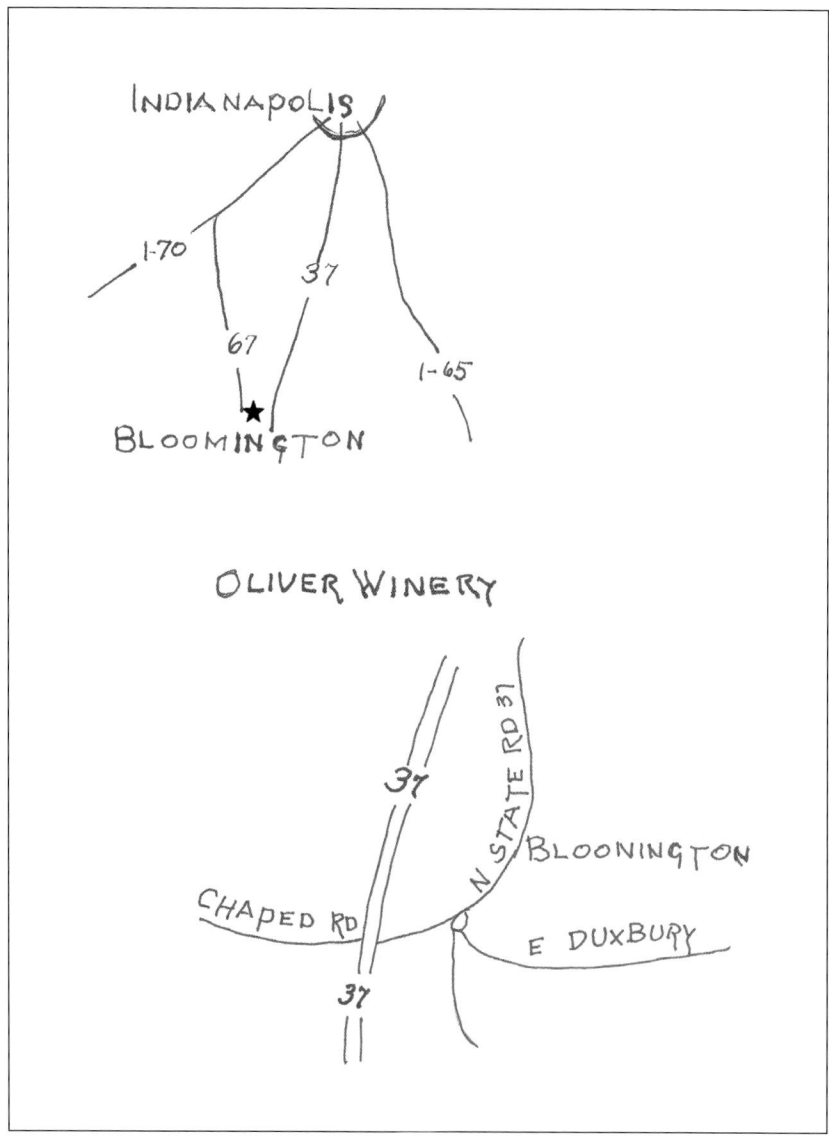

Oliver also produces Vignoles, Traminette, and Vidal Blanc that can compete against the best of the Hoosier varietals.

When visiting Oliver—especially on weekends or at peak seasons such as the Brown County fall foliage—one should expect large crowds at the winery. But no worries. Oliver offers plenty of parking and magnificent grounds. Regardless of the crowds, one can most always find a quiet corner on the back deck, or along the pond at a picnic table.

Oliver also offers a venue for live music and for wedding parties. The tasting room—which is frequently expanded into the production facility—provides ample area of hundreds of people to enjoy these fine wines. A meat and cheese fridge offers additional food choices, and Oliver encourages people to bring a picnic lunch to be enjoyed alongside an Oliver bottle. If you have not been to Oliver (or haven't visited recently) make it a point to include this stop in a weekend get-away or a side-trip the next time you travel through Bloomington. You won't regret the delight that Oliver Winery offers.

Information by the Glass

Owner: Bill Oliver

Hours: Monday - Saturday 10 a.m. - 6 p.m.
Sunday 12 p.m. - 6 p.m.

Amenities: Outdoor Seating, Gift Shop, Trails, Picnic Area

Tastings: Free

Price: $13 - $30

Recommendations:
Cabernet Sauvignon—this wine has big tannins and is a wine that will get better with age. Pair this one with lasagna and a mixed salad.

Chambourcin Rose—a subtle wine with raspberry and strawberry undertones, beautiful in the bottle, served chilled with barbecued ribs or glazed salmon.

Creekbend Catawba Sparkling Wine—one of the most beautiful sparkling wines anyone can find in a bottle, this dessert wine is perfect for an anniversary or wedding.

Activities: Live Music, Festivals, Weddings, Banquets, Wine Appreciation, Tours

Nearby Attractions: Monroe Lake, Indiana University

Estate Grapes: Chambourcin, Cabernet Sauvignon, Merlot, Traminette, Cabernet Franc, Vignoles, Cayuga White, Sauvignon Blanc, Catawba, many more.

Sweet & Sour Pork Chops

Pork chops (lean or boneless) Salt, pepper
¼ cup pineapple juice Pineapple rings

Cook and then sear chops in olive oil until cooked to taste and texture, sprinkle with salt and pepper on tops. Reduce heat and add pineapple juice. Simmer. Add a pineapple ring to the top of each chop. Simmer for 2 minutes more. Serve with Chambourcin Rose or an Oliver Sparkling Wine.

Owen Valley Winery

491 Timber Ridge Road
Spencer, IN 47460
812-828-0883
www.owenvalleywinery.com

The Owen Valley Winery in rural Spencer sports wines with a beautiful and distinctive label. Located on spacious grounds, along with some ten acres of vines, this rural winery hosts weekend live music and other entertainment, but also provides a relaxed and quiet setting for guests who simply want to enjoy a glass or bottle on the front porch. Ample parking makes any visit an ease.

The wines produced here feature some of the typical Indiana varietals that one would expect from Hoosier wines along with grapes brought in from California (think Zinfandel and Syrah). For those who enjoy the sweeter wines of Indiana, one can't go wrong with the Catabwa or Cauga—both of which offer a welcome, fruity taste with a clean finish. And for those who are looking bolder presentations, try the Owen Valley Timber Ridge—their version of the Marechal Foch grown on their grounds. This wine is not as deep as a Zin or Cab, but stands on its own legs with some of the best in the state produced from this varietal.

Owen Valley is part of the Indiana Uplands wine trail and can be included in a visit to the Butler, Oliver, and Cedar Creek wineries—all of which are within a 30 minute drive.

What visitors will appreciate about the Owen Valley Winery is the atmosphere and the laid-back appreciation of wines that the staff will offer. Likewise, the Owen Valley label is one of the most artistic and distinctive on any bottle. And because this winery offers a wide selection from dry to sweet, everyone is certain to find a taste that will appeal.

Indiana Wineries: The Ultimate Guide to Wine in Indiana

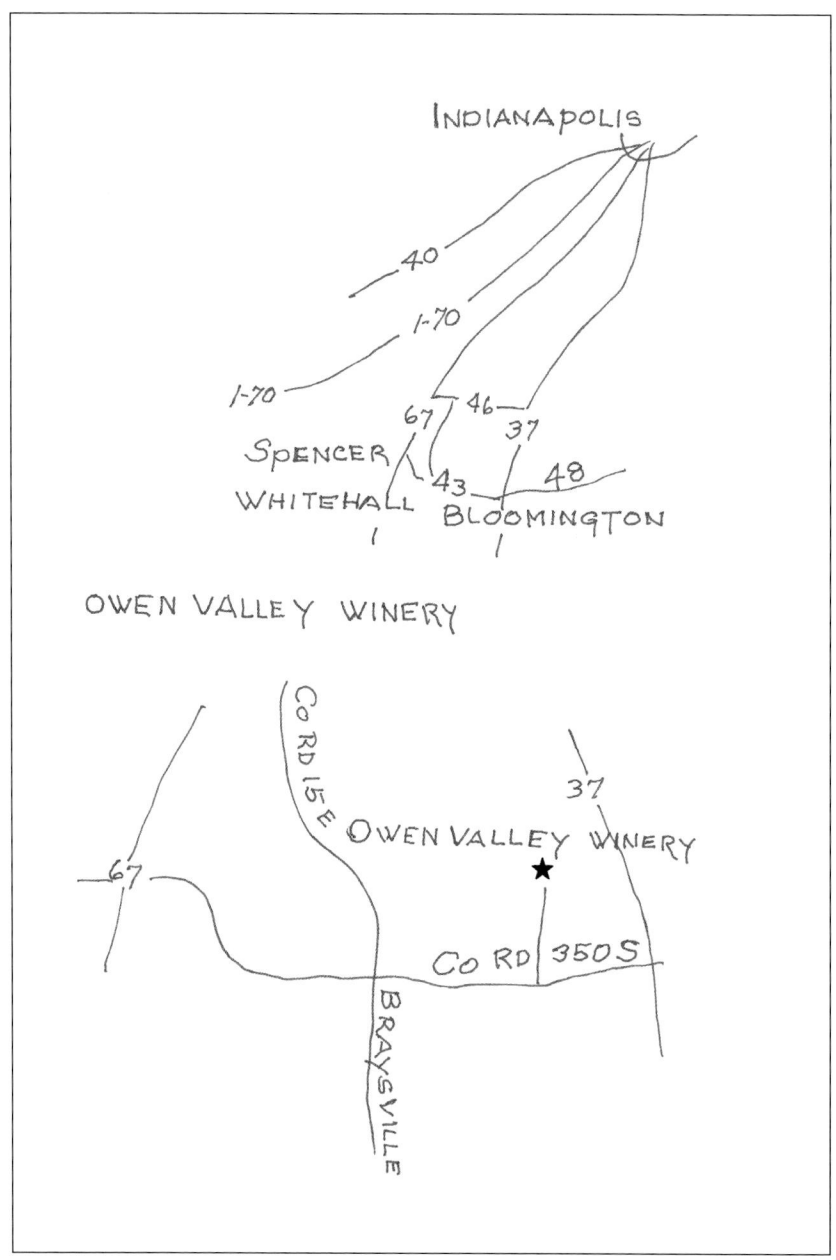

Information by the Glass

2nd Location:
Tivoli Theatre Tasting Room
2811 Washington Street
Spencer, IN 47460

Hours: Wednesday - Saturday 12 p.m. - 7 p.m.
Sunday 12 p.m. - 6 p.m.

Amenities: Outdoor Seating, Gift Shop

Tastings: $5

Price: $15

Recommendations:
Persimmon Bold—likely the only winery in Indiana producing a persimmon varietal in season. A spicy and bourbon barrel-aged wine that would pair well with (get this) persimmon pudding. With 16% alcohol, this persimmon wine has a portly taste, and could certainly be called a Hoosier classic.

Activities: Live Music

Nearby Attractions: McCormick Creek State Park

Estate Grapes: Vidal Blanc.

The People's Winery
414 S. Third Street
Logansport, IN 47947
574-721-0791
(see The People's Winery on Facebook)

Driving across the Wabash River from the south into old downtown Logansport, one can catch a glimpse of The People's Winery—an establishment located in the historic People's Bank building on the right. After a rocky start—in which most of The People's Winery inventory was lost in a fire in Carmel, Indiana—this winery demonstrates the resiliency of the human spirit and the determination to produce not only quality wines, but a superb winery. The People's Winery is just that.

Inside this winery patrons will discover a large wrapped bar perfect for tastings. Ample seating (with tables and chairs for forty) provides a relaxing setting amid a spirited display of original artwork and a small gift area where one can also purchase appetizers. The place offers a good vibe the moment you walk in and patrons will also discover friendly and knowledgeable folk behind the tasting bar.

Live music and other special events are sprinkled through the year—and a nearby comedy club has made the winery a popular pre-show warm-up. And from the winery, one can walk to several fine dining experiences, too.

As for the wines that The People's Winery is producing—no one should walk away disappointed. This winery has a far-reaching and full slate of labels, with wines being produced here from juices far and wide. Among the whites, how about Chardonnay, Bella Bianca, Pinot Grigio, Riesling, and Gewurztraminer. And The People's Winery also produces a fine Cabernet Sauvignon (which actually has 10% Syrah and 10% Zinfandel to add complexity). There is also a Rosso Grande—an oaky red with firm tannins and plenty of spice to complement the ripe berry and melon structures.

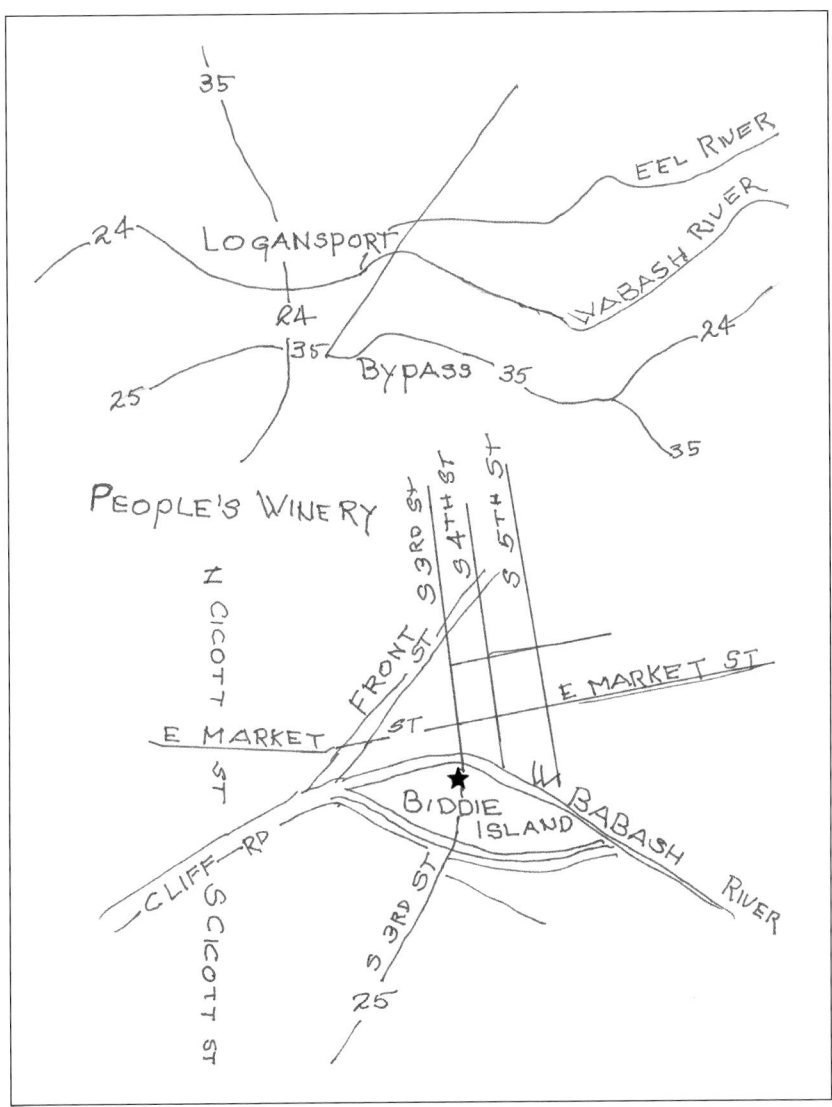

The People's Winery also produces an impressive array of sweet and dessert wines made with unique blends such as Viognier and pineapple, Chardonnay and peaches, and Shiraz and blueberry. These fruit wines are a bit more rich and complex than traditional fruit fare and as such are worthy of note.

If you have never been to Logansport, you won't have to travel far to take in a couple of other wineries, too—and the enclave of wineries in the area are attempting to form yet another wine trail. Let's hope they are successful. After all, as The People's Winery name implies—when people discover some of the wineries of Indiana, they make their way to others.

Look for more information about The People's Winery on Facebook or call ahead to check on their special events and activities.

Information by the Glass

Owners: Brad and Stacie Angle

Hours:
Tuesday - Friday 2 p.m. - 8 p.m.
Saturday 11 a.m. - 7 p.m.
Sunday 11 a.m. - 4 p.m.
Closed Mondays

Amenities: Gift Shop, Artwork

Tastings: Free

Price: $15

Recommendations:
Riesling—a very dry and fruity rendition of this German varietal, but well balanced with hints of Peach and Apricot. Drink this wine with crab, lobster, or with Chinese food.

The People's Choice—this honey-colored dessert wine is unique for its hazelnut and vanilla notes but has a velvety smooth finish. Well balanced and mellow. Pair this dessert wine with dark-chocolate ice cream and cherries.

Activities: Live Music, Art Shows

Nearby Attractions: Logansport Restaurants and Antiques.

Apricot Trail Mix

Package of dried apricots   Package of dried cranberries
Package of dried blueberries   Package of dried apples

Mix packages together, replace in zip lock bags for hiking or travel to wineries. Enjoy with Riesling.

Pepper's Ridge Winery
4304 North CR 200 West
Rockport, IN 47635
812-649-9463
www.peppersridge.com

Pepper's Ridge—the southern-most winery in the State, located in scenic rural Rockport—is a full-service establishment that features a spacious, wood-paneled tasting room and plenty of parking. The winery is also an appropriate gathering place for bridal showers, family gatherings, and events. And with a slate of live music, special events, and tastings, Pepper's Ridge is pure enjoyment.

Patrons here will be surprised by the expansive list of wines, too.

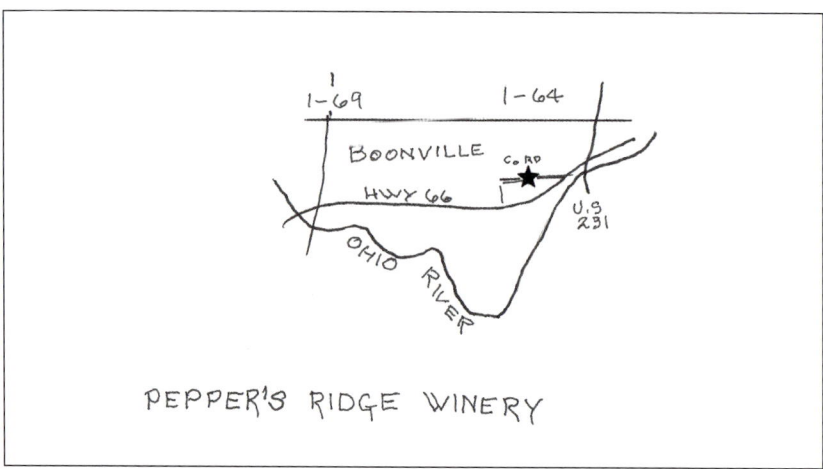

Along with those well-heeled Hoosier varietals such as Chambourcin, Catawba, Niagara, Vignoles, and Foch, visitors who respect the wine scenery will appreciate the Pepper's Ridge expressions to be found in their Reisling and Chardonnay—the latter of which has a smooth buttery finish but without the tartness of some. Pepper's Ridge also has bold red available in their Shiraz and a delightful Merlot which is, as one might expect, a very drinkable red with less tannins and, in this winery's hands, a smooth taste with some smokiness and blackberry notes.

Pepper's Ridge also sports a number of fruit wines, including Apple, Pear, Blackberry, Elderberry, and—with what seems to be growing in popularity—a rather tart Persimmon that will leave a pleasant memory of green apple in its wake. For those who like traditional sweet wines such as those made from the Concord grape—come early in the season. Concord—anywhere in the state—seems to be a popular vintage, and it is not less the case here in the deep south.

Here's the thing: Pepper's Ridge is just a fun place to visit. And with a growing number of wineries cropping up around the Hoosier state, it's good to know that wine lovers along the Ohio River valley can count on Pepper's Ridge to make a good showing. Great entertainment here, to boot—so be sure to visit the web site often enough to calendar your favorite singers and events.

And in season—enjoy the wrap-around porch with a glass or a bottle. Just relax. That's the ambiance of this place, and visitors should never be in a hurry to leave.

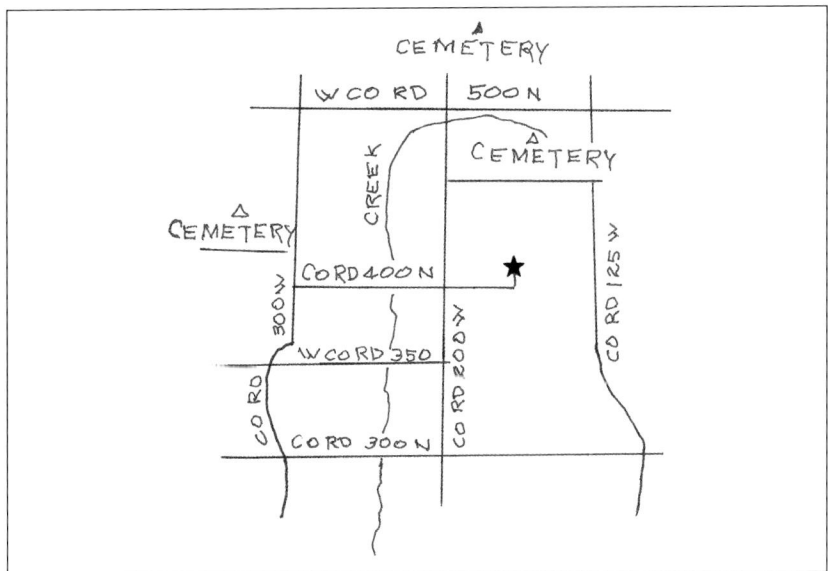

Information by the Glass

Hours:
Wednesday - Sunday 12 - 6 p.m.

Amenities: Outdoor Seating, Stage Area for Live Music

Tastings: Free

Price: $15

Recommendations:
Plum—a beautiful wine the glass with high notes of sweetness that don't overpower. Enjoy the plum wine with salted nuts or trail mix.

Hoosier Red—a Chambourcin offering that's semi-dry, fruity, and amazingly hearty. Hoosier Red should be enjoyed with spicy Chinese cuisine or with beef stew.

Activities: Weddings, Parties, Live Music

Nearby Attractions: Scales Lake Mountain Bike Trail, Ohio River

Estate Grapes: Chambourcin, Catawba, Niagara, Vignoles, Marechel Foch.

Powers Winery
10651 SR 262
Dillsboro, IN 47018
812-432-3620
www.powerswine.com

When Pat and Connie Powers began making wine as a hobby, they didn't envision turning their pastime into a business. But in the Hoosier state, this often happens. What they discovered was that other people enjoyed their wines and so the family farm in Dillsboro became a full-fledged winery with quaint tasting room, gift shop, and warm conversation. The Powers Winery also offers a unique design-it-yourself gift basket, for those who are so inclined to share their wines with others.

This winery offers a relaxing atmosphere on a family farm setting, and patrons will enjoy the peace and quiet that this winery affords. But the drive into the countryside will also provide plenty of time to discuss the wines.

Among the list that Powers produces, there are numerous dry reds and whites, named after family members, that offer varying tastes and complexities for every palate. The "Dry Red" wine is the boldest of these offerings, but the Brisa and Mertle are also quite tasty and present fruit-forward expressions that can be enjoyed with pasta dishes or with roasted chicken.

Among the sweeter varietals, Powers has combined a number of berries and fruits with grape to produce some interesting sweet labels, including Kiwi Pear, Pomegranate, and several wild berry flavors. Straight fruit wines here include Peach, Blackberry and Apple.

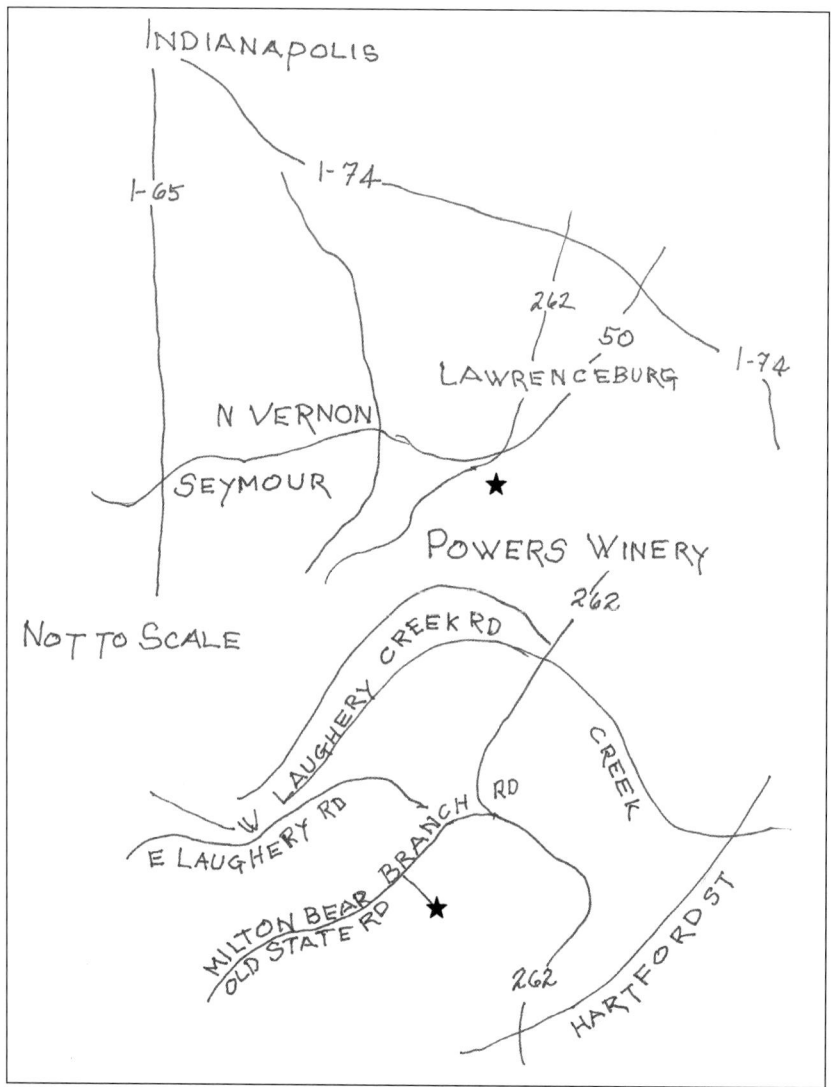

Look for Powers to begin showing up at some of the Indiana wine fairs, as their fruit wines, in particular, will certainly be a catch for those who enjoy the sweeter, fruit-forward, drinkable wines.

Powers is carving a niche for itself and patrons will enjoy this family-owned winery.

Information by the Glass

Owners: Pat and Connie Powers

Hours:
Monday - Wednesday call ahead for times
Thursday - Sunday: 12 - 6 p.m.

Amenities: Gift Shop

Tastings: Free

Price: $12 - $15

Recommendations:
Powers' Summer Ice—this ice wine is incredibly sweet and delicious but also has a wonderful ambiance of warmth (hence the "summer") that would pair well with vanilla bean ice cream or bread pudding.

Activities: Special Events

Nearby Attractions: Clifty Falls State Park.

Indiana Wineries: The Ultimate Guide to Wine in Indiana

Vanilla Wafer Treat

Vanilla and chocolate ice cream
Chocolate syrup

Vanilla wafers, crushed
Whipped cream

In dessert dishes serve up one scoop each of vanilla and chocolate ice cream, sprinkle with crushed vanilla wafers, syrup and whipped cream. Enjoy with Summer Ice.

Quibble Hill Winery

338 Gowers Lane NW
DePauw, IN 47115
502-424-9559
www.quibblehillwinery.com

Information by the Glass

Owners: Steve & Jamie Kraft

Hours:
Wednesday - Sunday 12 - 7 p.m.

Amenities: Outdoor Seating

Tastings: Free

Price: $12 - $15

Activities: Special Events

Nearby Attractions: Clifty Falls State Park

Estate Grapes: Concord, Chambourcin, Syrah, Moscato, Niagara, Vidal.

Rettig Hill Winery
2679 E. Hwy 350
Milan, IN 47031
Phone: 317-460-0542
www.robertpesce.com/rettighill

The Rettig Hill labels, produced by Jeff Hill, is available in several restaurants and outlet stores around the state, and it is best to check out the Rettig Hill website (above) in order to obtain the best overview of these wines. The Rettig Hill vineyard, located in Ripley County, was originally owned by the Sisters of St. Francis—and the Rettig Hill labels premiered at the Indy Wine Festival in June of 2012.

The wines of Rettig Hill include grapes such as Cab Franc, Catawba, Chambourcin, Norton, Syrah and Traminette—but this is less than half of the varietals on this estate.

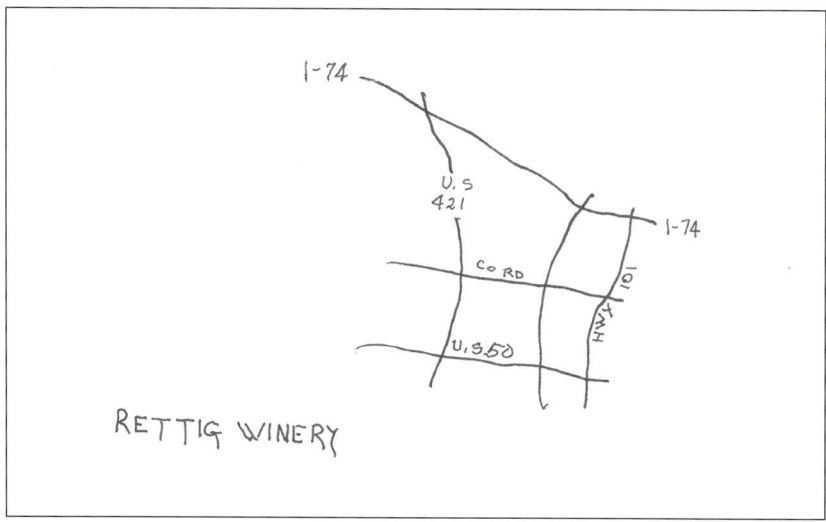

Among the best wines produced by this newer winery, enjoy the Cab Franc/Syrah blend—which is a fruit-forward wine that has been aged in oak has does have spice and depth to it. The Grand Rouge, also a blend of Norton and Villard Noir, is another oak-aged red that has some wonderful raspberry and pipe tobacco notes to it.

To find the Rettig Hill labels, look for them at wine festivals or ask for them in your favorite wine shop.

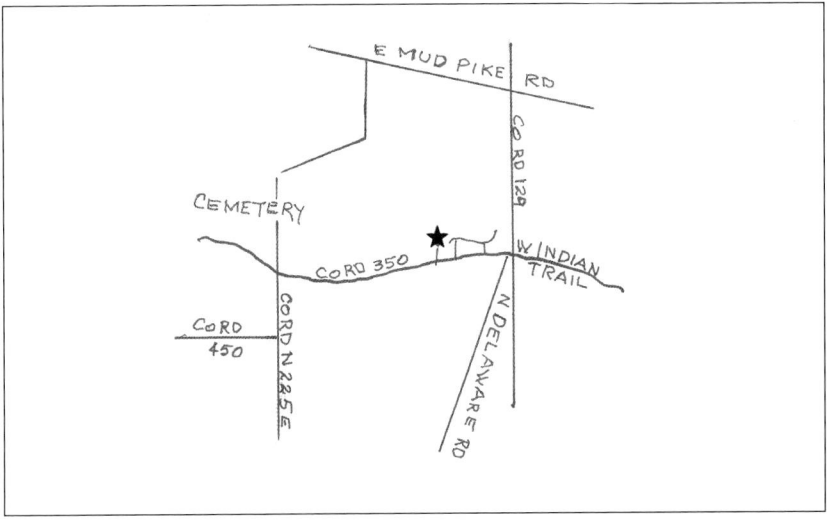

Information by the Glass

Owner: Jeff Hill

Hours: see website/facebook page

Amenities: Tasting Room

Tastings: Free

Price: See facebook page

Activities: Special Events

Nearby Attractions: Historic Milan/Antiques

Estate Grapes: Cab Franc, Catawba, Chambourcin, Norton, Syrah and Traminette.

The Ridge Winery
11048 E State Road 156
Vevay, IN 47043
812-427-3380
812-599-3473
ridgewinery@netpenny.net
www.theridgewinery.com

Drive toward the southeast corner of the state and you can't miss The Ridge Winery on State Road 156 out of Madison. Since 1995, this winery has anchored the historic Swiss wine heritage located in southern Indiana—touted as the oldest winemaking tradition in the United States. Indeed, one can see why this region would have been promising to Swiss immigrants and why they would have planted vineyards in Ohio valley.

This winery, located on a farm, overlooks the Ohio River—and one can sit on the spacious decks of The Ridge Winery and enjoy both the wine and fare produced by this family-owned and operated establishment.

Because of its location, the winery also doubles as a restaurant and entertainment center, and visitors can plan to have a lunch or dinner on the premises: food that ranges from Italian cuisine to salads and even sea food. The restaurant and covered deck area is also large enough for wedding receptions, parties or class reunions.

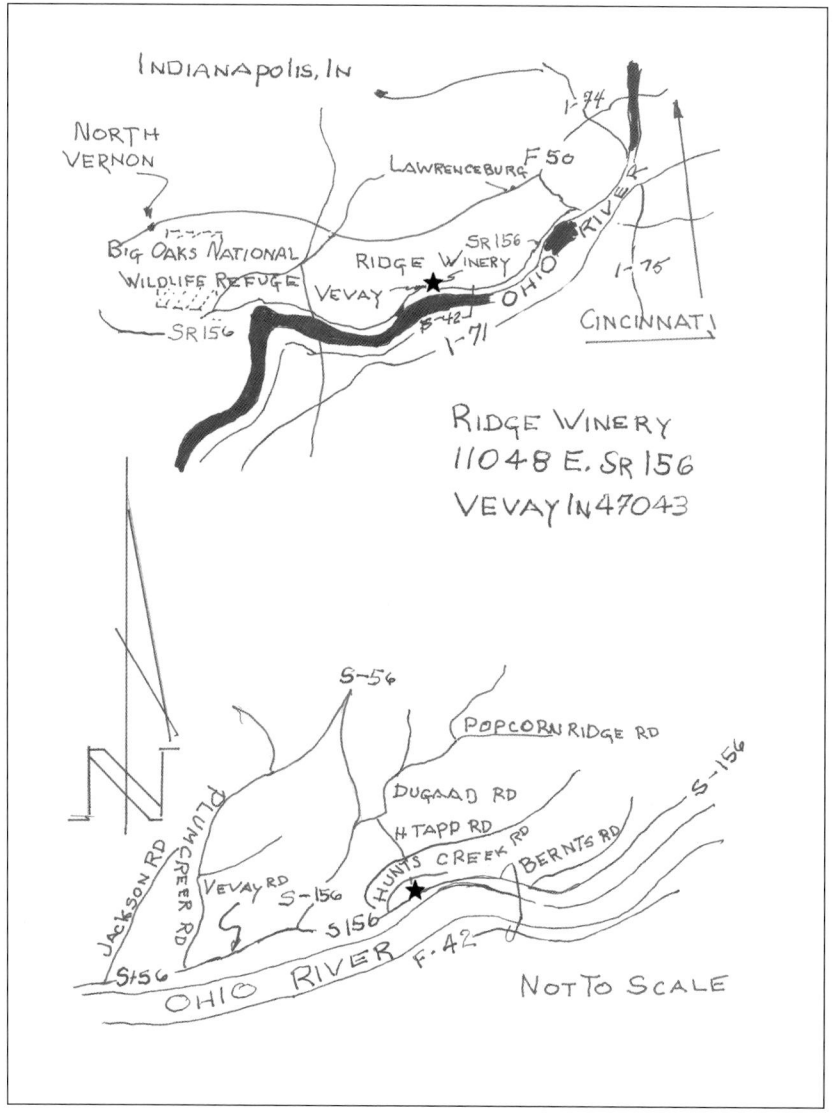

An expansive gift shop is also on site, featuring novelty wine-related items as well as serving the practical needs of the wine lover.

The wines produced by Ridge celebrate the Swiss wine-making heritage of the region and feature names like: Swiss Wine Festival (Shiraz), Classy Red (Merlo), Vevay Bicentennial (Sweet red table wine), Switzerland Country Red (American Concord). Most of this winery's selections are of the sweeter variety—likely reflecting the tastes of the area—but as with many Indiana wineries, one can also find Blackberry, Cherry, and Strawberry wines, too.

The staff at The Ridge Winery have a wealth of information about the Swiss wine-making heritage and the history of this area, and there are historical brochures and photos that one can pick up in a rack near the entrance. The Ridge is most certainly a destination winery—located in a unique Hoosier setting along the river.

As the locals might say, you have to want to arrive here. But once you do, plan to spend some time or enjoy a glass of wine (or a bottle) on the deck.

Information By the Glass

Owners: Tom and Mary Jane Demaree

Hours:
11 a.m. - 6 p.m. Sunday through Friday
10 a.m. - 8 p.m. on Saturday
Winter hours vary

Amenities: Gift Shop, Outdoor Seating, Gourmet Foods

Tastings: Free

Price: $12 - $15

Recommendations:
Peach Crush—a very sweet but delicate blend of peach and grape juices that, served chilled, makes a fine complement to a dish of vanilla ice cream.

Activities: Swiss Wine Festival, Special Events, Live Music

Nearby Attractions: Vevay Antiques, Schenk Mansion

Estate Grapes: Vinifera and Hybrids.

Date Pudding

3 eggs
¼ cup flour
¼ teaspoon salt
1 cup chopped walnuts

1 cup sugar
1 teaspoon baking powder
2 ½ cups of chopped dates

Beat eggs and add sugar while beating. Stir in flour, baking powder and salt. Add eggs then stir in dates and nuts. Pour into greased pan and bake for 30 minutes at 350 degrees. Add powdered sugar before serving with Switzerland Country Red.

River City Winery
321 Pearl Street
New Albany, IN 47150
812-945-WINE
Rivercitywinery.biz

This New Albany winery appeals on many levels. First, as a downtown New Albany establishment with old world charm, it is a destination of locals and travelers alike. The huge bar inside means that, if you've come to taste the wines, you won't have to wait—and tastings are free. Or, if you plan to visit southern Indiana wineries in group—be sure to visit here—as you won't be disappointed in the spacious confines of this charming facility.

The River City Winery has also made a name for themselves as a top-scale pizzeria and gourmet gathering place. Their brick-oven pizzas are some of the best in the area and they also have a menu replete with fare ranging from filet mignon to scallops to ravioli. So a bottle of wine with dinner could be the perfect close to a day-long wine tour in this area—and this writer would recommend you make River City your last stop of the day if you are looking to wrap up your tour with a delightful and relaxing evening.

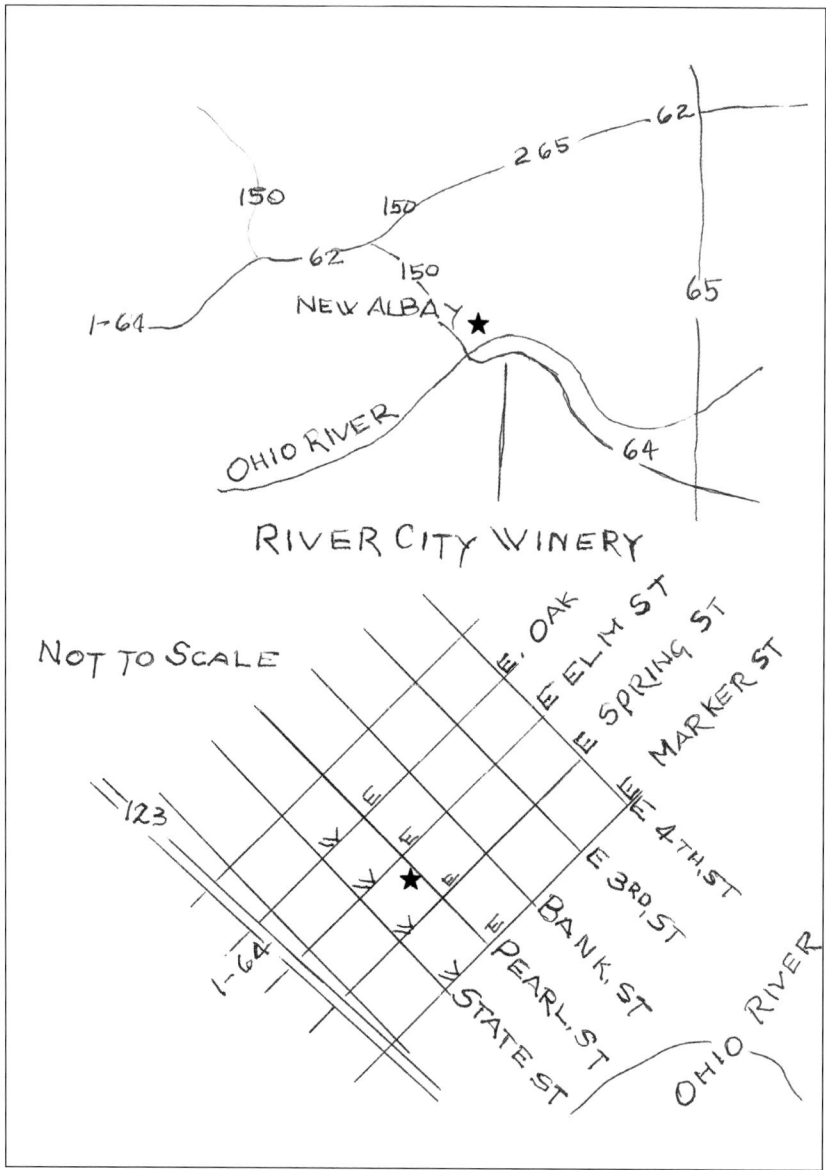

The River City wine lineup features dry, semi-dry, and a broad array of dessert and sweet wines—some of the latter, including the Tropical Storm, a mango wine, being unique to Indiana and to

River City in particular. The dessert wines are all under $15 and any purchase of three bottles or more saves an additional 10%.

Those looking for some bolder selection should give the Neyron Red a go. This blend of Marechal Foch and and Cabernet Sauvignon has the supportive depth to carry it past the tongue and offer the richness of the Cab. The Fire Engine Red is another medal-winner that the winery is proud to deliver, and this Chambourcin rose has the kind of tart, lovely crispness that one can appreciate as a chilled glass with some laid-back summer conversation. Visitors can also find choices here ranging from Traminette to Concord grape.

The River City Winery is in the heart of Pearl Street also—meaning that visitors can find ample opportunity for antique shopping or taking a stroll toward the river. A lounge near the front entrance also offers room for visiting and relaxing before or after ordering. For a deeper appreciation of the wine and fare offered by this hand-crafted wine-maker, visit their web site.

Information by the Glass

Hours:
Tuesday - Thursday 11 a.m. - 9 p.m.
Friday & Saturday 11 a.m. - 11 p.m.
Sunday 11 a.m. - 9 p.m.

Amenities: Gift Shop, Restaurant, Banquet Hall

Tastings: Free

Price: $15 - $25

Recommendations:
The Robert E. Lee—a hybrid blend of Cabernet Franc ($20 bottle), another signature Hoosier grape that sports a bold, dry taste,

here with hints of currant and blackberry.

Green Apple Flood—this super sweet green apple wine will serve notice that it is a force to be reckoned with and the some have described it as Jolly Rancher with a kick.

Activities: Live Music, Wine Shows

Nearby Attractions: Falls of the Ohio, New Albany Restaurants, Louisville Slugger (Kentucky).

Individual Pizza Squares

Individual refrigerated pizza crusts
Sliced jalapenos
Pizza sauce
Sliced green peppers
Sliced black olives
Sliced tomatoes
Grated cheeses
Sliced onions

Make an assembly line of ingredients in individual bowls and precut pizza crusts into horizontal strips. Back on pizza pan until crisp. Serve with Robert E. Lee.

Rowland Winery
8716 Rowland Lane
Dillsboro, IN 47018
812-432-5002

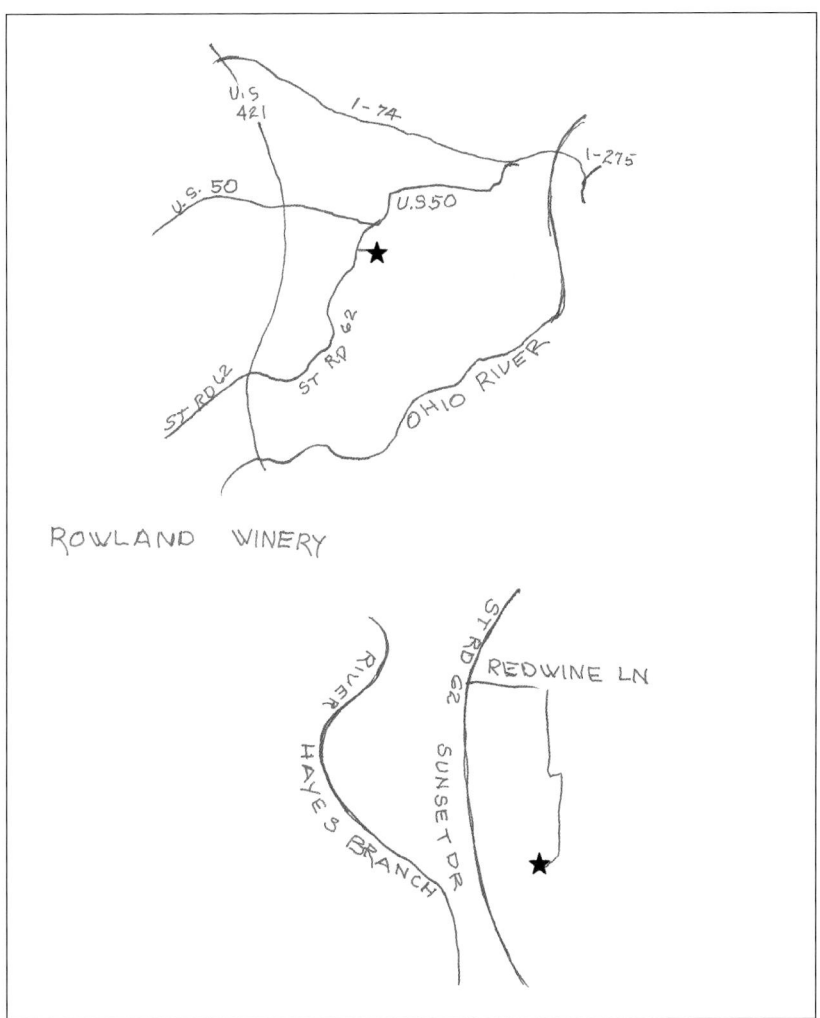

This family-owned and operated winery is located in Dillsboro, Indiana—and along with Powers Winery and Fiekert's Homestead Wines (Rising Sun), offers a respectable triangle of wineries for those desiring to make a quick run to the south-eastern region of the state.

Rowland offers a respectable list of wines, dry and sweet, red and white. Don't overlook their fruit wines and be sure to call ahead for hours of operation.

Information by the Glass

Owners: The Rowland Family

Hours: see facebook page or call

Amenities: Tasting Room

Tastings: Free

Price: see faccbook page or call

Activities: Special Events

Nearby Attractions: Rising Sun Casino.

Salt Creek Winery

7603 W. County Road 925 N.
Freetown, IN
812-497-0254
saltcreekwinery@gmail.com
www.saltcreekwinery.com

Established in 2010 as a hobby by Adrian and Nichole Lee, the Salt Creek Winery in Freetown, Indiana—about 30 minutes from historic Story, Indiana—is a destination well worth your time. Currently open on the weekends, Salt Creek offers a surprisingly expansive list of wines—white, red, dry, sweet and fruit varieties—that are to be enjoyed in this delightful and scenic atmosphere. It is safe to say that this hobby has now turned into a full-fledged business designed around customer satisfaction and top-flight labels. And the Salt Creek logos are distinctive and beautiful in their own right (take a look on the website).

Located among the rolling hills of southern Indiana, Salt Creek has the most amazing vista of any winery in the state—as on a clear day one can see seven to ten miles across the valley and take in the amazing colors in their seasons. The Lee's have also created one of the best outdoor live music venues of any winery as well.

When you do plan to visit, make sure you check out the live performance schedule on the Salt Creek website. Bring a lawn chair and sit a spell. Yes—this is that kind of place. And if you are in a rush you'll miss much of what this winery—and the Lees—have to offer.

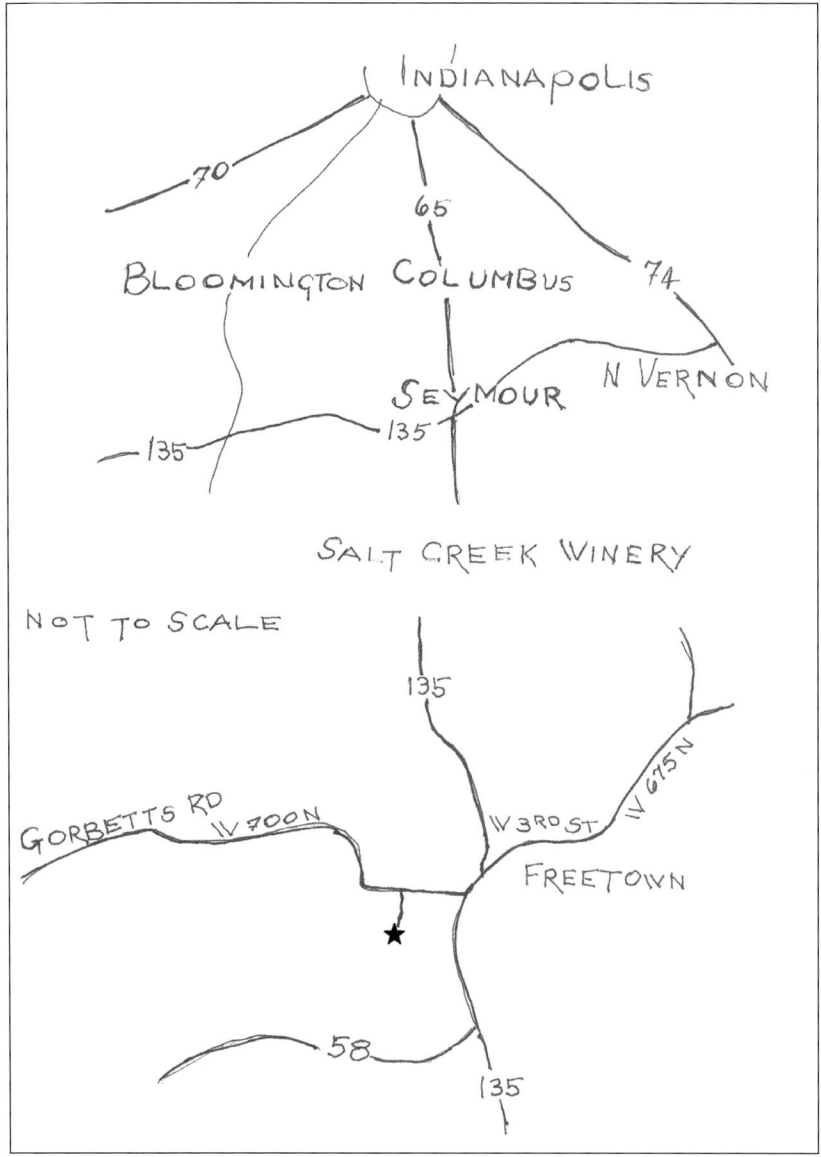

The winery itself is housed inside a bright and beautiful pole structure with a quaint tasting bar, a small gift area, and a refrigerator filled with Fair Oaks cheeses and crackers. A few interior tables and some Amish-made picnic tables round out the available seating, but there is plenty of well-tended hillside for a picnic blanket or a nap, too.

As for the Salt Creek wines, the Lees import juices from around the country (and the world) to produce an eclectic lineup. Local berries and fruits round out the list. And with Nichole's pharmaceutical background, the Lees have a keen taste for creating wines with distinctive aroma, body and taste.

Salt Creek produces both a Merlot and a Cabernet Sauvignon in dry reds, and each has been aged in oak. The Merlot is medium-bodied with black cherry and currant, while the Cab has a classic depth to it, with hints of plum and blackberry. Salt Creek also produces a wonderful Plum wine and a Wild Blackberry that will stand up well against the competition.

Among the sweeter varietals, look for some fine tastes in the Catawba and the Salt Creek Sweet Red blend. If you plan to enjoy a glass on site, look for these in the refrigerator case.

Salt Creek is a destination winery (weekend)—but is close enough to Columbus and Brown County that one could incorporate it into a weekend winery expedition. Make Salt Creek a last stop, however, so you can enjoy the live music and the vista at sunset—which is spectacular!

Information by the Glass

Owners: Adrian & Nichole Lee

Hours: March 30 - New Year's Day
Saturday 11 a.m. - 6 p.m.
Sunday 12 - 5 p.m.

January-end — March
Saturdays only 11 a.m. - 5 p.m.

Amenities: Tastings and Tours, Outdoor Seating, Stage, Natural Views, Gift Shop

Tastings: Free

Price: $10 - $15

Recommendations:
Riesling—an off-dry Riesling of old world quality with hints of apple and pear. Best served chilled and enjoyed solo or with salted nuts, white fish or pasta salad.

Blackberry—a Hoosier favorite and one that will have the taste of fresh picked fruit. Not overly sweet, this one, but with enough pizzazz to enjoy with dark chocolate or truffles.

Activities: Concerts

Nearby Attractions: Brown County State Park, Nashville, Lake Monroe, Story

Estate Grapes: Chambourcin, Riesling, Cabernet Sauvignon, Concord.

Grits on the Side

1 ½ cups grits in package
3 eggs
1 pound sharp Cheddar cheese
¼ cup butter
Salt and Tabasco

For an unique side dish, prepare grits. In a pan, prepare the grits by instructions on packet. Combine grits and other ingredients in a baking dish. Bake for 1 hour at 250 degrees. Add more cheese to top if desired. Serve with fish or chops, and Riesling.

Satek Winery
6208 N. Van Guilder Road
Fremont, IN 46737
260-495-WINE
www.satekwinery.com

In 1992, when Larry & Pam Satek planted their first vines on the family farm, their goal was to provide grapes to other wineries. They did not envision a working winery of their own until after retirement. But the Sateks demonstrated their capabilities as winemakers early on. With Pam's background as a school teacher and administrator, and Larry's PhD in Inorganic Chemistry, they were, in their practical and technical abilities, made for the task. The Satek winery opened in June of 2001 and, right away, became the leading northern Indiana winery—all with wines produced from their own vineyards.

As the vineyard expanded from two to four acres, and additional varietals were planted—including now DeChaunac, Steuben, Seyval Blanc, Vigal Blanc, Marechal Foch and Golden Muscat—the winery also expanded by purchasing product from other regions around the U.S. The result, today, is a winery with a large lineup possessing local and national flair, and wines that will appeal to any palate.

Satek Winery is located on spacious grounds that, for most of the year, offers an expansive and countrified, even relaxing, atmosphere for their patrons. Tents erected on the grounds make for plentiful seating for larger groups, and there are also patios and plenty of grassy area of picnicking. People who visit Satek frequently bring their own food baskets, select one of the fine Satek wines, and enjoy an afternoon or evening basking in the sun.

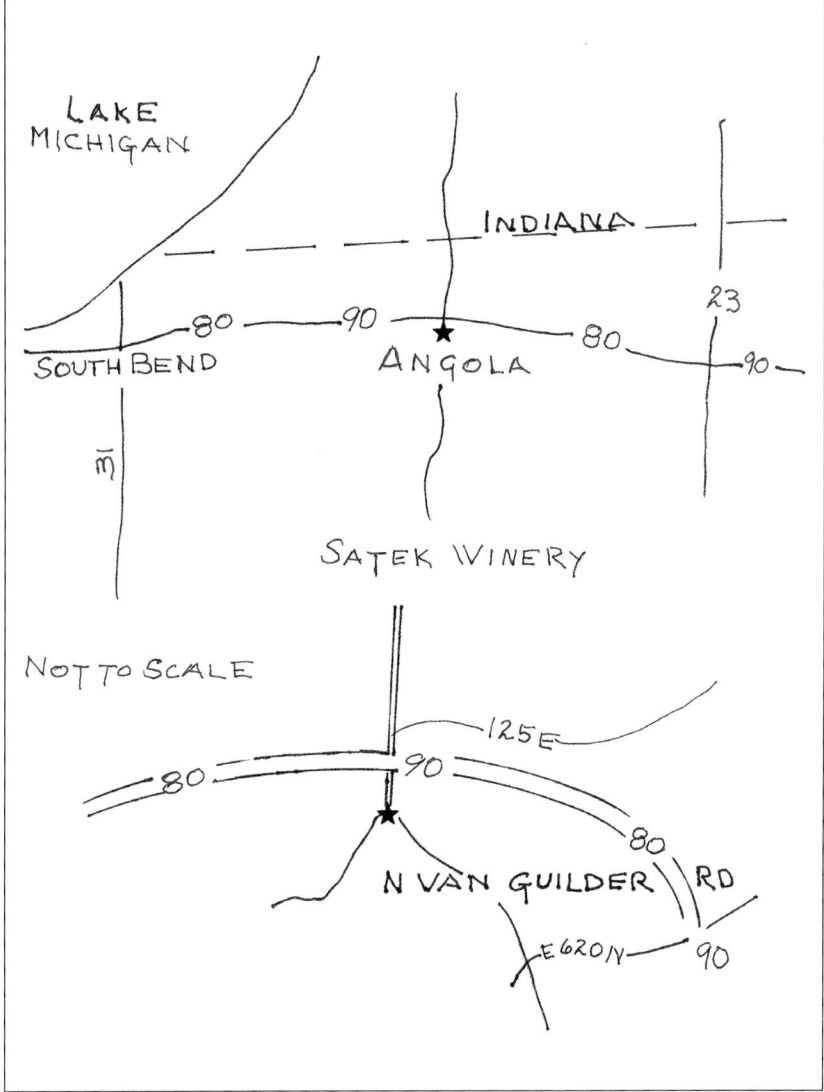

Visitors will also find the Satek staff knowledgeable, courteous, and helpful to a point. And don't miss the beautifully sculpted vineyard as you enter the premises—it's a wonderful place to take a family photograph.

This winery offers wines from all of the varietals noted above, as well as new ones made each year from grapes shipped in from around the country. Here you'll find everything from locally grown blackberry and raspberry wines to the rich, fortified Kreibaum Bay Port—which is one to enjoy either as a desert wine or just by relaxed sipping.

The Chardonnay is an excellent wine here, with overtones of pear, slightly buttery—but more dry than one might usually encounter elsewhere. Satak also makes a fine Merlot and a superb Syrah—which may be their darkest and richest wine, almost inky, but deep and rounded in taste. And each year, ice wine is usually produced—and these bottles go quickly.

Satek's production is on the rise, and they do ship to other states, too—so consider a bottle to ship to a friend. And if you get on the Satek mailing list, you can also receive word about upcoming wines, specials and discounts.

The Satek winery's proximity to the Braili Winery and Vineyard also makes these two a destination worth calendaring. Easy access from several major highways also makes Satek a draw for people in Michigan and Ohio.

Information by the Glass

Owners: Larry and Pam Satek

Hours: 10 a.m. - 6 p.m. daily

Amenities: Outdoor Seating, Gift Shop, Banquet Rooms

Tastings: Free

Price: $8 - $20

Recommendations:
Larry's Luscious Dry Red—this is a Meritage style French red that would pair well with red sauce pasta dishes.

Steuben—an award-winning Hoosier wine in Satek's hands, a rose that sits pretty in the stem but is even more delicious to drink. Semi-sweet and makes a superb summer evening wine, chilled.

Mango Mania—one of the more exotic wines you are likely to find in Indiana. Nothing more here but pure delight.

Activities: Weddings, Concerts, Special Events

Nearby Attractions: Pokagen State Park

Estate Grapes: Pinot Gris, Chardonnay, Vidal Blanc, Seyval Blanc, Riesling, Traminette, Cabernet Sauvignon, Chambourcin, Zinfandel, Syrah.

Cream Cheese Ball

2 8-ounce packages of cream cheese
¼ cup chopped green pepper
8 ounces of pineapple bits   2 cups chopped pecans
2 tablespoons chopped onions   Salt

Mix cream cheese well until very soft, add 1 cup of chopped pecans and other ingredients, continue mixing well. Shape into a ball and press remaining cup of pecans into exterior. Serve with Larry's Luscious Red.

Scout Mountain Winery and Bed & Breakfast

2145 Scout Maintain Road NW
Corydon, IN 47112
812-738-7196
877-351-8607
www.scoutmountainwinery.com

Among southern Indiana's treasures, Corydon (the old capital) possess both history and artistic flair. Not far away from the historic downtown area, a quick drive down highway 62 will land you in good stead at the Scout Mountain Winery. Accompanied by a full-service Bed and Breakfast, along with an orchard, a vegetable garden, and acres of forest, the Schad family have brought their 20-plus years of wine-making experience to bear upon this exceptional homestead. Along with the wine tasting patrons can obviously enjoy an overnight stay, but also the antique and art communities in the old capital itself, Marengo or Squire Boone Caverns, or even a canoe on the Blue River. There is also golf and plenty of exceptional restaurants nearby.

Scout Mountain has also taken to posting food recipes on its website—food to accompany their various wines. And the rates for the Bed & Breakfast—actually a stand-alone/private cottage—are some of the most reasonable one will find anywhere.

With nearly a dozen wines on the list, Scout Mountain will surely have a taste pleasing to any palate. There are plenty of home-grown vintages here to enjoy as well. The Chambourcin, Catawba, and Vidal Blanc all have their own benefits—mostly semi-dry in outlook and presentation. And the Traminette, as a traditional semi-sweet white has a beautifully crafted touch of vanilla and a delightful citrus tone to it.

Fresh from the vineyard, the Apple Cherry wine is fresh and inviting, too. A wonderful dessert wine for those who lean more toward the after-dinner experience. Scout Mountain also makes a delightful port from the Chambourcin grape.

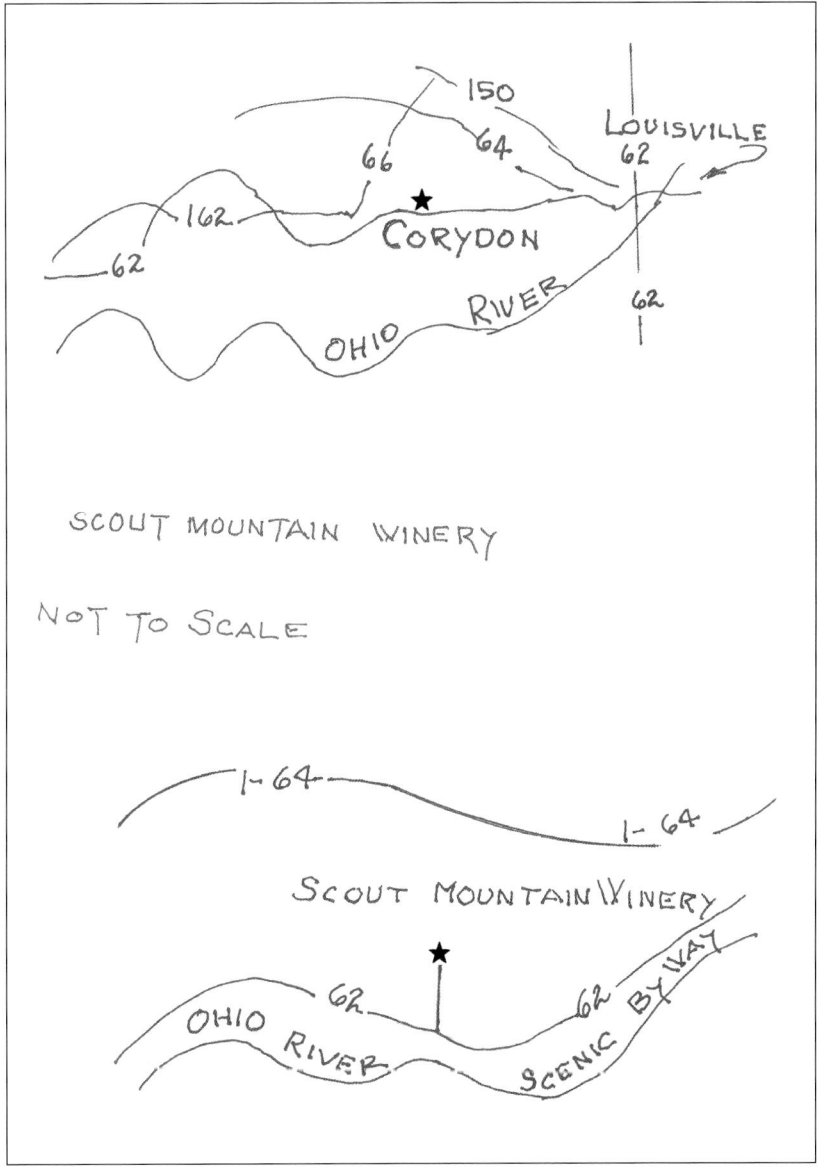

This winery offers a great many treasures and patrons should consider this a destination winery to be enjoyed alongside the old capital itself.

Information by the Glass

Owners: Schad Family

Hours:
Wednesday - Sunday 12 - 6 p.m.
Closed all major holidays

Amenities: Bed & Breakfast, Gift Shop, Outdoor Seating

Tastings: Free

Price: $15

Recommendations:
Chardonel—this dry white wine tells a story through its citrusy mix of peach and apricot overtones and would go well with a salt/garlic pesto on crusty white bread and salmon.

Buzzard Roost Red—a fortified Chambourcin wine that, at 22% alcohol, will hold up quite nicely on cold nights or as a back porch centerpiece with friends.

Activities: Live Music, Chili Cook-off

Nearby Attractions: Old Capital, O'Bannon Woods Park, Falls of the Ohio

Estate Grapes: Chambourcin, Catawba, Vidal Blanc, Traminette, Chardonel.

Shady Creek Winery
2030 Tryon Road
Michigan City, IN 46360
219-874-9463
info@shadycreekwinery.com
www.shadycreekwinery.com

Shady Creek Winery is one of the youngest wineries in Indiana (established in 2009). But this winery's youthfulness is most deceiving. In fact, Shady Creek is producing some of most complex and deeply satisfying wines in the Midwest—especially in the dry red varietals and premier blends.

Located just minutes off of the Lake Michigan shores (and minutes from Michigan itself), Shady Creek is located on 20 acres with a state-of-the-art tasting bar and show room. A wrap-around porch (with Adirondack chairs), screened seating area, and balcony round out the spacious show room, where one can also purchase local artists' works and enjoy the gift shop.

But as for wines—this is a destination worth the drive if one appreciates superior taste.

The winery, a family operation that caters well to guests and groups with equal hospitality, has a flair and panache that visitors will appreciate. Shady Creek also provides delicious food-pairing plates ($10) that can accompany one of their best bottles of wine.

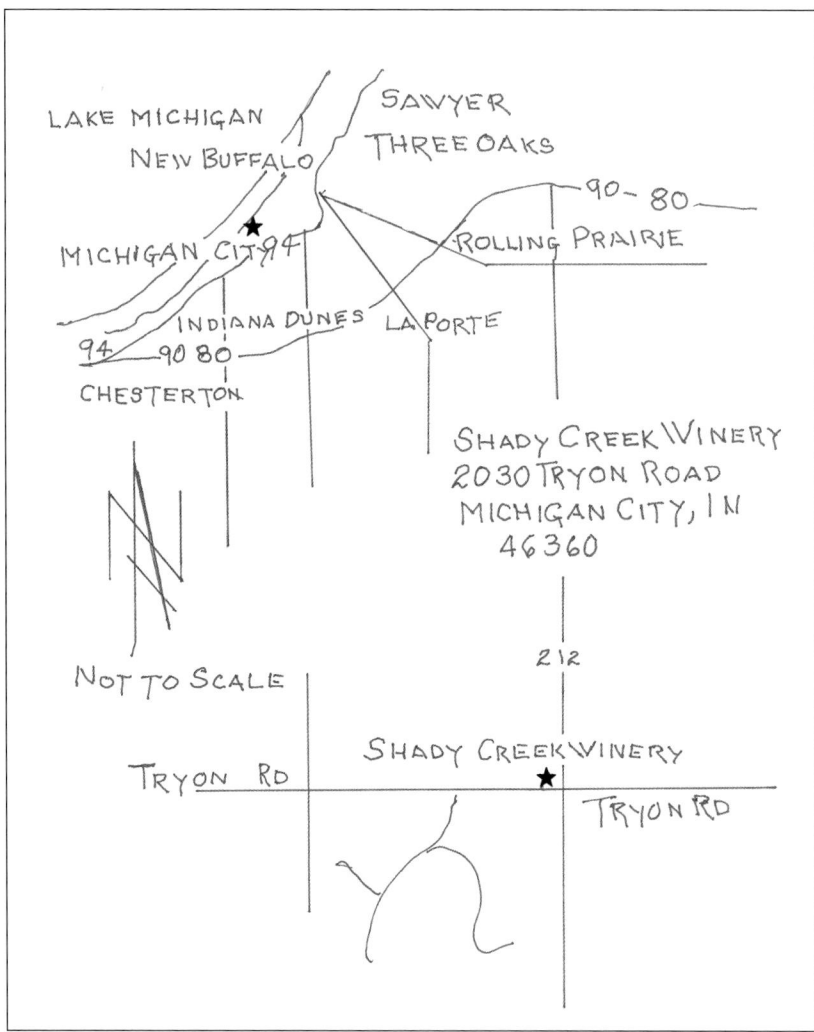

Shady Creek doesn't grow their own grapes, but the juices they ship in from the finest California vineyards are expertly crafted into fine offerings at surprisingly respectable prices. Among the best labels that Shady Creek offers are Rip Tide—a delicious red blend that provides a rich berry taste. The Cab Franc is also excellent, as is R.D.R. (Rescued Dog Red)—another medium-bodied blend with a smooth finish.

The Cabernet Sauvignon is also superior—well-balanced and filled with tannins. And the Syrah—perhaps the best offering of the lot—is a deep, rich and aromatic wine with smoky overtones. At any rate, these dry reds can stand up against any of the top labels in the state, and there is no doubt that this winery is still maturing along with their barrels.

A wine tasting trip to northern Indiana won't be complete without a visit to Shady Creek, and one a sunny day, be sure to make time to enjoy a glass on the porch. And take home some bottles, too.

Information by the Glass

Hours:
Spring Hours after March 6 (and Note Central Time—Chicago)
Wednesday - Friday Noon - 6 p.m.
Saturday 11 a.m. - 6 p.m.
Sunday Noon - 5 p.m.

Amenities: Outdoor Seating, Gift Shop, Banquet Facility, Tours

Tastings: Free

Price: $12 - $22

Recommendations:
Rip Tide—a dry American red with balanced taste.

Syrah—one of the boldest Syrahs in-state, well-crafted and spicy with a cherry-tobacco finish. Drink with red meats such as steaks and chops.

Pink Sky—a semi-sweet rose made for summer evenings on the back deck, pairs well with vanilla ice cream and wafers.

Activities: Music, Weddings, Appreciation Classes, Banquets, Art Shows

Nearby Attractions: Indiana Dunes, Lake Michigan

Estate Grapes: Riesling, Chardonel, Pinot Grigio.

Amazing Western Omelets

Eggs	Diced green pepper, onion,
Cream	Ham and mushroom
Paprika	Shredded Cheddar cheese

Beat eggs well adding a teaspoon of cream to each 5 eggs. Bring a large omelet pan to sear coated with olive oil. Add 3 eggs per omelet and before turning, add diced vegetables and a sprinkling of Cheddar cheese. Roll and continue cooking well. Remove from pan and add Cheddar to top along with dash of paprika. Serve as evening meal along with Syrah.

Simmons Winery
8111 E. 450 N.
Columbus, IN
812-546-0091
www.simmonswinery.com
www.450northbrewing.com

Established in 2000, the Simmons Winery and Farm Market (and now brew pub and restaurant) offers a near full-service tasting and dining experience in rural Columbus. In the fourteen years (at the time of this writing) that this winery has been in existence, it has continued to make improvements to the building and grounds, as well as to the wines themselves. Located on a 120+ year old family farm, the family planted 10 acres of grapes in 1998 as a start, and continues to produce wines from this family estate. In short, Simmons offers an eclectic array of wines and ample opportunities on the grounds for a longer visit.

The payoff to a Simmons visit may be in the variety. In addition to the spacious grounds—including a banquet hall and a beautifully landscaped flower garden area with wedding gazebo—visitors can also find fresh fruits and vegetables in season and a well-stocked gift shop. The newest addition—a restaurant and pre pub—features the Simmons micro brews (450 North Brewing Company) and a broad menu of appetizers, salads, sandwiches and brick oven pizzas.

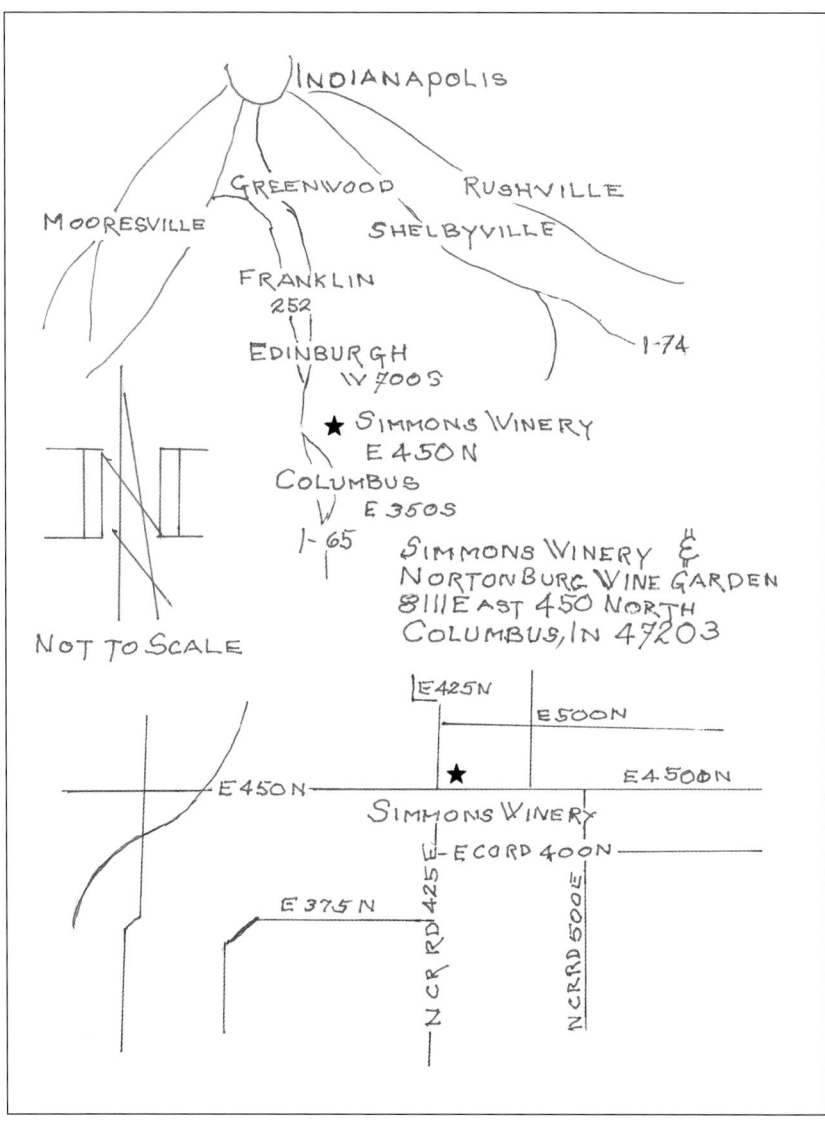

But if one is simply visiting for the wines, one won't be disappointed. Simmons offers a variety of reds, whites and blushes—

from dry to sweet—as well as some attempts in French-American hybrids and the usual Indiana grape varietals. The best estate wines here come from the Chardonel, Vidal Blanc, and Chambourcin grapes—but the winery does wines from grapes grown elsewhere as well.

Among the wines to taste are the St. Vincent, the Nortonburg Red, and the Autumn Rose. And if one has the time, or has planned to make a meal of it, the restaurant can offer some nice pairings for respective tastes.

Information by the Glass

Hours:
Sunday - Thursday 11 a.m. - 8 p.m.
Friday & Saturday 11 a.m. - 10 p.m.

Amenities: Gift Shop, Gardens, Banquet Hall, Restaurant, Gourmet Foods, Pizza

Tastings: Free

Price: $12 - $20

Recommendations:
Nortonburg Red—a nice blend with fruity undertones

Merlot—a favorite, medium-bodied wine that pairs well with pasta

Activities: Hayrides, Live Music, Special Events

Nearby Attractions: Brown County State Park

Estate Grapes: Chardonel, Vidal Blanc, Chambourcin.

Classic Deviled Eggs

Hard boiled eggs
Worcestershire sauce
Milk

Butter
Mustard powder
Paprika

Boil eggs and remove shells. Cut in half, removing yolks. Mix yolks with melted butter, Worcestershire sauce (to taste) and dashes of mustard powder (to taste). Place mixture back into egg halves and dash with salt, pepper and paprika. Enjoy with Merlot.

Stoney Creek Winery
10315 CR 146
Millersburg, IN 46543
574-642-4454

www.stoneycreekwinery.com

Gary and Jan Plank have created in Stoney Creek a quaint but exciting place for conversation and wine tasting. Their oak barrel tasting bar inside this barn tasting room and production facility offers an intimate place from which to taste their wines and engage in friendly talk. With their wine-making and Mennonite heritages, the Planks have blended some old-world and traditional practices into a place of hospitality—and with taste.

Now with a couple of years under its belt, Stoney Creek Winery is also planting its own vineyard and we can expect that they will soon have a new trove of Hoosier tastes built around Indiana grapes.

Currently, Stoney Creek offers primarily fruit wines, but some of interesting tastes and combinations. The Kiwi Pear wine is one of the most unique blends in the state, as is the Stoney Creek Peach Apricot—which, as the label implies, holds a citrusy zest along the lines of a White Zinfandel. Some of the red sweet wines here are Strawberry, Blackberry, Blueberry, and a "Wildberry". And a popular wine at Stoney Creek is their peach dessert wine.

Stoney Creek also produces a grandfather white and red wine: a Chardonnay and a Cabernet Sauvignon, respectively. So visitors can also feel that they have access to some of these bolder vintages if they so desire.

Tastings are free at Stoney Creek, and patrons can soak up some of the rural landscape as they make their way to this northern destination.

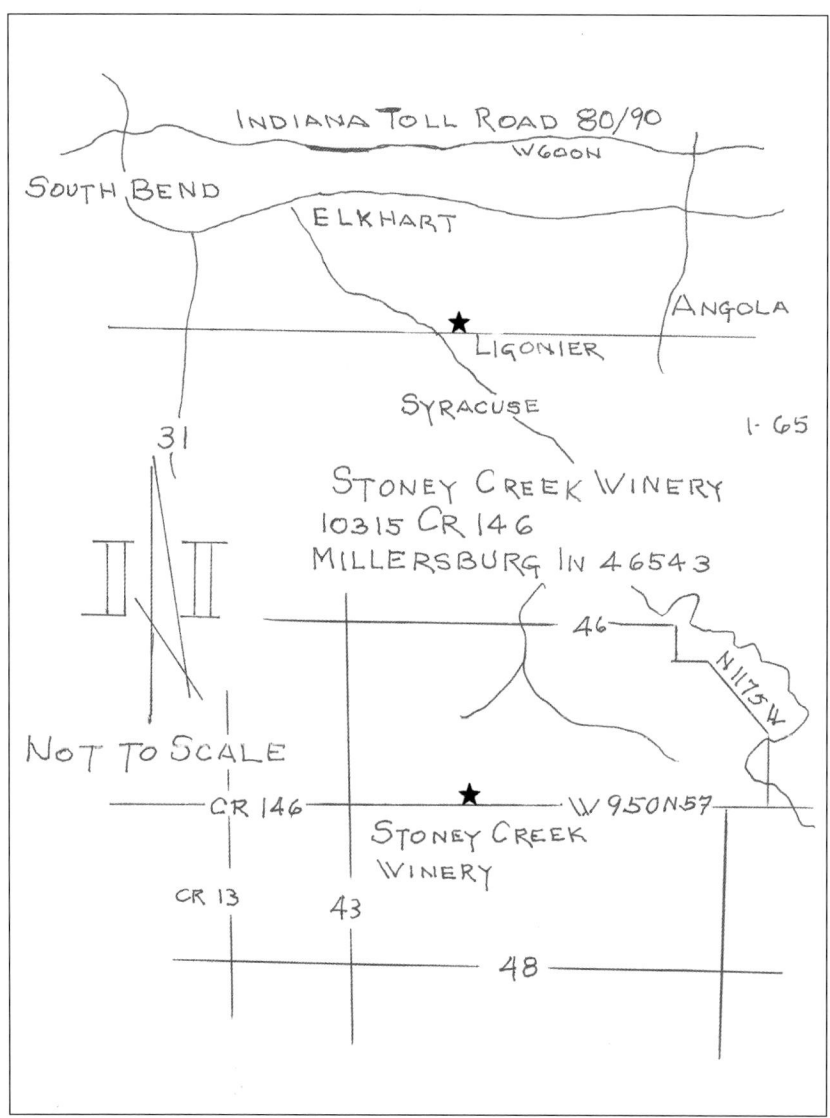

Information by the Glass

Owners: Gary & Jan Plank

Hours:
Saturdays 11 a.m. - 7 p.m.
Sundays 1 - 6 p.m.
Other days and hours call ahead (usually closed after Christmas for the winter)

Amenities: Outdoor Seating, Gift Shop

Tastings: Free

Price: $15

Recommendations:
Kiwi Pear—this sweet white has a tartness that sits well on the tongue and can be paired very nicely with a fruit salad or with cottage cheese.

Activities: Special Events

Nearby Activities: Elkhart Shopping, Notre Dame University.

Stream Cliff Farm Winery
8225 South CR 90 West
Commisky, IN 47225
812-346-5859
www.streamclifffarm.com

As its name implies, Stream Cliff Farm Winery is a working farm—and as soon as one drives onto the premises one realizes that this winery holds a special charm and rustic beauty all its own. Unique among the Hoosier wineries, Stream Cliff Farm offers the largest selection of herbs and flowers (for purchase) that one is likely to find anywhere. And, although there is no vineyard on the premises (the winery produces from grapes and juices purchased from across the country) this winery is part of a larger complex reminiscent of a quaint country village complete with general store, craft shop, restaurant, and barnyard animals that include goats and chickens.

Essentially, visitors to Stream Cliff will want to arrive with plans to purchase flowers (don't miss the large greenhouses behind the winery itself), stroll in the countryside, or enjoy a full course meal. And, as a cursory glimpse at the map will reveal, this winery is truly a country experience.

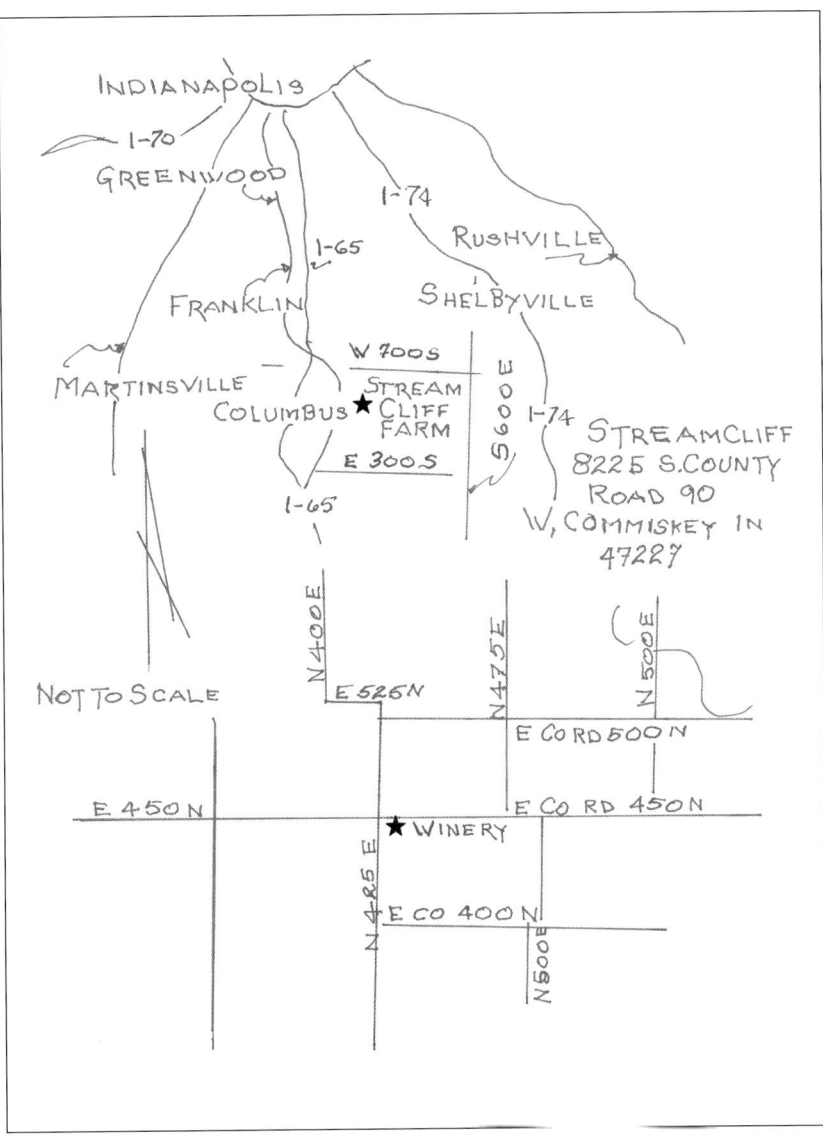

Stream Cliff's restaurant plays host to many different types of seasonal events and it is apparent that this is a local destination for lunch and dinner. In terms of ambiance and approach, Stream Cliff would certainly appeal to women who enjoy beauty and charm in their wine-tasting experience.

Among the wines that Stream Cliff offers with their free tastings—all served up in country flair at a saloon-style bar surrounded by red-checkered tables—are the Running Horse Red, a Merlot with medium-bodied fruit and clean finish and My Dolly, a Chardonnay with decent oak that underscores the usual buttery tone of this grape.

Stream Cliff's blackberry wine—their best-seller—is going to be one of the better fruit wines to be found in the state, and tastes as though one has plucked the berries fresh from the bush. This wine would be perfect with a bowl of vanilla ice cream.

One can also write to the winery (online) to receive free email reminders of upcoming events and/or a subscription to the annual newspaper—published in turn-of-the-century format as the Tearoom & Winery News. This winery deserves to be an option for those traveling from Madison to destinations north and is easy to find. And better yet, if you are in the market for flowers and herbs, you can't go wrong with shopping in the vast marketplace of this botanical farm.

Information By the Glass

Owner: Betty Manning

Hours:
April - October, Wednesday through Saturday, 10 a.m. - 4 p.m., Sundays 12:00 - 4 p.m.
October - December, Wednesdays-Sundays Noon - 4 p.m.
January - March, open Saturdays Noon - 4 p.m.

Amenities: Gift Shop, Tea Room, Gourmet Foods, Flower Shop, Gardens

Tastings: Free

Price: $15 - $20

Recommendations:
Rawhide—a Pinot Noir with a rich fruity flavor, dry but not overpowering.

Prancing Horse—a cranberry wine with a touch of orange juice and spiced cider.

Activities: Dinners, Garden Days, Cooking Classes, Quilt Shows

Nearby Attractions: Clifty Falls State Park.

The Thomas Family Winery
208 East Second Street
Madison, IN 47250
812-273-3755
800-948-8466
www.thomasfamilywinery.us

This winery is located in historic Madison, in close proximity to the river and all of the action and ambiance of Main Street. As with all of the other shops and businesses of this area, The Thomas Family Winery has a true Hoosier hospitality evident from the open door to the saloon-style bar where free tastings are served up by very knowledgeable staff. The winery interior features fine art by various local artists (for purchase) and the country store shelving offers local crafts and wine accessories.

While The Thomas Family Winery does offer a limited selection, the wines here are produced from both Indiana grapes and other regions (such as the Zinfandel from California). One can expect some quality tastes from Thomas Family—and the Seyval Blanc and Chambourcin offer some of the better tastes from Indiana vineyards. The latter has a very earthy scent, with flowers and spice evident in the fruit and just enough tannins to make this Chambourcin a nice wine to pair with grilled beef or chicken.

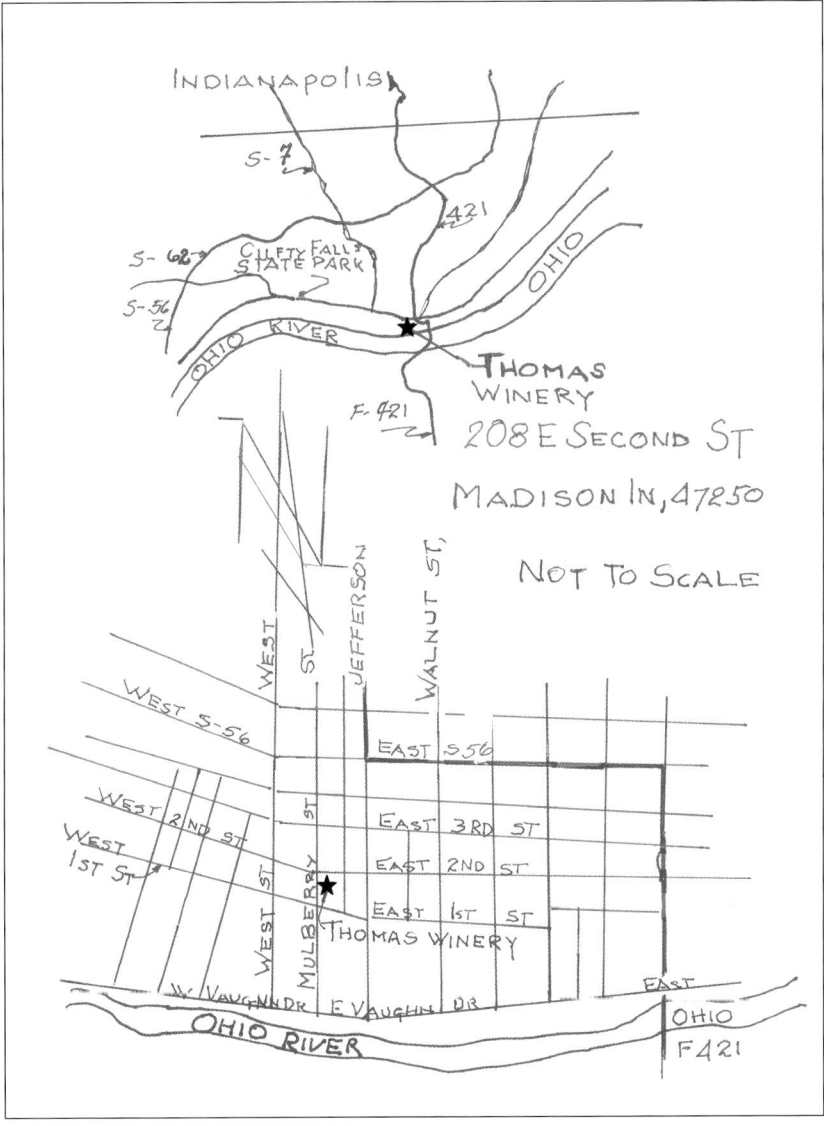

The winery also offers sandwiches and cheeses, so visitors can feel that they can enjoy a bottle of wine with some traditional fare, either indoors, or outside on the patio deck and courtyard that features a lawn-sized checkers set and a shelter house.

In addition, the winery is in the heart of the historic Madison shopping area, so patrons can make a weekend here by shopping for antiques, crafts, or by enjoying one of the many street fairs and festivals that grace the riverfront every few weeks.

Information By the Glass

Owners: Steve & Elizabeth Thomas

Hours: Monday - Thursday, 11 a.m. - 6 p.m.
Friday - Saturday, 11 a.m. - 9 p.m.
Sunday, Noon - 5 p.m.

Amenities: Gift Shop, Gourmet Foods, Outdoor Seating, Restaurant

Tastings: Free

Price: $12 - $20

Recommendations:
Chambourcin

Vidal Blanc—under-scored with apricot, melon and apple, a light desert wine that won't bend toward the sweet side too heavily.

Activities: Music and Special Events

Nearby Attractions: Historic Madison, Bed & Brekfasts

Estate Grapes: Chardonnay, Carignane.

Sugar Drop Cookies

1 cup brown sugar
¼ cup buttermilk
1 ¾ cups flour
½ teaspoon salt

½ cup shortening
1 egg
½ teaspoon baking soda

Mix ingredients, then cover and refrigerate for one hour. Afterwards, drop dough dollops onto cookie sheet and bake for 10 minutes at 400 degrees. Remove from oven and top with powdered sugar. Serve with Vidal Blanc.

Tonne Winery
101 West Royerton Road, Suite B
Muncie, IN 47303
765-896-9821
www.TonneWinery.com

Guests of the Tonne Winery (rhymes with "sunny") will immediately feel the "down home" atmosphere. Just 10 miles off of I-69 north of Muncie, this winery is tucked into the Hoosier landscape but offers some state-of-the-art winemaking—a nice gift given the dearth of wineries in the Muncie, Marion, central-eastern corridor of the state. One will find the ambiance here to be welcoming and hospitable, and the tasting bar area is spacious enough for a large group of friends. Add outside decks, ample parking, and adjustable seating arrangements in both the main foyer and rear production area, and Tonne assumes an even greater capacity for parties and weekend gatherings.

Like many Hoosier wineries, Tonne features some of Indiana's finest varietals, with Chambourcin, Steuben, and Traminette rounding out the field. The Traminette, in particular, is of the old-world German variety, and has won awards for this vintage. Rather than the sweet-T that many are accustomed to, the Tonne Traminette is crisp, exceedingly dry, and well-rounded. Tonne also produces a variety of sweet wines that are delicious—

including Blueberry and Catawba.

From year to year, Tonne also brings in California grapes to produce some satisfying dry reds—including Cabernet Sauvignon and Merlot. The latter has a fruity blush and sits well on the palate, but would also make a fine cooking wine.

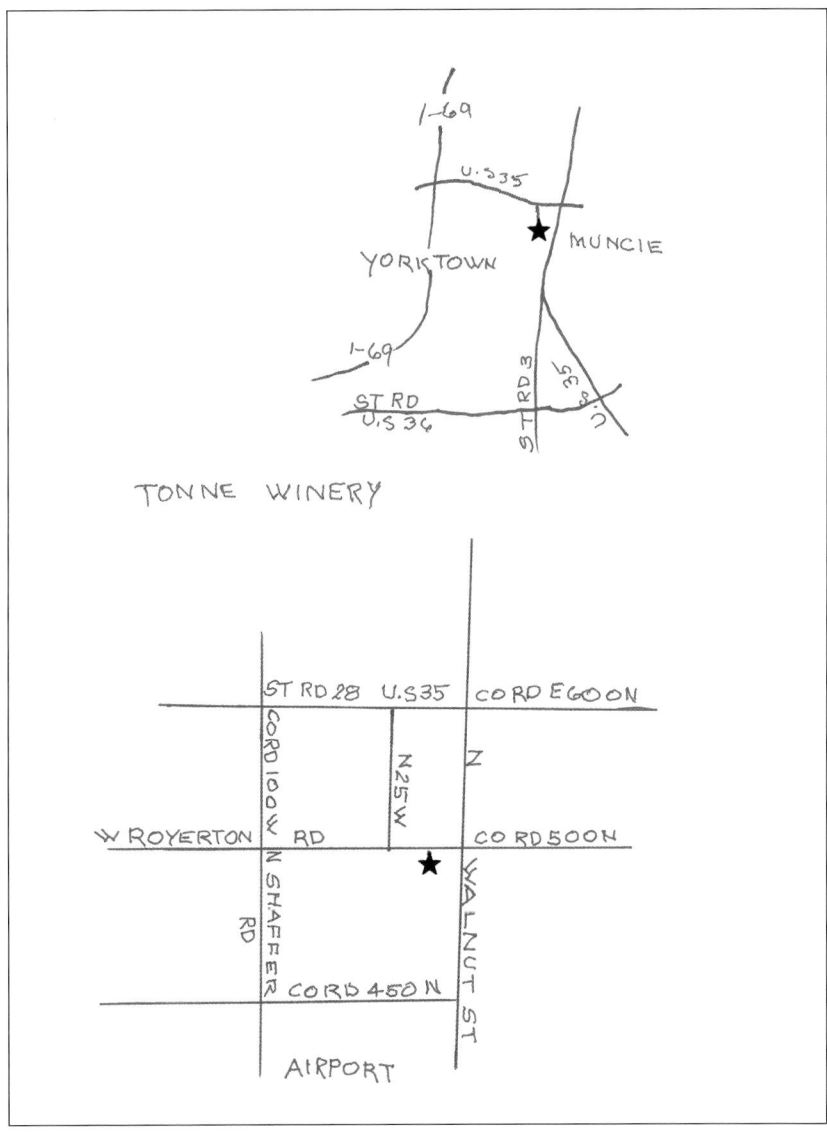

What makes the Tonne Winery extra special are the friendly staff. A lot of pride in this place, and the entire experience is airy and filled with light. Various gift items and the Tonne line of labels is available in racks lining the perimeter of the room. And the winery is easy to find and well-marked.

The next time you drive through the Muncie area, give this winery some time. It will grow on you.

Information by the Glass

Owners: Larry Simmons & Kevin Tonne

Hours: 10 - 6 daily, Sunday 12 - 5 p.m.

Amenities: Gift Shop

Tastings: 5 free

Price: $12 - $18

Recommendations:
Merlot—makes a great cooking wine, and could also be paired with lamb.

Traminette—a very enjoyable white, dry to a statement, that can be served with fresh salad and strawberries.

Activities: Special Events

Nearby Attractions: Ball State University

Estate Grapes: Pinot Grigio, Traminette, Catawba, Riesling.

Strawberry Chocolate Bars

Fresh strawberries　　　　　Milk chocolate
Oreo cookies　　　　　　　Marshmallows

Remove cream centers from Oreo Cookies and crush. Add melted marshmallows to the Oreo cookie crumbs and form into bars. Add fresh strawberries on top. Melt Milk Chocolate in a pan and pour over the top of the strawberries. Sprinkle powdered sugar on top. Let sit in the fridge overnight. Enjoy with Traminette.

Trader's Point Winery
5520 W. 84th Street
Indianapolis, IN 46268
317-879-9463
www.TradersPointWinery.com

As one of the newest wineries in the state, this family owned and operated winery found a niche market in an industrial park just south of 86th street. But the history of the area—more commonly known as Trader's Point—offers this winery and these wines a rather promising beginning. Given the heavy traffic of this area, the winery need only make a name for itself for people to find it.

Trader's Point is a beautifully designed storefront with a large back space for production, and the staff/owners here are courteous, knowledgeable and hopeful. Electing to the purse the wine tastes of the majority of Hoosiers, Traders Point offers a rather incredible lineup of sweeter wines, and given the length of time this winery has been in operation, this alone is commendable.

Nothing old or stodgy about a tasting experience here. Be sure to drop by for the full lineup of dryer to sweet, and plenty of fruit.

There's something for everyone though, from Chardonnay to Syrah, and dessert wines that even include a traditional Mulberry wine.

Also, watch for the Traders Point label at some of the larger wine festivals around the state. Traders Point is mixing it up and they are making a fast name for themselves.

Information by the Glass

Hours: Tuesday - Saturday 12 - 6 p.m.
Sunday 1 - 5 p.m.

Amenities: Gift Shop

Tastings: Free

Price: $12 - $15

Recommendations:
Syrah—a very nice Syrah with tannic edges and hints of spice and cherry, pair this one with flank steak or barbeque chicken breasts.

Activities: Special Events and at festivals

Nearby Attractions: Eagle Creek State Park, Indianapolis Restaurants.

Turtle Run Winery
940 St. Peters Road NE
Corydon, IN 47112
812-952-2650
www.turtlerunwinery.com

Increasingly, as Indiana wineries discover the unique potential and landscape for growing varietal grapes, more acres of vines are being planted. Some southern Indiana wineries such as Huber, Oliver, and Butler—are mainstays in the production scene. Others, such as Turtle Run, are principal players but may be less-known that the larger wineries.

Owner and wine-maker Jim Pfeiffer has continued to populate his acreage with an increasingly diverse cast of grapes, and with over fifteen acres, now ranks in the top five or six wineries (in acreage planted) in the state. His vineyard would read like a Who's Who of popular Hoosier offerings—including Cabernet Franc, Cabernet Sauvignon, Traminette, Vignoles, Chambourcin, and a host of others, including Catawba.

Turtle Run, located in Corydon, Indiana, produces wines of remarkable character and breadth, and a quick perusal of their price-per-bottle would also reveal a level of bargain and affordability not always found in smaller, boutique wineries. The wine production, which can range from steel tank to oak barrel, is well-studied and academic—and one is always going to taste a wine here of some sophistication, though joined to the locale.

Among the best wines that Turtle Run has to offer, the Traminette—a grape produced as a cross between Gewurztraminer and a French American hybrid—sits a light amber in the glass and has both aroma and flavor of orange peel, melon, and lemon. Furthermore, since the Traminette is in plentiful supply, Turtle Run has produced two labels: a steel aged variety and an oak barrel option that has a heavier, earthy taste if not a bit dryer.

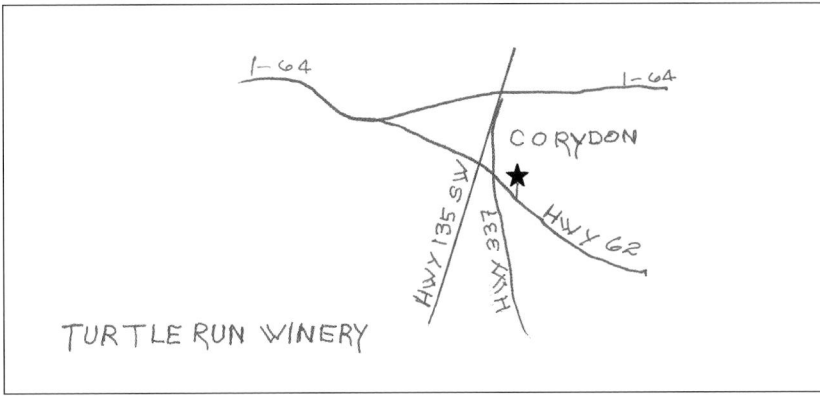

The Chambourcin is another nice wine with a fruity tongue—and at 13.9% alcohol is bold with hints of spice, cherry and black pepper.

Turtle Run is also a destination winery given the fact that on weekends, especially, one can often take in a live-music concert or some other event. Check out the calendar on the Turtle Run website for upcoming concert series and specials on wines and food events.

As the glass will tell, Turtle Run has made a name with Indiana grapes and is positioned to be one of the premier southern Indiana wineries for years to come.

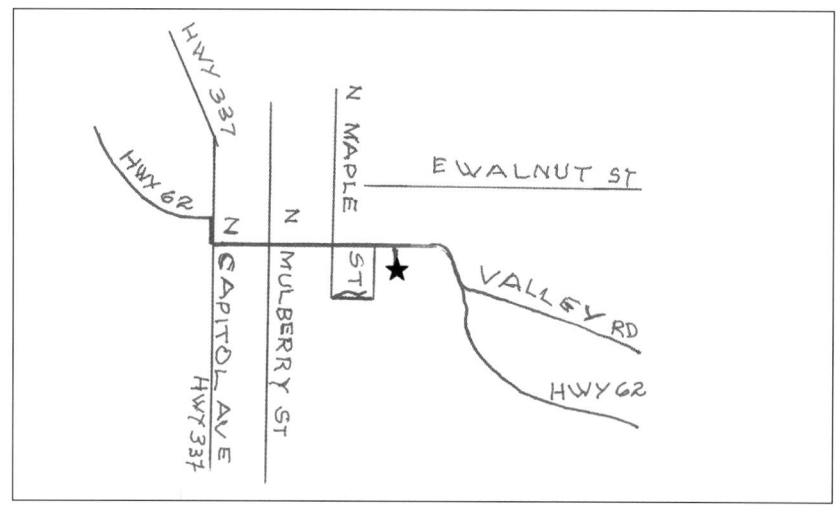

Information by the Glass

Owner & Wine-Maker: Jim Pfeiffer

Hours: Daily 12 - 6 p.m.

Amenities: Gift Shop, Gourmet Cheeses, Outdoor Seating

Tastings: Free

Price: $10 - $18

Recommendations:
Terrapin Red—a nice triad: Chambourcin, corot noir and noiret. This barrel-aged blend has a refined balance and a long, smooth finish to it. As blends become more popular for their depth and balanced taste, this red is unique both in substance and style.

Vignoles—a sweet wine with strong flavors of orange, lemon, and a touch of honey.

Activities: Concert Series, Bike Ride Tours, Jazz, Wine Talks &

Tours, Wine Appreciation Classes

Nearby Attractions: Squire Boone Caverns, Marengo Cave, Zimmerman Art Glass

Estate Grapes: Chambourcin, Vignoles, Traminette, Coret Noir, Noiret, Catawba, Diamond, Pinot Noir, Cabernet Sauvignon, Cab Franc, Chardonnay, Pinot Gris, Steuben.

Ham Loaf Supreme

½ pound ground beef
1 egg
½ cup chopped onion
¼ cup bread crumbs
Worcestershire sauce, salt, pepper

½ pound ground ham
3 tablespoons brown sugar
⅓ cup milk
¾ cup catsup

In large bowl mix beef, ham, along with onion, celery, milk, bread crumbs and the egg and Worcestershire sauce. Shape the ball and place in a baking pan. Mix brown sugar and catsup and pour over top of ham loaf. Bake 45 minutes at 350 degrees. Serve with Terrapin Red.

Two EE's Winery
6808 N. US 24 E.
Huntington, IN 46750
260-672-2000
www.TwoEEs.com

Two EE's is one of the newest wineries in the state, but from the outset has taken up the daunting task of carving out a unique niche in the Hoosier scene. Opening in May of 2013 in a remarkable stone facility easily accessed from US 24, Two EE's (Eric & Emily Harris) has created a Napa-like atmosphere in this spacious winery decorated in the colorful labels they produce. The winery's location on forty acres, with rolling hillside and spacious parking and patio/decking, will draw you in immediately. Inside, one can taste at the bar while looking through a glass wall at the production facility—and watch the winemakers as they go through their paces at the brightly-polished tanks. All in all, it's a captivating experience and the staff will make you feel at home. Visitors will also have no problem finding a place at luxurious tasting bar—and the experience here is young and invigorating.

Although Two EE's is, in fact, a young winery, they have already produced a full line of fine wines. For those who love fruit wines, there is pear and plum . . . and also Sangria. Whites include the local Traminette—which is remarkably grapefuity with some hints of key lime. And the Vignoles and Catawba are excellent as well.

But what makes this winery super-cool is its dedication to big, bold reds. And listen, guests to this winery are going to find a few old world Italian wines that they are not going to encounter anywhere else in the state. Two EE's has a Dolcetto, a wonderfully rounded and robust wine, and an Aglianico, which is full and rich and slightly reminiscent of the Zinfandels found among the old vines of Amador County, California.

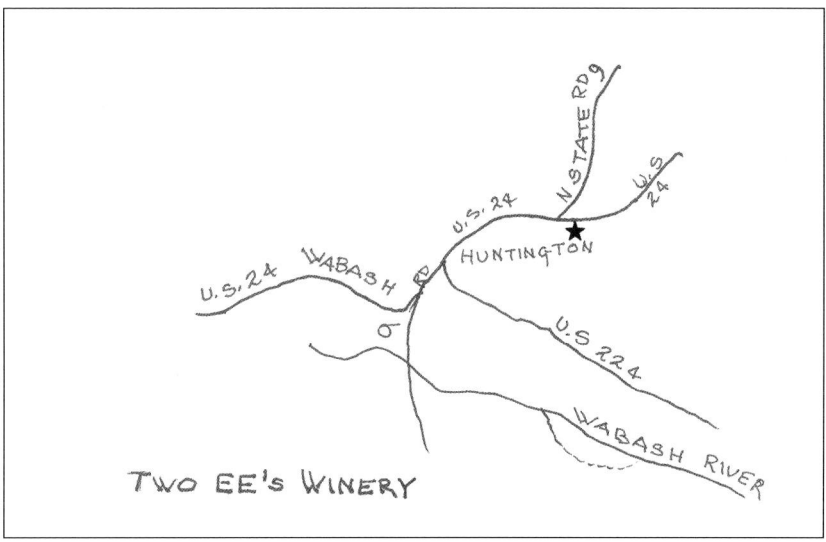

Other unique varietals here include Teroldogo (which is truffly with an inky appearance in the glass), Norton, Durif, and Plonqe—a semi-sweet red that can double as a desert wine if one isn't inclined to sip it.

The premier wine of Two EE's is the Tannat, which won gold in a Wine Channel competition and is a marvelously inky wine with a balance of fruit and tannin. This wine is deeper than Cab and has layering and complexity enough to keep a person studying the pleasure for hours.

Make a point to visit this winery soon.

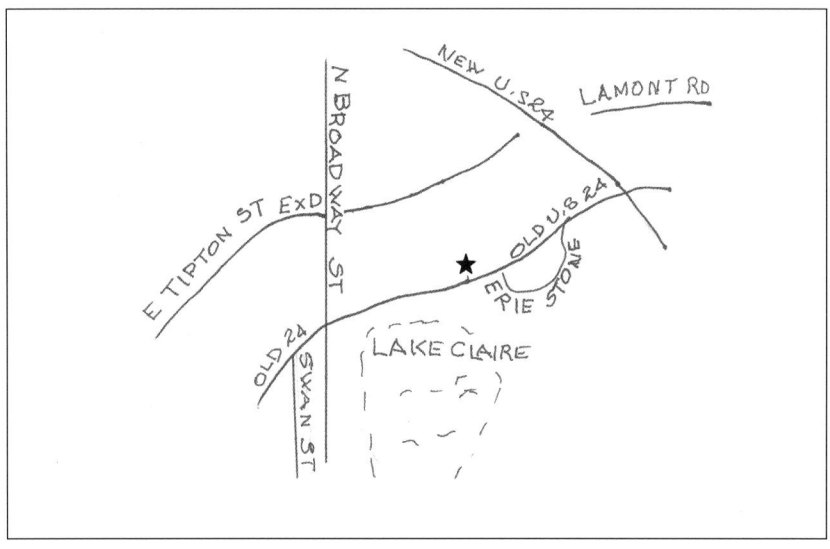

Information by the Glass

Owners: Eric & Emily Harris

Hours: 11 - 7 p.m. daily

Amenities: Gift Shop, Outdoor Seating

Tastings: Free

Price: $18 - $30

Recommendations:
Aglianico—a dry, expresso-like wine with hints of bittersweet chocolate, pairs well with lamb and pork.

Tannat—a superb dry red with notes of blackberry and cigar.

Late Harvest Chardonnay—a marvelous dessert wine with all the buttery notes combined with drams of sweetness. Drink it with peach cobbler.

Activities: Special Events

Nearby Attractions: Huntington Reservoir

Estate Grapes: Traminette, Muscat, Diamond, Blaufrankish, Norton.

Whyte Horse Winery

1510 S. Airport Road
Monticello, IN 47960
572-583-2345
info@whyhoursewinery.com
www.whytehorsewinery.com

There are some Indiana labels with a distinctive flair for branding and iconography, and the Whyte Horse is an emblem that most people will remember. The winery, located on the outskirts of Monticello, is a full-service boutique in an upscale 1886 farmhouse, complete with an old-world oak interior, cherry bar, and a full line of Indiana varietals as well as classic Cabernet and Italian Sangiovese.

The Pampels (Larry & Connie; Don & Denise), standing on the foundation of four generations of wine-makers, tend acres of vineyard featuring Indiana varietals along the Big Creek in White County such as Traminette and Vignoles, and have also grown their wine-making expertise by completing certification at U.C. Davis and tending to the intricacies of their own labels. Larry

Pampel, winemaker, has created some intriguing blush wines as well as some award-winning blends such as the Whyte Horse Rhapsody (Cabernet, Zinfandel, Sangiovese and Temprarillo).

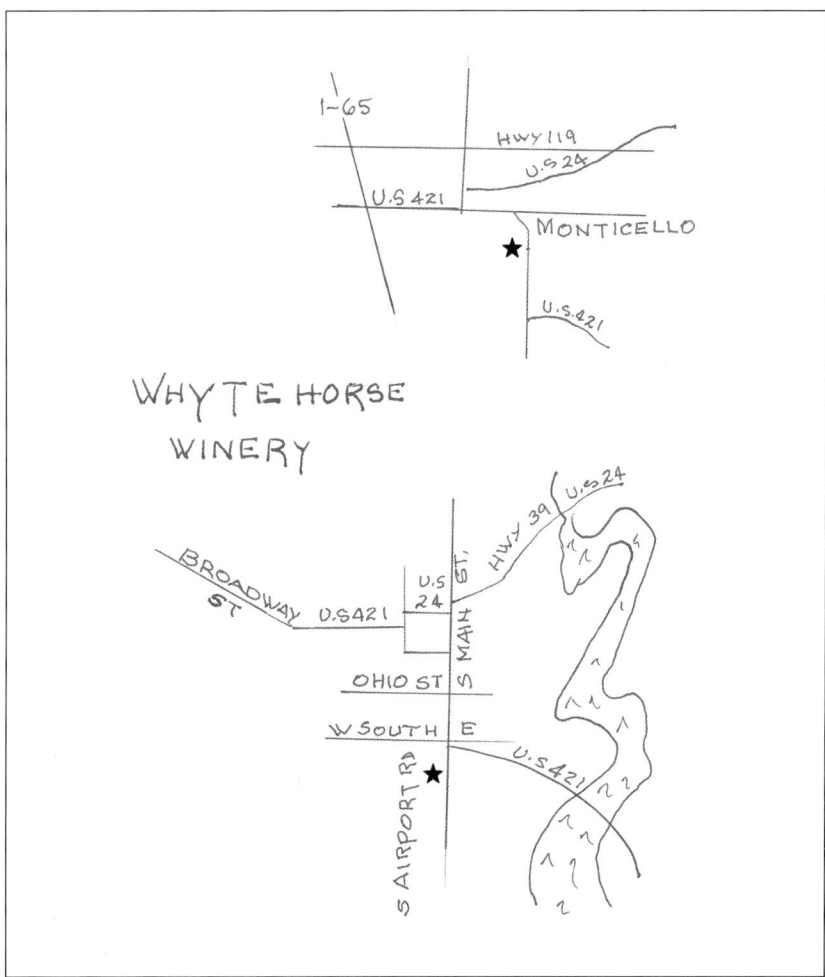

The Whyte Horse has created a brand for itself in the greater Monticello area, partnering with many local restaurants, which carry the Whyte Horse label on their lists. One can find the label from Lafayette to Logansport, from Merillville to Valparaiso—with the winery offering a nice wine club discount to members also.

Like other rural wineries, Whyte Horse has also made a strong play to become a location for banquets and weddings. The back half of the property on Airport Road features a gazebo at the center of the vines, with ample parking and broad walking paths leading to the seating area. For gatherings of two hundred or less, the winery's facilities would provide a scenic backdrop to events that are searching for a unique location. A picnic lunch also goes well with this place. Live music may also be found from time-to-time in the gazebo area.

As for cheeses and snack foods, the winery also provides these in the tasting area, and two rooms of gift shop items rounds out the ambiance of the place –making it one of the more decorative and architecturally-distinctive wineries in the state. And for families on the move toward fun, Monticello is home to Indiana Beach and a robust downtown area where shopping and food is easily accessible.

Whyte Horse has a unique approach, and one will experience a true Hoosier hospitality whether visiting or tasting.

Information By the glass

Owners: Larry & Connie Pampel, Don & Denise Pampel

Hours:
Tuesday - Saturday 11 a.m. - 7 p.m.
Sunday Noon - 6 p.m.
(Call for winter hours)

Amenities: Outdoor Seating, Banquet Facilities, Gift Shop

Tastings: Free

Price: $12 - $20

Recommendations:
Rhapsody (French oak barrels and a four varietal blend)

Dolce White (blend of Rieseling and Traminette for those who love a sweeter white)

Tawny Harbour (a heavy-bodied port-style wine made from five vintages of blackberry and aged in French oak barrels)

Activities: Weddings, Music

Nearby Attractions: State Parks

Estate Grapes: Chambourcin, Riesling, Chardonnay, Cabernet Sauvignon, Sangiovese, Traminette, Seyval Blanc.

You Know You Want It Chicken

1 whole chicken
2 eggs

Flour
Shortening

For this classic fried chicken, cup up the chicken and dip each piece in mixture of beaten egg and the roll in flour. Melt ample portions of shortening in a non-stick skillet to high temperature. Fry chicken as you turn down the heat, each piece turned 3-4 times after 15-20 minutes total, or until golden brown. Remove pieces and lightly salt. This chicken pairs well with Rhapsody.

Wildcat Creek Winery

3233 East 200 North
Lafayette, IN 47905
765-838-3498
www.wildcatcreekwinery.com

Rick and Kathy Black, owners of the Wildcat Creek Winery, have worked diligently to transform this 1900 farmhouse into a working winery and tasting room. Located in rural Lafayette, the winery is nevertheless very accessible from interstate 65 (watch for the signs) and maintains an ambiance of farming life while providing a down-home hospitality.

Visitors will not only be treated to a free wine tasting, but may also enjoy the ample indoor/outdoor seating areas (don't overlook the gazebo and garden deck in the back), periodic food and wine pairings, and the gift shop. The interior of the farmhouse—which serves as the tasting room—is quaint, but features some beautiful hand-made wine racks and mantle piece. Visit the web site to learn about upcoming special events—such as local band performances, parties, and food. The winery also offers its building and grounds for reserved occasions, and visitors may also enjoy this winery in conjunction with a weekend in the greater Lafayette area.

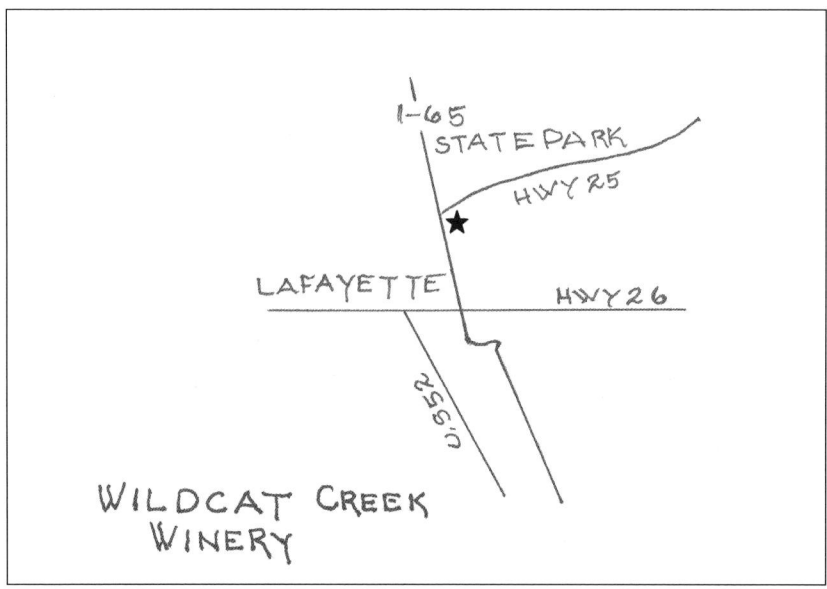

Although this winery is young—established in 2007—the owners are committed to creating some of the finest wines in the Midwest.

Currently the winery specializes in semi-dry and semi-sweet offerings, with traditional Indiana grapes as centerpiece. Chambourcin, Steuben, and Traminette are the heart-and-soul grapes here, but Wildcat Creek also produces a respectable Riesling with hints of apple, grapefruit and peach—and there are several blends, including Prophet's Rock Red and Peter's Mill White that spill over into the dry wine category.

As for dessert wines, don't overlook the Aunt Minnie's Cherry Tree—which is one of the few cherry wines produced in the state. Save a bottle of this for the holidays (with a box of chocolates) and one has the perfect chocolate-covered-cherry taste in a glass.

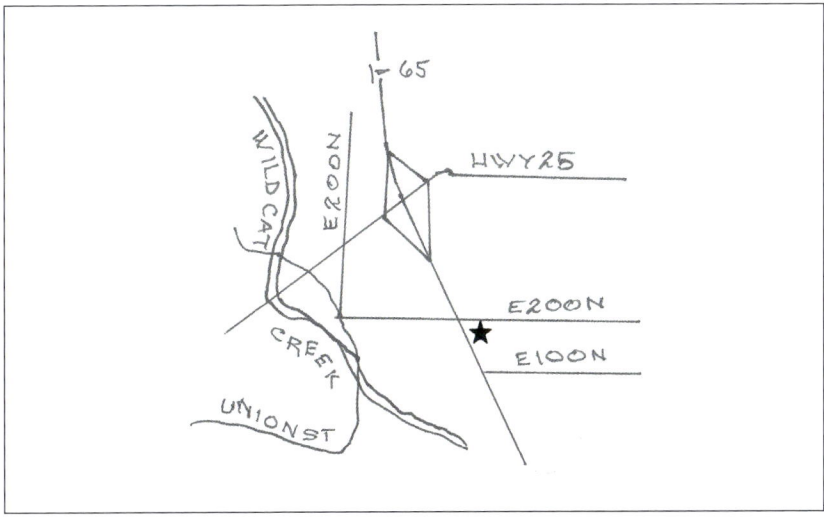

The winery offers discounts on cases, and even if one doesn't leave with a bottle, there is still plenty to enjoy here around a picnic lunch or a quiet evening on the back deck.

Wildcat Creek is one of those up-and-coming wineries that people will want to keep an eye one in the years ahead.

Information by the Glass

Owners: Rick & Kathy Black

Hours:
Monday - Saturday 11 a.m. - 6 p.m.
Sunday Noon - 5 p.m.

Amenities: Gift Shop, Outdoor Seating

Tastings: Free

Price: $12 - $19

Recommendations:
Chambroucin—a semi-dry wine that was selected as Indiana Wine of the Year in 2011. Hints of raspberry and cherry.

Aunt Minnie's Cherry Tree—unique dessert wine that should be paired with fine chocolate.

Activities: Live Music, Special Events

Nearby Attractions: Purdue University.

Wilson Wines

10137 S. Indian Trail Road
Modoc, IN 47358
765-853-5100
www.wilsonwines.com

Every now and again one comes across an Indiana winery that doesn't impress at first blush, but then turns out to be a diamond in the rough. That's Wilson Wines!

Your GPS is going hate you as you make your way to this family farm in Modoc, Indiana—you may even take a few wrong turns. But your persistence will pay off in fun and frolic and fine wine if you find the tepee sign along Indian Trail Road.

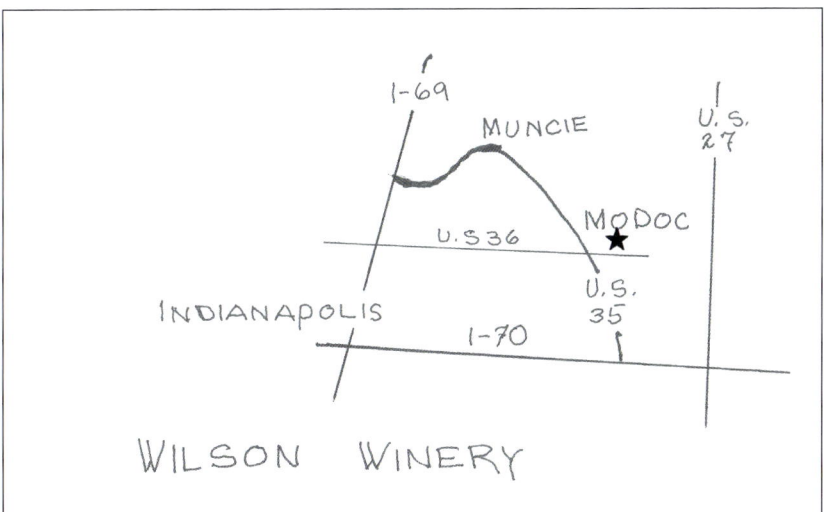

Jim and John Wilson have transformed this modest family farm into an adventure and throughout the summer and fall, in particular, carry on their top-class wine making in an air of entertainment and personalized attention. Nearly every weekend the boys also regale their guests with family and farming tales, as well as live-musical events, cook-offs, and barbecue nights. You don't have to be a local to regard this family farm as a fun place to spend a Friday or Saturday night—and if you are looking for a hoot, make your way to Modoc.

But listen . . . don't forget the Wilson Wines.

In addition to producing from their own vine stock since 2000, the Wilsons have also perfected some wine-making techniques that will make you appreciate what they can do with California vintages, including a super Cabernet Sauvignon that is more smooth and oaky, with the more recent vintage years being highly-drinkable and indicative of those California blends layered with smooth taste. And the Wilson Sauvignon Blanc is farm all-over—with hints of grass and grapefruit that, chilled, is perfect summer sipping.

The Wilson Winery is also known for the many fruit wines—including Elderberry, Cranberry, and a fresh Plum wine that is sweet enough to use as a dessert wine, but fresh enough to store away for a year or two for a special occasion.

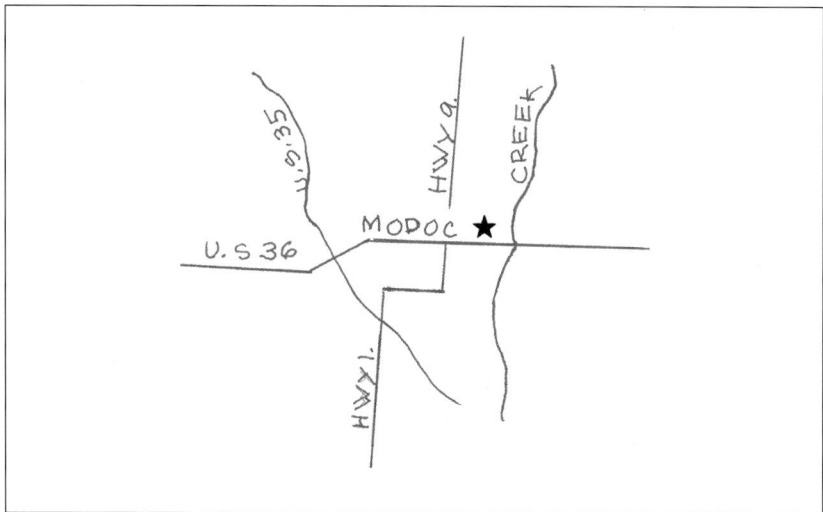

Wilson Wines also brings in top-name groups and individual recording artists and, although the wine-tasting room is on the smaller side, the spacious lawn at this country venue offers both a built-in concert arena and room enough to play croquet, lawn bowling, or space for a family gathering. Having served as leaders in the Hoosier winemaking community, the Wilsons are well-known around the state, but the accolades are best reserved for their top-tier wines. Their knowledge and expertise shine through in every bottle—and if you get to the winery for a tasting, you will be guaranteed to have fun. There might even be a croquet game happening on the lawn.

But don't forget the wines . . . some of the best to be found in the south-eastern corridor of the state.

Information by the Glass

Owners: John & Jim Wilson

Hours:
Thursday & Friday 6 - 9 p.m.
Saturday & Sunday 1 - 6 p.m.
Other times by appointment

Amenities: Gift Shop, Outdoor Seating

Tastings: Free

Price: $12 - $18

Recommendations:
Vignoles—a well-balanced white wine, Indiana varietal, that goes well with fish and fruit.

Modoc White—a nice-tasting wine with a sub-par coloration in the bottle, but at $5 each, one of the best values you'll find anywhere. Goes well with vanilla ice cream.

Sauvignon Blanc—a superb white varietal that Wilsons have perfected with an elemental flair. This one will table well with fish and fowl alike.

Activities: Crocket, Chili-cookoffs, concerts

Nearby Attractions: Hiking and Biking Trails

Estate Grapes: Chambourcin, Sauvignon Blanc, Traminette, Niagara, Riesling, Vignoles.

Potato Carrot & Pea Soup

Peeled and diced potatoes
Cream of mushroom soup
Milk & cream
Salt, pepper

Peeled and diced carrots
Small package frozen peas
Diced onion

Boil diced potatoes and carrots until tender. In a large pan add potatoes and carrots to ¼ diced onion, can of cream of mushroom soup, peas, and small amounts of milk and cream to make the stock to taste. Add salt and pepper to your liking. Enjoy with Wilson Sauvignon Blanc.

Windy Knoll Winery
845 N. Atkinson Road
Vincennes, IN 47591
812-726-1600
www.windyknollwinery.com
toby@windyknollwinery.com

Windy Knoll is a winery unto itself—especially when one considers that it is the only Indiana winery in the southwest part of the state, just miles from the Wabash River and the Illinois border. Located just five miles north and east of Vincennes—one of Indiana's most historic towns (state's oldest Cathedral, state's oldest university, George Roger's Clark national monument, Grouseland home of President William Henry Harrison)—Windy Knoll Winery is the perfect place to top off a day-trip with some relaxation.

This winery has been producing wines for fifteen years, and most of their labels are bottled direct from the grapes and fruits they grow on premises. And, while Windy Knoll is best-known for their sweet fruit wines, they do sport a full lineup of wines from sweet, to semi-dry, to dry.

This winery's atmosphere is laid back—but visitors will enjoy this countrified aura of a farmstead reminiscent of warm summer days, with vines and fruit trees dusting the rolling landscape. Livestock and a family home round out the experience. And visitors arriving at Windy Knoll from highway 50 will have no trouble locating the winery. Signs abound, and the directions are clear.

The winery showroom is a quaint ranch house that is predominantly gift shop and display, with some crackers and cheeses available for afternoon or pre-dinner fare. Tables inside and outside provide plenty of seating, though parking may be tight on certain high-traffic days. Most unique for those extremely hot country days, a slushy machine in the gift shop allows patrons to turn their glass of wine into a refreshing ice mix.

As for the wines . . . no doubt guests will discover Windy Knolls' strengths to be in their sweeter stock. And there are some unique wines here that one may not find anywhere else.

The Wabash Mist, for example, is a Rose reminiscent of White Zin, with some notes of strawberry, peach and cherry. A pomegranate wine is another unique offering, and so is the pear wine—a crisp, citrusy selection that will stand up well in the glass and is a perfect after-dinner dessert wine.

For those looking for reds or dry, the winery does offer a couple of traditional Indiana-grown selections in the Traminette (which may best be categorized as semi-dry), the Foch, and the Cabernet Franc—which has a soft, smooth finish, lightly smoky, or perhaps with a hint of almond.

Visitors will discover that Windy Knoll has over twenty wines—very likely something for everyone—and is a place to visit when driving through south-west Indiana.

Information by the Glass

Owners: Rick & Gwen Lesser

Hours: Daily Noon - 6 p.m.

Amenities: Outdoor Seating, Gift Shop

Tastings: Free

Price: $12 - $15

Suggestions: When it season, try the summer strawberry or the pear wines. The Pinot Noir is another semi-sweet wine that may have a broader appeal—particularly with Pinot fans. And the Cabernet Sauvignon—grapes from California—serves at the high-end red at $35 a bottle.

Activities: Special Events, Social Gatherings

Nearby Attractions: George Rogers Clark National Memorial, Grouseland (Home of President William Henry Harrison)

Estate Grapes: Vidal Blanc, Seyval, Muscat, Chambourcin, Pinot Noir, Cab Franc, Marechel Foch, DeChaunac, Merlot, Cabernet Sauvignon, Vignoles, Traminette.

Grilled Swordfish with Olives, Tomatoes and Marjoram

Six 6-7 oz. swordfish steaks. The thicker the steaks the better.
1 28 oz. can diced Italian tomatoes, in juice
⅓ cup large green or Kalamata olives. Pitted and halved
1 tablespoon chopped fresh majoram
3 tablespoons extra virgin olive oil   2 garlic cloves
Zest from one orange   1 bay leaf
2 tablespoons of Sherry Vinegar   2 tablespoons dry vermouth

Heat 2 tablespoons of olive oil. Add garlic and cook over medium heat for no more than 2 minutes. Add orange zest, vermouth and bay leaf. Boil for 1 minute. Add tomatoes and juice. Simmer for 10 minutes. Add olives, marjoram and sherry vinegar. Set sauce aside. Start grill and set to medium high. Wash fish steaks and pat dry. Rub olive oil on both sides of fish. Sprinkle both sides with salt and cracked fresh pepper. Grill 3-4 minutes on one side and 3 minutes on the other. If the steaks are thin, reduce the cooking time on the second side to no more than 2 minutes. Place steaks on plate and spoon sauce on top of swordfish steaks. Pairs nicely with Windy Knoll Pinot Noir.

Recipe courtesy of Steven Libman.

Windy Ridge Vineyard & Winery
3998 N. 150 W.
Cayuga, IN 47928
765-492-9550
www.windyridgewinery.net

The Windy Ridge Winery is Indiana's only central-western located winery (near the Wabash River). Established in 2012, it also one of Indiana's newest wineries. This family owned and operated winery grows much of their own grapes—which includes six acres of common Indiana varietals such as Cayuga, Concord, and Traminette.

This winery doesn't have a large wine list, but with the dozen labels they produce they have enough selection to warrant a visit, especially for those who lean toward the sweeter spectrum of wines. Here you'll find some good reds (made of Concord grapes) and an award-winning white, made of the Cayuga grape, that has hints of grapefruit and apricot.

As a weekend getaway, the Windy Ridge Winery is laid back and offers free tastings. Check the web site for upcoming special events and musical guests, too.

Windy Ridge is also experimenting with some unique fruit wines, too. On your next visit, be sure to try their Persimmon selection, or perhaps the Paw-Paw—the fruit often describes as the "Hoosier Banana".

When you visit Windy Ridge, come prepared to relax and enjoy the sunshine. This rural winery is known for its friendly and personable atmosphere.

Information by the Glass

Hours:
Saturdays & Sundays 12 - 6 p.m. (call ahead for holiday hours)

Tastings: Free

Price: check website or facebook page

Recommendations:
Desperado—the Windy Ridge award-winning sweet white, hints of grapefruit and apricot with fruit body.

Estate Grapes: Cayuga, Concord, and Traminette, Concord.

Wine Shak Vineyard
8765 SR 37
Tell City, IN 47586
812-547-7700
www.wineshakvineyard.com

The Ohio river basin of Indiana provides some of the best vineyards in the state, and the Wine Shak in Tell City offers their superb grapes in a small, but respectable, lineup of wines. In fact, while the Wine Shak produces all of their grapes, they are also growing some varietals that cannot be produced in other parts of the state—including Cabernet Sauvignon, Merlot, and Syrah. All told, this winery is making waves in the Hoosier winery-landscape and continues to bottle some remarkable vintages and blends.

The Wine Shak staff has also made a deep and detailed study of the climate and topography of southern Indiana—especially as it relates to the latitudes of the great winemaking regions of Europe. And with this in mind, vineyards were established years ago that are not producing the yields necessary for their top-flight lineup.

The fourteen vintages represented in the vineyard are what produces some of the following:

- Sugar Creek Gold—a crisp white wine, layered with fruits.
- Winter Blush—an excellent rose of textured and blended varietals, not overly sweet.
- Cynthiana (also known as Norton)—a dry red wine staggered with tastes of blackberry, licorice and overtones of cherry.

The Wine Shak is a destination winery that can also be combined with a visit to Monkey Hollow (St. Meinrad) and Blue Heron wineries and other fun along the Ohio River. Visit the Wine Shak website for details on special activities, entertainment, and deals.

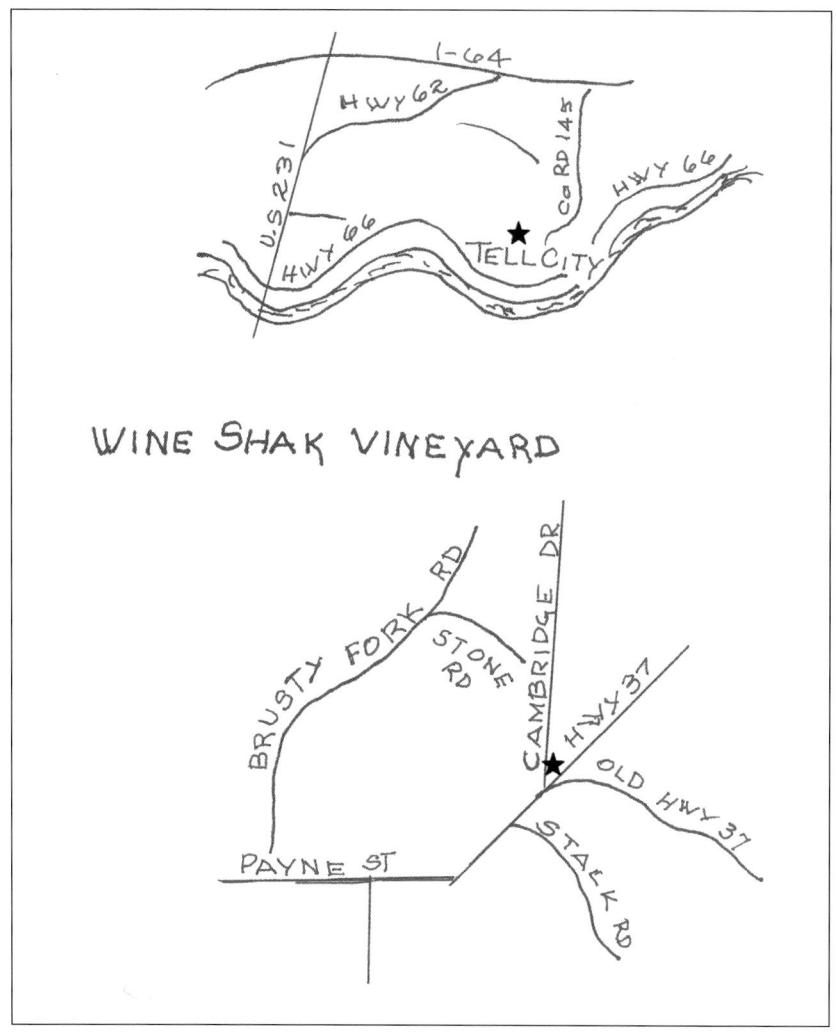

Information by the Glass

Hours: Call ahead for hours

Price: Check facebook page

Recommendations:
Old World Red—the top vintage here, an old world aged blend in the Bordeaux tradition, with complex textures of Cab and Merlot, deftly crafted. Should be paired with a New York strip or Rib-eye steak, au-gratin potatoes, Caesar salad. This is one that can enjoyed in the glass and has ageing potential

Estate Grapes: Cayuga, Concord, and Traminette, Cabernet Sauvignon, Merlot.

Pan-Seared & Oven-Roasted Filet Mignon

4 to 8 oz. filet mignon	Coarse salt and fresh cracked pepper
Olive oil	1 tablespoon butter per steak

Remove meat from refrigerator one hour before cooking. Pre-heat oven to 425 degrees. Season meat with olive oil, salt and pepper – on both sides. Use hands to rub olive oil on meat. Melt butter in large skillet or saucepan over medium high heat. When the butter has melted and the pan is hot, sear filets. 3 minutes on one side, 2 minutes on the other. Place pan in oven for 8-9 minutes for medium rare, longer for medium or well-done. Remove meat from pan, place on a plate and cover with foil for 4-5 minutes, then serve. Pair it with the Wine Shak Old World Red.

Recipe courtesy of Steven Libman.

Winzerwald Winery
26300 North Indian Lake Road
Bristow, IN 47515
1-866-694-6937
www.winzerwaldwinery.com

Dan and Donna Adams, who epitomize the Swiss and German wine-making traditions through their exceptional wines, have created the Winzerwald winery as a celebration of this same spirit. Moreover, they have marketed the Winzerwald label far beyond their southern-Indiana location (with tasting rooms in Bristow and Evansville), as their wines can be found in venues and stores from Fort Wayne to Valparaiso to Indianapolis.

Winzerwald sports a full slate of wines, most created from these old world methods, with traditional white vintages such as Riesling, Gewurztraminer and Lieblich comprising the core of their list. The winery also has created some of the best blush and rose wines in the state, including their signature Little Rhineland Blush—a beautifully textured and balanced wine that can hold its own with flavorful pasta dishes or stand alone as a refreshing back porch pastime.

Of course, the traditional German whites are where this winery excels, but one doesn't have to overlook the Winzerwald reds, either. Consider, for example, the Winzerwald Cabernet Sauvignon Reserve—a remarkable Cab with a unique and robust array of tastes as it aerates in the glass, including blackberry, currant, and even cinnamon undertones. Winzerwald also bottles Pinot Noir, Merlot, and yet another one of the traditional Hoosier varietals in the Chambourcin—a wine, that here, comes to life in the glass because of the longer growing season down south, and has a smoother finish and a more complex presentation than one commonly tastes in this varietal.

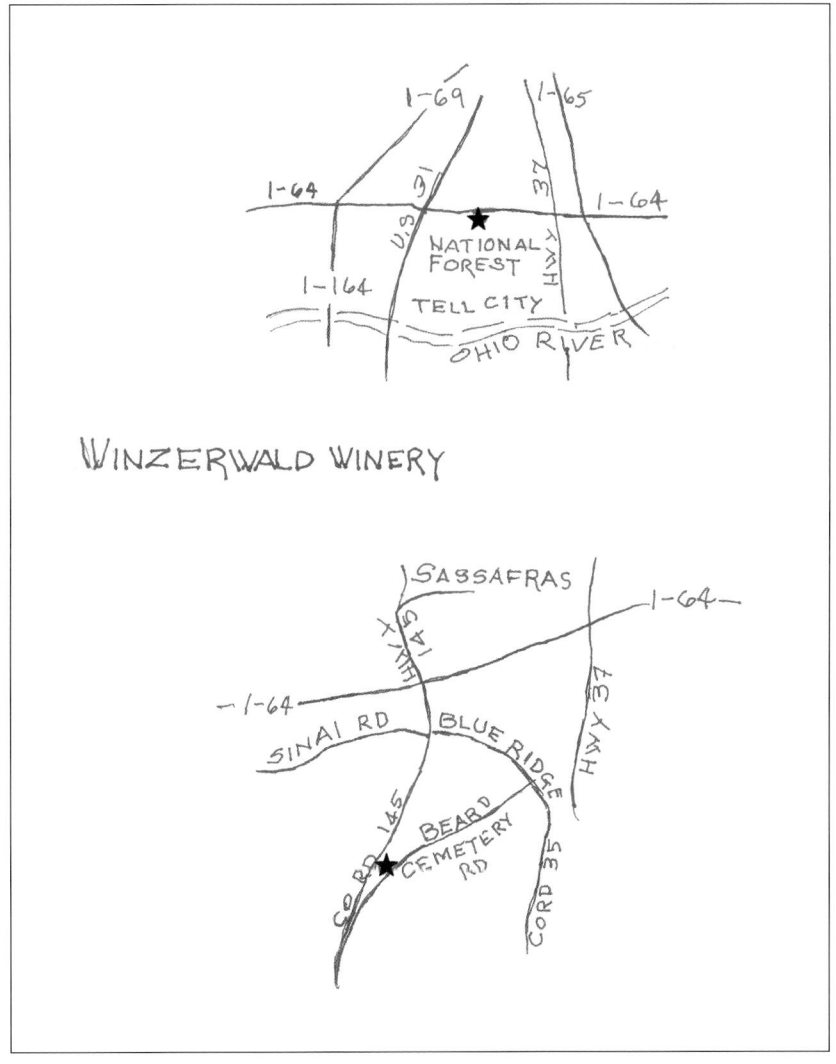

This southern Indiana winery has also created some fine sweet wines, including Cranberry and Stawberry, and offers yet more German specialties in their Schweizer spice wine, Gluhwein, and ice wines and port in season.

Make sure you check out the Winzerwald web site or call ahead for special dates and events. There is frequently live music and other German-heritage events throughout the year. And don't forget the tasting room in Evansville.

Information by the Glass

Owners: Dan & Donna Adams

Alternative Tasting Room in Evansville
2021 West Franklin Street
Evansville, IN 47712
812-423-2427

Hours:
Tuesday - Sunday 11 a.m. - 6 p.m.
Closed Mondays and holidays

Amenities: Gift Shop, Outdoor Seating

Tastings: Free

Price: $12 - $24

Recommendations:
Riesling—this semi-dry white can jump out of the glass and surprise you, but should be enjoyed, of course, with traditional German fare such as schnitzel (pork) and boiled potatoes.

Schillerwein—a traditional German white that can be enjoyed with a hot pretzel or with baked bread and butter.

Cabernet Sauvignon Reserve—likely the Winzerwald tops as far as bold, complex reds are concerned. Enjoy with red meat or with shrimp salad.

Activities: June Wine Bash, Wein Klub

Nearby Attractions: Holiday World, Hoosier National Forest, Mesker Zoo (Evansville)

Estate Grapes: Cabernet Sauvignon, Chambourcin, Gewurztraminer, Traminette, Chardonel, Pinot Grigio, Riesling, Liebich, Blaufrankish.

Traditional Leg of Lamb

6-7 pound leg of lamb
2 large onions, sliced
⅓ cup olive oil
2-3 lbs. potatoes, peeled and sliced
Salt, pepper, thyme, rosemary
4 cloves garlic, chopped
5 summer tomatoes, sliced
⅔ cup white wine

Prepare a large baking dish layered with potatoes and the spices (a pinch of each) along with the garlic cloves. Add leg of lamb. Add white wine and oil over the top of the full mixture and then roast uncovered for 90-minutes to 2 hours or until tender. Serve the lamb in slices along with the vegetables and a glass of Schillerwein.

Other Hoosier Wineries

Belgian Horse Winery
7122 West 625 North
Middleton, IN 47356
765-533-7000

Evangeline Orchard and Winery
10737 North 800 East
Monticello, IN 47960
574-278-6301

Kapp Winery
8716 West State Road 56
Jasper, IN 47546
812-482-6115

Vinetree Farm Winery
8343 W. Hardinsburg Road
Hardinsburg, IN 47125
812-472-3580

Indiana Grapes

In the U.S. we bottle wine according to varietal of grape. For example, wine producers identify a Pinot Noir as a Pinot Noir. A Chardonnay is a Chardonnay. A Zinfandel is a Zinfandel. In Europe, wines are traditionally identified by region: hence names like Chianti, Champaign, or Bordeaux.

What makes wines and wine-making so interesting and enduring, however, is the variety of tastes that can come from the same type of grape. There are many factors, of course, that go into these depth and breadth of tastes that wine makers can create from the same variety of vine. The latitude, altitude, type of soil, sunlight, water, fertilizer, and even the length of the growing season—all of these factors and more play a role the wine-making process.

Like any region, Indiana has its unique soil, sunlight, exposure, climate and growing season. A Hoosier vineyard may produce the same varietals as, say, a vineyard in Napa Valley or Bordeaux, France—but these grapes will all vary slightly in taste and complexity due to these many variables.

Unlike some regions where the growing season is longer, Indiana vineyards do have certain limitations when it comes to production and survivability of certain grapes. Not all grapes will thrive in our soil and seasons. Not all varietals will develop the taste and depth required to make great wines.

But that is not to say that Indiana is without great vineyards or complex wines. Far from it. Indiana may not be on a par with Napa or the finger lakes region of New York state, but Hoosier vintners are growing some phenomenal grapes and bottling some first-rate wines built on varietals that fare well in these parts.

Likewise, we dare not forget that all wineries—even the ones in Napa and in all points around Europe—buy grapes and juice to either supplement their own vineyard production, or contract with vineyards to produce their entire supply. We dare not judge any winery, or any winemaker, solely on the basis of whether they grow their own grapes. In fact, most wineries do not. And just as there are expert winemakers, so are there exceptional vintners. Some farmers simply excel in the vineyard, sell their commodity (grapes), and leave the end result to the expertise of the winemaker.

Perhaps, as you have traveled throughout Indiana and visited wineries, you may have noted that there are certain varietals that appear more often than others. Grapes like Chambourcin, Cabernet Franc and Traminette, for example, appear on the lists of nearly all Hoosier wineries. These grapes—along with several others—fare well in the Hoosier climate and shorter growing season. Indiana is premier in these vintages. These grapes thrive here.

For these reasons then, it can be helpful to understand these varietals—and we've prepared here a brief guide to Indiana Grapes to help explain the taste, textures and possibilities that these grapes afford. Moreover, as you read about them, you can then begin to form a clearer expectation of how these grapes should taste in the glass—and you may begin to form an opinion about, say, a Traminette, and how it varies from winery to winery. You will learn how these grapes are used, and begin to place them in "families" of taste or complexity. In time, you may also be able to identify these vintages from the taste alone, without having to refer to a winery's description of them before forming your own opinion.

Our hope is that this guide will be a starting point for your own wine appreciation, and may also accompany you on your wine tastings.

Most of all, we hope you will discover the grapes and vintages that you enjoy best. For as they say, the best wine for you is the wine that you enjoy drinking best. Wherever your taste leads you, keep exploring the best that Indiana wineries have to offer. In time you will no doubt discover those wineries around the state that build their labels around the tastes you enjoy the most. You'll find yourself returning to those wineries time and again. And you'll have a deeper appreciation for that winery's labels, too.

So, here are the Indiana grapes. We hope you'll enjoy them most in the bottles you love. This list is by no means exhaustive, but these would be the principal vines that one would encounter in the vineyards of the Hoosier state.

Red Wines

Chambourcin

Chambourcin is a French-American grape variety that is one of the most prominent grown in the Hoosier state. Available since 1963, Chambourcin does well in Indiana because it is resistant to disease but is also full of promise—both in its potential taste and aroma. The grape is dark, and can be produced both as a dry wine with certain complexities of taste, but also as a semi-sweet wine if the residual sugars are left in the grape during the fermentation.

Nearly all southern Indiana wineries will produce a Chambourcin label. This is because Chambourcin does better in the shorter growing season than does, say, a vine such as Cabernet Sauvignon. Therefore the Chambourcin harvest will usually offer winemakers a panoply of possibilities—and it should be noted that Chambourcin is usually produced here as a dry red option, in taste and depth reminiscent to a Merlot, but can also be produced as a semi-dry or even semi-sweet also. Chambourcin sometimes makes its appearance in Hoosier labels as a rose. Again, this is a grape that offers options—and winemakers will sometimes double their labels from this single varietal.

Marechal Foch

This grape, sometimes referred to simply as Foch by many wineries, is a very hearty grape (small and very dark as it ripens on the vine) and can fare well in the northern region of the state. Because of its rich red color and deeper tones, many winemakers will consider Foch a full-bodied red, not as deep and complex as a Cabernet or Zinfandel, but will often speak of it on a par with Syrah or Malbec. And in the hands of certain winemakers, it can be.

Most of the Fochs that one will taste in Indiana, however, will have a fruitier taste than dry. But Foch is a highly-drinkable vintage that should be considered across the possibilities it affords. Foch can be a superb table wine if given the chance to shine.

Norton

Sometimes known as Cynthiana, this grape tends to ripen late in season with smaller clusters and, therefore, has a smaller yield. Norton produces excellent reds with handled well, and in the glass this grape trends to the fruitier side of the scale with a certain tartness on the edges of the tongue. Because of its smaller yield, Norton is not as readily encountered as, say, a Chambourcin—but when you do find a Norton in a lineup, give it a try. Most wineries in Indiana do not feature a Norton, but when handled correctly this varietal can sit well in the glass. Likewise, Norton also makes an excellent fortified wine, with some Indiana wineries using the Norton as their port of choice.

Noiret

Offering more complexity than the Norton, Noiret grapes are a hybrid varietal with heartier tannins. Noiret can also produce wines reminiscent of Zinfandel, with pepper and spice notes in it. Most people who taste Noiret also note its structure along the descriptive lines of blackberry, green pepper, and sometimes mint. Again, because it fares well in harsher climates, this grape is found more often in the northern part of Indiana and can also be used in red blends.

Steuben

Many vintners describe the Steuben grape, on the cluster, as being the most beautiful of all grapes on the vine. Indeed, when you visit vineyards around the state, you may note the Steuben grapes for their depth of color and robust, almost picturesque, attraction on the trellis. Steuben can appear in the glass as anywhere from a dark red to a rose, and many wineries around the state are finding this grape to be a popular varietal among those who enjoy semi-dry to semi-sweet options.

Concord

Perhaps the most well-known grape in America, Concord grapes have a large, round appearance on the vine, and are used to produce most grape juices. The grape is sweet and fruity, and for this reason many wineries include a Concord-based wine among their offerings.

Behind the scenes, many winemakers will admit that wines made of the Concord are among their best-selling. Concord wines are highly recognizable, and for those who enjoy sweet wines, the Concord is one of the most popular and easily recognizable of grapes. Think grape jelly and you have a general idea. In the glass, Concord stands out as deep purple, but is also used widely in sweet blends to add distinction and color to other sweeter grapes—even among the white varietals (to form rose or blush).

White Wines

Traminette

This is a fairly recent hybrid grape (produced from Gewurztraminer) that has often been described as *The Indiana grape*. Common throughout the state, nearly all wineries produce a Traminette—and even some of the smallest wineries and vineyards will plan this varietal first when they are establishing a planting. Like the Gewurztraminer grape, Traminette is a heartier cousin, and can produce wines of character and depth. Those enjoying Traminette often speak of this wine in terms of its nose (floral) and its spicy tones that can range from cinnamon to black pepper to clove.

Many Hoosier wineries are especially proud of the labels they produce with this grape, and it is not uncommon to see award-winning Traminettes that have been bottled in Indiana. Still, there is enough variety and complexity in this grape that one can find a range of tastes from winery to winery. Among whites, Traminette is often touted as a semi-dry wine, but frequently has a fruity, even honey exposure, that insures its popularity. One could have a lot of fun in Indiana by comparing Traminette from winery to winery—and there would be dozens to compare.

Cayuga White

Another common Indiana grape, Cayuga White is a hearty grape—more robust and pale as the name implies—that grows well in all regions of the state. Along with Traminette and Chambourcin, Cayuga White can be found in most Hoosier wineries. This grape can become a semi-sweet wine that has a beautifully balanced spectrum from acidic to sugary, but can also be aged in oak to transform it into a drier wine. Hence, its versatility and appreciation among winemakers.

Chardonel

This is a hybrid of the Seyval and Chardonnay grapes, and therefore has some of the characteristics of the latter when it comes to the buttery, layered and complex notes that is Chardonnay. Chardonel, however, is widely grown in Indiana and among the better winemakers can trend toward an excellent dinner wine that goes will with fish and cream-based sauces. These wines are also excellent as a cooking wine.

Seyval

This is a very hearty grape—one of the most widely planted in this region of the United States—and is a grape grown by many wineries even if not used exclusively as a varietal in the bottle. Many winemakers use this grape to add flavor and complexity to their whites, but it can also be found bottled under its own name. In the glass, most people describe Seyval in "earthy" terms—with descriptions of "apple", "honeysuckle", "sweet hay" or even "cut-grass" commonplace. For this reason, Seyval is to be appreciated for its roots to the soil, and its ability to suggest the climate and surroundings from which it sprang. Wines made from this grape tend to grow on the tongue and have a more lasting impression.

Vidal

Not as common as Seyval, nor as hearty, the Vidal grape requires a longer growing season and longer time on the vine. But for this reason, a lot of ice wines and specialty wines in the state will spring from the Vidal grape. Those enjoying ice wines made by Hoosier wineries will often find this grape in the bottle. It is sweet, delectable, and sits well across the spectrum of sweet to acidic. More difficult to find as a stand-alone wine, it holds promise also as a sparkling wine option and is sometimes used to make Brandy.

Catawba

A grape growing in popularity in the Midwest, the Catawba is often bottled along the lines of a White Zinfandel, and has some of the same pink to rose exposure in the bottle. At any rate, it makes beautiful wine, and most Catawba will be found in the sweet category to strict dessert wine.

Niagara

Another popular grape, the Niagara makes superb sweet wine of distinctive character. Many wineries will feature a Niagara label, or under other name, as their premier sweet wine. Niagara, for those enjoying sweeter wines, tends to be a favorite after-dinner option and from the length and breadth of Indiana, one would not have a difficult time finding wineries who produce their own version of it.

Other Indiana Grapes

Increasingly, Indiana wineries (and farmers) are stretching the boundaries and experimenting with varietals that, up until a few years ago, were regarded as impossible to grow in this climate. Now, it is not uncommon to find any of the following on Hoosier wine lists: Riesling, Chardonnay, Pinot Gris, Cabernet Franc, and Cabernet Sauvignon.

What makes these varietals so extraordinary in Indiana is that, grown in state, these grapes can blossom with new tastes and boundaries—far different than the traditional descriptors associated with these grapes as they are encountered in other regions. As stated, a Cabernet Sauvignon grown in Indiana is going to taste much different than a Napa Valley grown Cab.

When tasting certain varietals in Indiana, it is often helpful to ask about the source of the grape. A Cabernet wine produced by a Hoosier winemaker doesn't always mean that the grapes were grown in state. Sometimes they are. Sometimes not. But you can find some excellent Cabs grown in state, especially in the southern regions of the state.

Most of all, learn to appreciate the differences among these grapes. Every region—and Indiana is no exception—offers its own unique tastes.

Indiana Wineries: The Ultimate Guide to Wine in Indiana

Wine Trails of Indiana

One of the pluses of living in a smaller state like Indiana is the relative ease of travel. And when it comes to visiting Indiana wineries, this is made all the easier if one follows the wine trails. Currently, there are five such trails—and they can be described by region.

Each of these trails offers a group of wineries who have partnered together to make the trail a fun and enjoyable experience. These partner wineries often have passport-style punch cards that tourists can use on the trail and, once completed, exchange for a wine glass, information on wine clubs, or other assorted gifts. Sometimes, driving a wine trail and visiting all of the wineries makes for a perfect weekend—and if one is traveling in the summer or, perhaps, through the autumn colors, a wine trail can be an unforgettable experience.

For those who live in the Indianapolis area, all of these wine trails are accessible in just a few hours—another plus—and, while it may not be possible to visit all of the wineries on a given trail in a single day, each wine trail offers a taste of its respective region, and wine lovers are sure to find some new sights and possibilities that will make them pine for a return visit.

A wine trail also offers another plus: and that is the ability to compare wines.

In fact, as you plan your next wine trail excursion, let us offer a few helpful tips and pieces of advice that can make your experience all the more enjoyable (and safe).

- Ten Wine Trail Tips

- Work up a plan before you set out on your excursion. This plan should help you locate the various wineries in the best use of your time—both on and off the road. For example, you may choose to visit the winery that is farthest from your home first, and then backtrack along the trail, visiting those wineries that lead you back to your front porch.

- Be aware that a GPS system doesn't always help you find a winery. This is especially true for rural wineries that may be located on country roads. In fact, a visit to the various winery web sites can often be most helpful in terms of direction. Some have interactive maps, or suggestions or landmarks that can help you navigate your trip.

- Bring all contact information (phone numbers of the wineries) with you. You can call ahead and check on the winery hours (don't assume all wineries have the same schedule).

- When you visit the first winery on the trail, pick up your "passport" card and be sure to get it checked or punched at each subsequent winery. Be sure to claim your gift if you do visit all of the wineries in a single season.

- Bring cash. Most wineries will accept credit and debit cards, but often it is faster and easier to pay as you go.

- Bring a travel box for your wine purchases. If you don't have a wine box, you can often find one for free at a liquor store or supermarket. Just ask. Having slots for each bottle is helpful, and the wine will travel back home more safely and easily if you secure them in a box instead of tossing them in the back seat of the car. A box is also helpful on hot days, when summer sun can "boil" a bottle or hasten its demise. As you can, keep your purchases in a box with lid closed, and be sure to crack the windows of your car so your wine won't bake.

- Keep a record of your wine purchases along the trail—including the vintage, year, and any descriptions of each bottle provided by the winery. These notes can be helpful later, when you take out a bottle and wonder: "what was special about this one?"

- As time allows, don't be in a hurry. Enjoy each winery and appreciate the nuances.

- Enjoy the scenery, but drive carefully.

- Safety Tip: Please remember that a wine trail is perfect for sampling many wines. Be aware of how much you are sampling (these tastings add up quickly to full glasses!). And as general rule, it is always better to taste the wine (and either spit or pour out the samples after you've tasted) if you are driving a wine trail. Wineries are not offended by this—that's why they have urns on the bar! So—taste responsibly—and plan to purchase a bottle or two of your favorites from each winery which you can then enjoy in the weeks ahead.

As you plan for your next wine trail excursion, keep these tips in mind and you will have a more enjoyable experience. Now . . . let's hit the trails.

The Indiana Wine Trails

As noted earlier, there are currently five wine trails in Indiana. Each offers a sampling from a different region of the state. And so, let's begin north and move south as we traverse the trails and describe them.

WINE Tour, The Wineries of Indiana's North East Tour

http://www.winetourin.com/#info

Traveling north on I-69 toward the northeast corner of the state, one can pick up the trail and enjoy both new and established wineries (and some great wines, we might add). This part of the Hoosier state offers a different taste than the south (as you will discover), and with the shorter growing season and harsher winters, the wines in this region are often more rugged and enduring—in all the right ways. You will also discover some unique varietals up this way and more than enough expert winemakers to bring you back time and again. Currently, this wine trail hosts the following wineries:

- Briali
- Satek
- Tonne
- McClure's
- Country Heritage
- Fruit Hills
- Two-EE's

Indy Wine Trail

http://www.indywinetrail.com/trailmap/

In and around the metro area, there are some exceptional wineries. Don't let urban appearances fool you. This trail can take some planning, but if you think of the beltway (465) as your primary route, you can easily drop off at various points to make these visits. Others are in the Indy-metro area, just a short drive down other highways. Some of the oldest and most established wineries are on this trail and if you live in the Indy-metro area, you should always be able to complete this full tour in a season.

- Mallow Run
- Easley
- Chateau Thomas
- Buck Creek
- Simmons
- Cedar Creek
- New Day Meadery

Indiana Uplands Wine Trail

http://www.indianauplands.com/

This central and southern Indiana trail has some amazing venues. And, while some of these wineries are located near larger metropolitan areas, others will offer a taste of rural Indiana. Be sure to pick up a passport for this trail, as you may have to make a weekend of it, or continue your drive. You will want to linger in these wineries—they are all that good.

- Best
- Brown County
- Butler
- French Lick
- Huber
- Oliver

- Owen Valley
- Turtle Run

Hoosier Wine Trail

http://www.hoosierwinetrail.com/

A drive to the south and east will yield some remarkable sights as well as some top-flight wineries. As you make your way toward Louisville, Kentucky, or the Ohio River valley you can easily drop off the I-65 interstate for a visit to these spectacular places.

- Chateau de Pique
- River City
- Indian Creek
- Scout Mountain
- Blue Heron
- Monkey Hollow
- Pepper's Ridge
- Mystique

Indiana Wine Trail

http://www.indianawinetrail.com/

These wineries, all located in the Madison-to-Richmond corridor of the state, each have a flavor and flair of their own. There is also much to do and see along this trail—including some spectacular vistas and rolling countryside. Great wines, too.

- Madison
- Lanthier
- Thomas Family
- The Ridge
- Ertel
- Stream Cliff Farm

Wine Festivals of Indiana

Wine festivals provide a panoply of wineries and experiences that can be savored at a single event. As such, they are something of a showcase for Hoosier wineries, but offer far more than just a wine-tasting experience. These festivals also offer a forum for wine lovers and wine makers to meet and to discuss new and old wines, revel in the wine-making art, and sign up for newsletters and special offers. In short, festivals provide a showcase for the great wines being produced in state—and a visit to one or more of these festivals each year is, indeed, a superb way to grow in appreciation and knowledge of wines in general.

There are new festivals cropping up each year—and no doubt by the time this book goes to press there will be the inevitable additions that are not found in this listing. However, there are several premier festivals that can be found around the state, and we will make a valiant attempt to describe each one here. (Alphabetical order.)

Big Red Liquors Wine & Food Festival

This one is held in Bloomington, Indiana, in late March at the Bloomington Convention Center. While there are wines from around the world featured in this gigantic showcase, there are also local wineries, too. A cover charge makes this tasting affordable, but also one of the broadest exposures to wines (worldwide) that one is likely to encounter in state. Big numbers, bold tastes, and a smart crowd make this wine festival one of the best showcases in the state. Visit the Bloomington Convention Center web site for more details (dates, times and cost).

Carmel Wine Festival

Every July the Carmel Wine Festival offers a summer showcase for both local and national wines. Food booths, arts and music round out the event. The Carmel Wine Festival plays host to a number of Indiana wineries every year and the representation continues to grow year by year. And because it is located in central Indiana, the festival does pull from areas beyond Indianapolis.

Harvest Festival

Held in Madison, Indiana, each fall in conjunction with other river attractions, the Harvest Festival features the Lanthier Winery as host. Other wineries are usually present and accounted for, and the beauty of the river walk this time of year can't be beat. Too many attractions to list—but there is plenty of antiquing, dining and music to enjoy.

Also, look for the winter fests here that also feature wine. Southern Indiana is host to several and if you are looking for a winter wine experience, you can find one in Madison.

Indiana Wine Fair

This wine showcase—traditionally held the last Saturday of April in Story, Indiana (at the Story Inn)—features many Indiana wineries and the best of their upcoming vintages. Organized in this small town ambiance, the IWF offers one of the earliest opportunities to taste the newest offerings of the Indiana winemakers. Nashville, Indiana is not far away, so visitors can make a full day of this Saturday excursion while sampling the best of the best.

Story is little more than a village (some might say a "stop in the road") along highway 135, but this event has grown proportionally to the point where buses are now bringing people in. Parking is scarce here, so look for these alternative transportation options if you go. The event is a bit pricey ($30 a head, or $10 for a designated driver), but visitors will get to sample from many Indiana wineries. Live music and other booths round out the day.

The Story Inn also provides a small restaurant option and, believe it or not, overnight lodging in the upper level. A large hitching post area adjacent to the Inn offers "parking" for those who prefer to ride in on horseback. At last count there were some 4,000 people who attended this wine fair, making it, perhaps, the most densely populated wine fair in state for the venue. Quaint and charming, if you've not been to Story, Indiana, you'll get there if you drive south out of Nashville, Indiana on highway 135. You may not find this place on the map—and if you "blink" you'll miss it at the turn—but if you like country, turn-of-the century charm, you'll want to be a part of this story.

Southern Indiana Uncorked
(www.southernindianauncorked.com)

This annual event on the Harrison County Fairgrounds offers an exposure to Indiana wines that is both fun and exciting. With the cover charge, visitors usually receive wine glasses and a full slate of entertainment options. This includes live music and activities. Many southern wineries make this a place to showcase their labels. And even with the crowds, the fairgrounds provide a spacious experience.

Swiss Wine Festival
(www.swisswinefestival.org)

Held in Vevay, Indiana, in August, this festival celebrates our Hoosier roots and place in the winemaking history, but offers far more than just a wine experience. In addition to the many Indiana wineries that make this an annual tasting event, there is a parade, food booths galore, and live music. A grape stomp, amusement rides, and dancing is also a part of the festivities. And with fireworks to cap off the evening, this annual festival is a spectacular mix of sight and sound. The daily schedule can be found online (see web site above) and there is a small admission charge. If you have not been to the Swiss Wine Festival, or have a desire to sample wines from across the state—this festival offers an exposure unlike few others. Make this the year to drive south.

Vintage Indiana
(www.vintageindiana.com)

This festival has become the premier showcase for Hoosier wineries in the capital city. Each year this festival seems to be bigger and bolder than the year before. Held on the Military Park grounds in downtown Indianapolis, one should expect to see between a third and a half of the Indiana wineries represented at this festival. Each winery holds court in its own tent, clearly marked with the winery's logo and information, and winery staff clearly enjoy the interaction with patrons.

Looking to gain a greater appreciation for Indiana wines or a broader exposure to the wineries in state? This festival won't disappoint. The entry fee more than pays for the experience itself and all purchases can be stored at the gate and boxed by able and willing staff.

Vintage Indiana can be a full-day, as a variety of food is available across the grounds and visitors are treated to a slate of entertainment—live music, presentations, and educational seminars. It's all here. And Vintage Indiana offers the bonus of being able to taste and select wines from across the state—all from one location. This is, however, more than a winery showcase—but a wine experience.

Weekend Wine Trips

One of the best ways to explore Indiana wineries (and the Hoosier state itself) is to create a weekend excursion. This allows plenty of time for relaxation as well as prime time for exploring some of Indiana's local haunts and hotspots. There are, in fact, great places to eat, to shop, and to recreate in every corner of the state—and by creating a weekend trip you can also add a handful of wineries to the mix without feeling rushed.

Here we've created seven weekend wine trips. We feel that you'll find one or two in this mix that would offer some unexplored corner of the state for your enjoyment. But don't just take our itinerary and suggestions for granted, either. Use these trips as outline only—if you do a bit of your own research on the internet you will no doubt discover other off-road destinations, restaurants, shopping, or sights that would fit neatly into these basic regional schemes (and be more exciting *to you*).

We have also attempted to create trips that would provide access to wineries in every region of the state. Not all regions are covered—but by looking north, south, east, west and central, you are sure to see the possibilities in these outlines.

Have fun traveling. But remember to be safe, to drink responsibly (or just taste like a pro), and enjoy those new wineries that you discover off the beaten path.

North

Traveling north along the I-69 corridor one has easy access to many wineries. Regardless of whether one is traveling from central Indiana north (or traveling north to south), I-69 is going to provide a main thoroughfare. A weekend trip in this north-east region of the state can include the following:

Sights and Recreation

Pokagen State Park (www.in.gov)
Foellinger-Freimann Botanical Conservatory—Fort Wayne
   (www.botanicalconservatory.org)
The Embassy Theatre—Fort Wayne
   (www.fwembassytheatre.com)

Accommodations

Inn at Windmere—Auburn (www.innatwindmere.com)
The Inn at Pokagen State Park (www.in.gov)

Dining

Biaggi's Ristorante Italiano—Fort Wayne (www.biaggis.com)
Baker Street Steakhouse—Fort Wayne
   (www.bakerstreetfortwayne.com)
Timbers Casual Dining and Lounge—Angola
   (www.timberscasualdining.com)

Wineries

Tonne Winery—Muncie
Two EE's Winery—Huntington
Country Heritage Winery—LaOtto
Satek Winery—Fremont
Briali Winery—Fremont

South-East (1)

Traveling south-east out of Indianapolis (I-74) will provide a landscape of possibilities. Consider Rising Sun your final destination. With I-74 as your main artery for travel, you can easily drop off for these side trips to the wineries listed here.

Sights and Recreation

Dagaz Acres Zipline Adventures—Rising Sun (www.dagazacres.com)
Red Wolf Sanctuary—Rising Sun (www.redwolf.org)
Courthouse at Greensburg

Accommodations

Nana's House—Greensburg (www.nanashousebb.com)
Mary Helen's Bed, Breakfast and Fine Dining—Batesville (www.maryhelensplace.com)
Tuggle's Folly Bed & Breakfast—Rising Sun (www.tuggles-folly.com)

Dining

Storie's Restaurant—Greensburg (www.urbanspoon.com)
Ertel Cellars Restaurant (www.ertelcellars.com)

Wineries

Ertel Cellars Winery—Batesville
Chateau Pomije—Guilford
Powers Winery—Dillsboro
Rowland Winery—Dillsboro
Fiekerts Homestead Wine—Rising Sun

South-East (2)

A trip to the origins of Indiana wine will always be a great adventure. This trip will take you back to Vevay, Indiana where it all began, and to Madison, where there is plenty of antique shopping and dining possibilities. No easy way to get to Vevay, but you'll enjoy the countryside and this weekend adventure.

Sights and Recreation

Madison River Walk
Historic Vevay

Accommodations

The Schenck Mansion—Vevay (www.schenckmansion.com)
Azalea Manor Bed & Breakfast—Madison
(www.theazaleamanor.com)
Hendricks-Beall Home Bed & Breakfast—Madison
(www.hendricksbeallhome.com)

Dining

Madison Lighthouse Restaurant—Madison
(www.urbanspoon.com)
The Red Pepper—Madison (www.urbanspoon.com)

Wineries

The Ridge Winery—Vevay
Thomas Family Winery—Madison
Lanthier Winery—Madison
Madison Vineyards—Madison
Stream Cliff Farm Winery—Commiskey

Central

There are several new and established wineries in the Indianapolis area, and using I-465 as the primary thoroughfare, one can easily drop on and off the belt to visit the wineries listed below. Of course, many sights in Indianapolis as well as superb entertainment. Many possibilities for a weekend in the capital city.

Sights and Recreation

The Indianapolis Museum of Art (www.imamuseum.org)
The Children's Museum of Indianapolis
(www.childrensmuseum.org)
Old National Center (Murat Theatre)
(www.oldnationalcenter.com)
Circle Center Mall

Accommodations

The Canterbury Hotel (www.canterburyhotel.com)
The Westin (www.westinindianapolis.com)

Dining

R Bistro—Indianapolis (www.rbistro.com)
St. Elmo Steak House—Indianapolis (www.stelmos.com)
Bazbeaux Pizza—Indianapolis (www.bazbeaux.com)

Wineries

Easley Winery—Indianapolis
New Day Meadery—Indianapolis
Chateau Thomas—Plainfield
Buck Creek Winery—Indianapolis

South

Traveling due south down I-65 out of Indianapolis, consider New Albany your final destination. Using I-65 as your artery, you can drop off the interstate to visit some superb wineries. One of the premier weekend trips if you are looking to make wine the centerpiece of your experience.

Sights and Recreation

New Albany River Walk
The Falls of the Ohio
Architectural Tour of Columbus, Indiana

Accommodations

The Brown Hotel—New Albany
Admiral Bicknell Inn—New Albany
 (www.admiralbicknell.com)

Dining

La Bocca—New Albany (www.laboccarestaurant.net)
Feast BBQ—New Albany (www.feastbbq.com)
Habana Blues—New Albany (www.admiralbicknell.com)
Bistro 310—Columbus (www.bistro310.com)

Wineries

Simmons Winery—Edinburgh
Chateau de Pique—Seymour
Huber Orchard Winery—Starlight
Indian Creek Winery—Georgetown
River City Winery—New Albany

South-west

South—and to the west—you'll be able to make a nice weekend excursion to the French Lick—West Baden area, using this destination as your hub. There are some good wineries in this southern region of Indiana, and some of the most spectacular accommodations you'll find anywhere in the state. This trip will be a relaxing wine excursion. Let the pace refresh you.

Sights and Recreation

French Lick Golf Course (www.frenchlick.com/golf)
French Lick Scenic Railway
    (www.indianarailwaymuseum.org)
French Lick Resort (www.frenchlick.com)
Patoka Lake (www.patokalakeindiana.com)
Marengo Cave (www.marengocave.com)

Accommodations

The French Lick Resort (www.frenchlick.com)
West Baden Springs Hotel (www.frenchlick.com)
E.B. Rhodes House Bed & Breakfast
    (www.bedbreakfasthome.com)

Wineries

Carousel Winery—Mitchell
French Lick Winery—French Lick
Vinetree Farm Winery—Hardinsburg
Winzerwald—Bristow

South-Central

Traveling south from Indianapolis, find Hwy 37 south toward Bloomington. This south-central leg is loaded with some of the best wineries in the state. You won't have to go far off the beaten path here to find some top wines.

Sights and Recreation

McCormick's Creek State Park
Hoosier National Forest
Little 500—Indiana University Annual Event
Nashville, Indiana shopping

Accommodations

Showers Inn—Bloomington (www.showersinn.com)
Brown County Getaways—Nashville (www.browncountygetaways.com)

Dining

The Irish Lion Restaurant and Pub—Bloomington (www.irishlion.com)
Grazie Italian Eatery—Bloomington (https://grazieitalianeatery.com)
Nashville House—Nashville (www.browncountyinn.com)

Wineries

Brown County Winery—Nashville
Butler Winery—Bloomington
Oliver Winery—Bloomington
Owen Valley Winery—Spencer
Cedar Creek Winery—Martinsville
Mallow Run Winery—Bargersville

Helpful Web Sites on Hoosier Wines

There is a growing list of helpful web sites and blogs that wine lovers can, and should, visit regularly. Indiana is also home to many of the most respected and appreciated wine experts in the United States.

Along these lines, here are some sites that will get you started on your wine education.

www.indianawines.org

This site, operated by the Purdue University, Indiana Grape Council, is a wealth of information about Indiana wines and her wineries. News, events, calendar . . . it's all here. You'll even find a listing of award winners at various wine competitions. Plenty of photos, too.

This web site also features a listing of other Indiana-wine-related web sites and phone numbers. Bed and Breakfasts, restaurants, Hoosier travel tips—it's chocked full.

This is the place to begin as you plan a trip or a wine tour.

www.indianawineries.com

One of the most helpful web sites related to Indiana wines. The primary feature of this site is an interactive map of the state, which shows the location of each winery and, with the click of the mouse, takes visitors to the respective winery web sites. All told, it's a remarkable piece of technology and one can easily gain a perspective on winery location from a glance at the map. Once you visit here, you'll return time and again (just as you will to this book!).

www.indianawinery.blogspot.com

The authors' showcase and information celebrating all Hoosier wineries. Interviews, photos, and new wine selections make this a blog that should be visited frequently. Travel tips, wine appreciation, and the latest information on Indiana wineries . . . it's all here.

www.indianawines.blogspot.com

This superb blog, written and maintained by Jeanette Merritt, profiles Indiana wineries in photo and upcoming events. A timely blog, it is a great place to learn about what is happening on the Hoosier wine landscape. Jeanette has a knack for interviews also—and there are many insightful personalities here who share their ideas about wine and winemaking.

www.hoosierwinecallar.com

I love this web site and blog hosted by four wonderful ladies. Each one has something to offer by way of comment, insight, or appreciation along the Hoosier wine experience. In fact, this site goes well beyond Indiana in terms of its expertise and commentary—think global with a touch of Hoosier hospitality. Once you begin reading this site you always come back for more.

www.midwestbeerandwine.com

A site devoted to news and profiles of wines and wineries (among others). Great photography, profiles of new (and newer) wineries, and fantastic journalism. A fun read, and an accessible way to get at the pulse of Indiana wineries.

https://ag.purdue.edu/foodsci/extension/winegrapeteam/Pages/default.aspx

This recent Purdue agricultural web site and blog is remarkable. With information about vineyards, grape horticulture, and even descriptions of Hoosier vines—this site is a must for anyone who is hoping to become a vintner, or who simply craves a more detailed exposure to the world of vine-tending. And better yet, profiles and interviews with great wine masters, too.

www.vintageindiana.com

A full color and interactive site devoted to the summer wine festival in Indianapolis—but also provides a listing of many Indiana wineries. The site provides information, well in advance of the festival, about the winemaking industry in state and provides superb visuals that bring the weekend to life. The many links from the site also make it a prime source of information from across the state.

Wine Shops Around the State

In addition to the Hoosier Wineries profiled in this book, one can also discover Indiana labels at some of the finest wine shops around the state. In addition to some of the "big box" stores or national chains, there are some very fine local stores that wine lovers should discover. These stores not only offer selection, but expertise among the staff. Several of these shops host wine tastings, even wine appreciation classes, on a regular basis. The best way to get a feel for these shops is by visiting their respective web sites initially, but nothing beats being on the premises and perusing the racks one-on-one.

We have our favorites, but here we are going to list the shops in alphabetic order and offer a brief description of each. In no way is this an exhaustive list of wine shops, but these are among the best in-state establishments that often carry Hoosier labels while also offering a personal touch and a knowledge about the Hoosier wine-making scene.

Bottle

5131 U.S. Highway 41 & S. 7th Street
Terre Haute, Indiana
www.bottle41.com

One of Indiana's newest wine shops located on Highway 41 in Terre Haute, owner Jeff Hock brings his California experience and wine critic taste to his quaint but wonderfully selective wine shop. He also has beers and fine olive oils, too. Travelling west on US 70, stop off for a visit.

Cork and Cracker

2126 Broad Ripple Avenue, Indianapolis
www.corkandcracker.com

This shop features a wide selection of wines (along with beers and cheeses). The owners are knowledgeable and welcome conversation about your favorite wines. A visit to the Cork and Cracker might also pair well with an evening at a favorite Broad Ripple restaurant.

Crown Liquors

150 N. Deleware, Indianapolis
www.crownliquors.net

Several locations around the state, but be sure to visit the beautifully-designed store on North Delaware in downtown Indy. Wines are in the basement—and one of the largest selections in state—all categorized by vintage. A climate-controlled room here also plays home to some of the finest wines in the world (if you are so inclined by the hefty price tag for collecting), and Crown offers Hoosier labels, too. Wine tastings (and classes) can be had on certain evenings, so check out the web site for times.

Grapevine Cottage

61 S. Main Street
Zionsville, Indiana
www.grapevinecottage.com

This wine shop has it all: enormous selection, expert staff, value, and plenty of wine accessories, gift baskets, and cheeses to make this a one-stop wine-lovers extravaganza. When you visit the Grapevine Cottage, plan to ask questions about the wines—which are mostly racked by vintage and by Parker Scale identification. If you shop well, you can find some excellent value here, especially in those boxes marked, "We Bought a Bunch".

Kahn's Fine Wines

5341 N. Keystone Ave.
Indianapolis, Indiana
www.kahnsfinewines.com

Sometimes referred to as a "superstore", Kahn's has one of the widest selection of wines one will find anywhere in the state. Yes, they have Hoosier wines, too—just ask. A great many wines from around the world here and plenty of advice to help even the most discriminating wine buff.

Vine and Table

313 East Carmel Drive
Carmel, Indiana
www.vineandtable.com

This shop has the look and feel of a winery—but with far more selection than one can process in an afternoon. Indiana labels can be found here, but the worldwide presence on these racks is astounding. Vine and Table offers a perfect opportunity to compare some of the top Indiana wines with some of the world's finest. Ask for advice. Many friendly and helpful people here.

Vino Villa

200 N. Madison Avenue
Greenwood, Indiana
www.vinovilla.com

A beautiful family-owned bistro (upper level) with full racks of assorted wines. Vino Villa is a fine choice for those who simply want to enjoy their wine shopping experience while also discovering some other Hoosier labels.

Common Questions for Wine Appreciation

Do good wine glasses make a difference in tasting?

Our experience is that good wine glasses can certainly enhance the experience with wine. This is true in several ways. First, a good glass that provides clarity will enable one to actually see the wine in the glass, study it, and ascertain much from its appearance (clarity, depth, color). A good glass can also reveal a wine's "legs"—which are the streaks that the wine leaves on the sides of the glass and have to do with the alcohol reacting to the air. Likewise, a good glass—and one that enhances the type of wine one is drinking (open bowls for bold reds, for example) will allow more oxygen, or less, to get into the wine as you swirl it. Wine does indeed change in taste and experience as it sits in the glass. So, purchase the finest glasses you can, but don't let the type or style of wine glass inhibit you in your enjoyment.

What wine accessories should I own?

First, you will want to own a good corkscrew. There are several styles, but a traditional hand corkscrew that also contains a small knife blade for cutting the foil top, works as well as some of the more expensive screws. Owning one or two wine decanters (for allowing the wine to "air" or "breath") can also be helpful, and these can also help with catching sediment when you are drinking certain finer wines (especially reds). Other wine accessories could include a strainer, coasters, and a wine chart (listing varietals, regions, and common descriptors).

What does sediment in a bottle mean?

Many wines naturally have organic matter that settles on the bottom of the bottle as it matures. This is true for both whites and reds. Sediment can also be an indication that, because the wine has matured, it will have a more tannic taste. In other words, this is not a bad thing. Never judge a wine by its sediment, however.

How long will a bottle of wine "keep" once I open it?

As a general rule, wine should be drank within a day or two of opening. Lighter wines will also begin to deteriorate faster than, say, a bolder wine with more alcohol content. If you do "re-cork" the bottle after you open it, we have found that most wines will keep in this fashion, even without refrigeration, for a day or two without compromising too much taste. You can refrigerate wines after opening them, but plan to do this only if you are going to go longer than two days. Also, there are now products designed to create a new "vacuum" in the bottle and, presumably, return the open bottle back to its former uncorked state. The verdict is still out on whether these actually work. Also, keep in mind that a fortified wine (sherry or port, for example) will keep for weeks after you open the bottle due to the higher alcohol content of the spirits. We have enjoyed certain bottles of port for weeks without noticing any compromise of flavor.

Is it true that a wine will improve with age?

This is not true of all wines. First, the majority of wines are bottled without vintages, meaning the year is not identified. These wines are meant to be enjoyed within a year or two of the bottling. Most wines with vintages would also fall into this category. However, vintage wines will usually improve with age—and some will greatly improve with long ageing in a climate-controlled cellar. For the average wine lover, we would recommend enjoying wine as one buys it, or perhaps enjoying it within a year or two of purchase. As most people are not wine collectors or wine connoisseurs, it doesn't make sense to invest in an expensive bottle if one can't store it properly. Let your wines age as you can—but don't become overly concerned about the age of your vintages. It is fun, however, to have a wine tasting of various vintages from the same winery, for example, or from the same year just to see how the tastes differ.

How can I improve my enjoyment of wine tasting?

We would recommend purchasing a simple wine chart or "wheel" that contains the various grape varieties and wine regions. These often contain basic descriptions of tastes, say, of a Pinot Gris vs. a Riesling or the differences between a Zinfandel and a Petite Syrah. And don't be afraid to really smell a wine before tasting it. Allow the aromas to first form your impression of a wine. Enjoy the bouquet. Learn from it. And once you do taste, don't always think that you have to drink a wine. Often you can appreciate a wine's taste without drinking it. This can be helpful, especially, when visiting several wineries in a day trip or when hosting a wine party in the home. You will eventually arrive at some of your favorite wines. It doesn't matter what others think. If you like these wines then they are your favorites. Enjoy them. Savor them. Serve these favorite wines with meals.

Do the names of wines indicate a certain style?

Not necessarily. In most countries, a wine identified by its varietal of grape (Zinfandel, Cabernet Sauvignon, etc.) does not mean that is 100% that grape. It must be predominantly that grape, but there are also wines built around blends of varietals or simply as "drinking" or "cooking" wines. Another example: most California Cabs, Merlots, Zinfandels and Syrahs are blends, but by law the bottle must contain 75% of the grape to be classified as the varietal shown on the label. Blending a bit of another grape into a wine actually deepens the taste, making it richer and complex, while still retaining the primary grape varietal as its identifying characteristic. In the U.S. wines are typically identified by the variety of grape—and this is what one will see on the label (Riesling, Syrah, etc.). In Europe, wines are typically identified by region.

Is it possible to mix various wines to create unique tastes?

Absolutely. In fact, we have discovered that it is possible to create some of your favorite blends by mixing two or more bottles of wine together in a decanter. Don't be afraid to experiment with some of your favorites . . . or to attempt to make an average wine better by adding a percentage of another vintage.

Is a cork superior to a screw top? Is there a difference in taste?

For most wines—those that one is going to drink within a year or two of bottling—there is really not noticeable difference between a cork and a screwtop. Many European bottlers who have long gone to screwtop presentation continue to add corks to their American distribution because Americans seem infatuated and concerned about the cork. Taste the difference if you can—but most people aren't going to note any difference between a cork bottle and a screwtop of the same vintage.

What can I do if the cork breaks off into the bottle?

This is sometimes a frustration with corks, and it can happen to the best of bottles. (Not long ago we had the entire glass top of a bottle break off during opening.) If this does happen, plan to push the cork all the way into the bottle and then decant the contents (use a strainer if you need to). You should be able to remove most of the cork bits and will find that this will not influence the taste of the wine. Besides, a little cork never hurt anybody.

What is an organic wine?

The organic wine market is certainly growing. These are wines made from grapes that have not been sprayed with insecticides, herbicides or fertilized with chemicals. In other words, the grapes are all natural and will contain only those elements taken from nature (sun, rain, soil, etc.). Organic wine can differ in taste from non-organic, but this is usually due to the fact that treated grapes have tendency to be fuller and more robust (healthier in appearance and fruitiness). But if an organic wine is important to you, you'll have no trouble finding some that you like—and many that are, indeed, excellent in every way.

When ordering a bottle of wine in a restaurant, how many people will one bottle serve?

Generally, a bottle of wine will give you four half-poured glasses. So, depending upon how many glasses of wine each person hopes to enjoy, order accordingly.

Which is better, white or red wine?

This is like asking "what is the best baseball team?" In truth, white wines and red wines can and should be enjoyed for the different tastes and experiences. Many people, for example, will pair a white wine with seafood or fish, while a red wine is generally served with red meat or pasta dishes. These are simply rules of thumb, however, and are not hard and fast rules. Drink what you like. And perhaps more importantly, you should create your own list of favorite reds and whites and the meals they might accompany. Everyone is different. Also, seasons can play an impact. We enjoy rose wines, for example, more in the summer as a chilled experience rather than our typical bold reds, which we prefer at night. We also enjoy white wines, especially Rieslings, with sea food. But these are our preferences. Make your own.

Is it okay to drink water when enjoying wine?

Yes. In fact, water can actually enhance the wine experience—cleansing the palate and keeping the wine from drying out the mouth too much. Also, water can reduce the impact of the alcohol content of wine on the body. Historically, wine was actually used to purify water—and we can forget that in ages past, it was often dangerous to drink water (which could contain bacteria). On long voyages across the ocean, people typically drank wine, beer or spirits. Water was regarded as unsafe unless taken from fresh water sources or wells—and these were not always readily available.

What are the health benefits of wine?

There are now many studies indicating the wine (reds especially) have numerous health benefits—when drank in moderation, as wine should be enjoyed. Red wine has been shown to reduce the risk of heart disease, cancer, high blood pressure and strokes. Likewise, the antioxidants present in most red wines, including most fruit wines, has been shown to have numerous health benefits, including weight loss. Many Mediterranean diets, with wine as a centerpiece, are some of the healthiest on earth—and people who drink a glass of red wine each day generally have longer life spans and a zest for life. Also, a small glass of wine before bedtime can serve as a natural sleep agent and give one a refreshing night's sleep.

Are there really differences between vintages?

Absolutely. As you think about how each summer and winter varies from one another, consider how these variations will affect the development of the vines, their fruit, and the flavor of those grapes. Then consider how, in the process of winemaking, that fruit impacts the flavor of the wine produced. As one winemaker told me, "If you begin with great fruit, there's a very good change you can make a great wine. If you begin with bad fruit, you have to work miracles to produce a good wine." The taste of wine is in the details. And that is why you should learn as much as you can about wines, and be aware of those years when the vintages are celebrated. Keep those years in mind and watch for them on the labels. It all makes a difference. And again, it can be fund to do a ladder tasting—where you compare various years from the same winery. Nature speaks through wine.

What is port wine?

A port is a fortified wine—meaning that a spirit (greater alcohol content) has been added to the wine to stabilize it and preserve it. Some of the best port wines can be enjoyed for weeks after the bottle is opened, and port is generally enjoyed in smaller glasses, or just sipped, perhaps as a dessert wine or a nightcap experience. There are various types of port wines (and various hard spirits added to taste)—so check the labels and be aware of the differences. There are some great ports out there—and many wineries, even in Indiana, have a port wine offering. You might try a few of these to see if you like them. And then, if you do, plan to enjoy a bottle during the winter months—when port if optimally enjoyed.

Is an expensive bottle of wine better than a less expensive one?

What we have found is that there are good bottles of wine in all price ranges. We have purchased expensive bottles of wine and been blown away by their complexity and taste—but also been disappointed in others. And likewise we have found some of our favorite wines (especially from other countries) that are also some of the least expensive, in the $5-$10 range. So, price isn't necessarily the most important factor. In fact, even if you go by the Parker Scale and look for bottles in the high 80s up to the low 90s, you are going to find a broad range of prices here. In other words, there are excellent wines that one can find on the cheap. Just keep an eye peeled, learn the market, and talk to those who know wines. They can direct you do some great wines for a low price.

Do Indiana wines taste different north to south?

We think so. Again—soil, temperature, sun, rain, all of these and more play a factor. A winery in the northern part of the state will produce a Traminette that tastes a bit different from a southern winery's Traminette. That is not to say that one is better than the other, but you will no doubt experience the difference as you visit wineries, taste, and become familiar with the variations. Also, a wine produced in Indiana is going to taste different than the same varietal produced in another part of the country. That's why California, for example, has become a world-class Cab Sauvignon and Zinfandel producer, along with Chardonnay, and is also why Indiana is one of the tops in Traminette and Chambourcin. Climate talks. And as wineries use the grapes that mother nature provides best in those settings, it is no wonder that these differences can be tasted.

What is the Parker Scale?

No doubt you have seen various ratings for wines—or, if you have visited a wine store with a large inventory, you may have seen a numbering system employed. The most common of these in the U.S. is the Parker Rating system, which was created by wine critic and enthusiast Robert Parker (who also publishes the magazine, *The Wine Advocate*). *The Wine Spectator* magazine also employs this rating system, and is perhaps the most widely-respected and impactful wine magazine in America.

Essentially, the Parker scale uses a 50-100 points system, with points given to each wine based upon the color and appearance of the wine as it sits in the glass, the aroma, the flavor and finish, and the wine's potential for ageing. Although this scale does not indicate everything there is to know about a wine (including personal preference) the scale can be used by both critics and the casual wine advocate to assess wines, or even to compare one to another.

As we have tasted wines in the Parker system, a rule of thumb to go by might be the following:

88-90 points—a wine of quality and value
91-94 points—a great wine of character and depth
95 points or more—an exceptional wine

If I am planning a wine tasting, how much wine will I need?

Consider a tasting (if your guests are going to drink and not simply taste) to incorporate one glass per hour. So, in three hours, most guests will consume three glasses.

A 750 ml bottle will usually provide four to five 5 oz.- 6 oz. glasses. A case of wine (12 bottles) will then yield 60 glasses of wine.

You may also buy bottles in the following sizes at some wineries:

Magnum—equal to 2 bottles
Jeroboam—equal to 4 bottles
Methuselah—equal to 8 bottles
Salmanazar—equal to 12 bottles (make sure you have help to lift this one!)

Should different wines be served at different temperatures?

Yes—generally different wines have optimal taste at different temperatures. You might use this temperature guide below (from coldest to warmest). And remember, your refrigerator is typically about 40-43 degrees F:

Champaign—42-46 degrees F.
Sauvignon Blanc, Pinot Gris, Riesling—45-50 degrees F.
Chardonnay—tastes best at 52-55 degrees F.
Tawny Port and Dessert wines—57-62 degrees F.
Pinot Noir—60 degrees F.
Most other reds—65 F or room temperature.

Why is cheese so often paired with wine?

Actually, this is an American infatuation and is not so in many other countries, as cheese (fat) coats the palate and makes tasting of wine more difficult. However, that is not to say that the wine/cheese experience is a bad combination. When pairing wines and cheeses, you might consider the following to hold true for the best pairings: a whiter and fresher cheese will pair well with a white, crisp wine—and a darker/stronger cheese will pair better with heavier reds.

Can you cook with all wines?

One thing that you will notice in most recipes is that superb dishes often call for superb wines. The reasons for this are simple: if the wine tastes sub-par when you drink it, it will not improve as a cooking wine when added to a recipe. In other words, any wine will still hold its characteristics in the pot. You don't want to ruin a fine recipe by trying to add a tasteless wine.

Are Indiana wines improving?

Many people want to know if their Indiana wine experience will be different over time—especially if they have tasted certain Indiana wines in the past and were not that impressed. Here's our answer: like all wineries (regardless of region) Indiana wine makers continue to improve with age, just like their vintages. Practice makes perfect, as they say. And our experience has been that, as we have re-visited Hoosier wineries through the years, most continue to get better. Likewise, keep in mind that vintages do oscillate in taste and complexity from year to year, and for those estate wineries in Indiana who are growing their own, some years are better than others. If you have had a bad experience, give it another shot. You will likely be surprised at what you will find upon a second or third visit.

Do any Indiana wineries have wine clubs?

Yes. In fact, most do. These clubs offer discounts to members, can often ship wine directly to the home, and a few carry exclusive wine club newsletters that are distributed (usually by email) to their members. A wine club can be a way to keep your favorites stocked, but you should check about the details, as these vary from winery to winery. Most of the winery web sites also carry this information and can tell you more about how their respective clubs operate.

Can Indiana wineries ship in state and out of state?

As a general rule, yes. But Indiana continues to be a state with morphing food and beverage laws, and if you read the history of Indiana wines (in the front of this book) you will note that Indiana has come relatively late to the party as far as some of the wine laws are concerned. There continues to be discussion about shipping wine—both in and out of state—and it is not always a given that wineries *can* to do this. The laws are, at best, complex—and most of the winemakers can give a fuller reasoning behind why they can (or cannot) ship.

Do you have Indiana wines that you would recommend

The purpose of this book is to profile the wineries of Indiana—and to celebrate what our Hoosier wineries are doing. But we will would be happy to make recommendations (and will) if you contact us at our blog—which will feature a more critical palate, along with interviews and profiles—in the coming years. We will be glad to tell you what we think.

Contact us at: www.indianawinery.blogspot.com

I don't have a wine cellar—so how should I store my wine?

One doesn't need a wine cellar if one intends to enjoy the wine within a year or two after purchase. A bottle of wine will keep quite nicely stored on a small kitchen wine rack. Or, if you prefer to store certain bottles in a colder, darker place, consider the floor of a closet, or perhaps in a basement corner. You should be able to purchase some low costs wine racks or storage units (or look for them in antique stores) that will serve you well if you have less than 50 bottles.

Even if you are storing your wine for just a few months, however, don't forget to store the bottles in a horizontal position, or tipped slightly toward the cork. For corked bottles, it is important that the cork be kept moist by the wine (inside). Otherwise, the cork will dry out and allow the wine to breath—thus ruining it if it sits for too long in this condition.

More Favorite Wine Recipes

Two Wine-Based Mixed Drinks

Summer Sangria

This is a fantastic summer drink, refreshing and clean, with plenty of citrus zest. Can be chilled in the refrigerator, but is best served soon after mixing. Also, best served in tall cylindrical glasses, but ice tea glasses could also be used. Make sure the ice is pure—small cubed ice works best.

1 bottle Spanish red wine (of quality)
3 measures brandy
¼ pint orange juice (no pulp)
1 pint lemonade

Pour contents into a large bowl for mixing, with ice to taste. Stir thoroughly until ice cold. Pour into tall cylindrical glasses and garnish with twists of lime, lemon and orange.

Winter Mulled Wine

If you have never had mulled wine, it is an old-world drink that has much history and many traditions associated with it. Mulled wine is a winter experience, a real body warmer for extra cold nights or a romantic evening by the fire.

1 bottle of Bordeaux red wine (claret)
1 wineglass of orange curacao
1 wineglass brandy
Sliced orange
12 lumps sugar

A Brief Guide to Wine Tasting and Appreciation

People have been making and drinking wine for thousands of years. Evidence of winemaking dates as far back as 4000 B.C.E. in the Mesopotamian area (modern day Iran/Iraq), and in Egypt and China. And we know that the ancient Egyptians had a highly-sophisticated system of vine cultivation and production—knowledge and expertise that eventually made its way into Lebanon, Greece, and Italy. Wine was prevalent in most areas of the world and winemaking was one of the principal crafts of ancient societies.

The Bible—as well as most other ancient literature—is replete with references to wine. The fruit of the vine was celebrated, and wine was associated with health and life. This is not surprising, though we often forget that one of wine's most important functions in the ancient world was as a water purifier. During ancient times wine was often the only safe drink, as many people did not have access to wells or a source of safe drinking water. Adults and children alike, we know, drank wine—especially among those who were wealthier (common folk drank beer).

These ancient wines, however, would have typically been lower in alcohol than today's wines, and would likely have had a more vinegar-like or cider taste. The ancient Greeks were the first to create a culture around wine and also came to appreciate wine's other attributes—it's storage capabilities (typically stored in clay jugs), its usefulness in health and healing, its variety of tastes (especially when water and herbs were added), and its place in religious rituals.

The Romans picked up this appreciation of wine and advanced

both wine-making and wine-appreciation considerably, introducing the first wine classifications and charts to their culture. This early work of the Greek and Romans was, in fact, the beginning of contemporary European expertise in the vineyard.

Wines, in fact, were appreciated across the Mediterranean world, and in the Bible we find references to a first vineyard planted by Noah (Genesis 9), to wine used in sacrifices and celebration, and even wine-appreciation instructions (Ecclesiastes 9:7). Wine was used in the Passover celebration and Jesus acquainted his sacrificial death with wine as a perpetual remembrance (Luke 22:15-20; Mark 2:22). References to vineyards, wine skins, and methods of vine cultivation (pruning) are abundant and the gospel of John records the first of Christ's miracles as turning water into fine wine.

In time, winemaking became a craft of the church, first in Europe and later in the New World—and the Spaniards, the Portuguese, the English, and seekers such as the Pilgrims and the Puritans all brought their winemaking skills the shores of America, each with varying degrees of success. During the long voyages across the Atlantic, wines were vital to the health and survival of all souls onboard, as clean water could only be stored for so long in flasks, barrels or canteens.

The sacramental aspect of wine assured that vineyards would be established and the monks, in particular, created wines that brought old world practices to new world tastes. And as vineyards began to take hold in the regions of New York, California and the Ohio River valley in America, a new winemaking industry was born.

Today, whenever we speak of wine appreciation we are also referring to the history of wines—the geology, sociology, and geography of a craft that has its roots in the vine and the land and the winemakers who have passed along the techniques and knowledge from one generation to the next. Although most people will never be master sommeliers (those wine experts who can identify wines by region, history, smell and taste), anyone can learn to appreciate a wine's history, its tastes and experiences.

At first blush wine appreciation can seem absurd—after all, we are talking about fermented grape juice. But once enjoyed, wines deepen on the palate and in the mind—as culture, time and craft begin to elicit questions about a wine's origins, tastes and nuances.

Wine appreciation begins in the glass, but upon deeper study and reflection one can bring the various wine regions of the world (all with their varying varietals, tastes, methodologies) into play as well as a broader understanding of how wine works—how it is made, how it is aged, and all of the accompanying techniques that make a wine what it is. Likewise, the grapes themselves vary by variety and taste—and these individually across the world as the vines grow in various soils and how differing exposures to sun, rain and soil. Grapes are storehouses for their environments—and this is a key ingredient in the full appreciation for what a wine brings from barrel to glass.

And again, one doesn't have to know everything about wine to appreciate what one loves in a wine—even if just the taste. Many people who love wines don't necessarily drink all that they taste—for wine involves all of the senses. Everyone can begin somewhere—and then build upon that knowledge and appreciation. Or, perhaps, for the purposes of this book—a person might set out to gain a greater appreciation for Indiana wines, for the various grapes and nuances of tastes that populate this region. In time, one might actually become and expert on certain mainstay Hoosier varietals such as Traminette or Chambourcin. Or one could bring past experiences from other regions of the U.S. or the world to bear upon their experiences with the wines in-state.

Wine is complex—and as such offers a much richer experience than any other beverage. One does not have to be a wine expert, however, to engage in the full enjoyment of wine or to have an opinion about what one enjoys (or not) in a vintage glass. But for those who might enjoy a helpful guide to wine appreciation—or have never attempted to fully appreciate what is in the glass—let us offer the following guide to wine tasting in these easy steps.

Step 1—Visual

This first step—examining a wine as it sits in the glass—may seem arbitrary or unnecessary, but one can learn a lot from appearance. We are, after all, visual creatures, and this first impression in the glass will set the stage. Hold the glass up toward a light source and look through the wine. Note the clarity or "depth" of the wine. A wine that sits darker in the glass (not easy to see through) will likely have a bolder or more complex taste. Wines that are browner in appearance may have a greater age to them. And some reds—such as Petite Syrah or Tannac—may actually appear as "inky" in the glass, or almost black in appearance. Many wine experts, in fact, can identify the varietal in the glass based upon the color, density, sediment, or transparency.

Even if you are not anywhere close to being a wine expert, you can still learn to appreciate a wine in the glass, and in time you will be able to identify some wines simply by sight. But the primary point of the visual, of course, is to appreciate what the winemaker has done with the wine, making it a beautiful expression in the glass.

Step 2—Smelling

Even if you are in a tasting room and have less than two ounces of wine poured in your glass, you will want to begin the act of tasting your wine by first smelling it. Wine glasses are made for smelling (which is why most have larger bowls on stems), so don't be afraid to stick your nose into the glass and breathe deeply. Let your nose linger among these aromas and ask yourself a series of questions (this can be fun):

" What floral, earthy, or fruity aromas come to mind as I smell this wine?"

"Are there spicy aromas that I can pick up?"

"How would I describe the smell of this wine to another person?"

Once you have smelled the wine initially, you may come back to smell the wine later after you have completed some other steps.

Scents do change as you continue the experience.

Step 3—Swirling

Again, a wine glass has a large bowl for the express purpose of swirling a wine. Swirling "opens" the wine up, mixing it with oxygen in the air, and over time, the taste of a wine will change simply from being exposed to the air. Some wines can actually change in taste each time you mix more oxygen with the wine, so experiment and see what subtle changes you can detect using this method.

You can swirl and smell again . . . and again. But after you have swirled, proceed to tasting.

Step 4—Tasting

If you do know tasting rooms in wineries, or are an old hand at the wine tasting experience, you know that typically a tasting experience will move from white wines to reds, or from dry to sweet. (Sweet wines tend to close the palate to appreciating the dryer tastes, which is why dry is placed first in order.)

After you have observed, smelled and swirled your wine in the glass, taste it. Take enough wine into the mouth so that you can swish it between your teeth and tongue, or otherwise taste the full experience of it. Remember that different parts of the tongue pick up on certain tastes (sweet, bitter, dry, salty, etc.) so be sure to move the wine across the tongue completely. Enjoy this tasting and ask yourself some questions like:

"What tastes emerge that either affirm or expand upon the aromas: dry, sweet, floral, fruity, earthy, etc."

"What tastes come to mind: Peach? Strawberry? Bourbon? Spicy? Smokey? Earthy?"

"How would I describe the taste to another person?"

The taste of wine, naturally, is the most important ingredient in the wine experience. Your ultimate experience with the wine (whether you like it or not as compared to others) is what is most important. Keep in mind that people's tastes and preferences differ—so don't be swayed by another opinion if someone says, "You shouldn't like this." You will have plenty of tastes you enjoy more than others, and many you will not appreciate as well as your favorites. And remember: there are many wines to taste. It is perfectly acceptable to think, "I don't like this wine." Keep tasting.

Step 5—Swallowing, Spitting or Pouring

When you do attend a wine tasting—particularly if you are going to visit several wineries in the same day—keep in mind that you don't have to swallow the wine. Of course, if you are enjoying wine at home or with a restaurant meal, you have purchased your wine to drink—so enjoy it! But if you doing a tasting, don't feel obligated to drink all of the wine—and you won't want to. Rather, all wineries provide receptacles for pouring wine after you have tasted it. And in some wineries and cultures it is acceptable to spit the wine into a receptacle. (You will usually pour!)

Pouring the wine during a tasting allows you, also, to taste more often and to taste more vintages. If you were drinking all of the tastings your senses would soon become impaired and you won't have the ability to discern the nuances of the wines—which is why you've come to taste. Winemakers are not offended by tasting and pouring—it is to be expected—so make this a part of your experience and appreciation.

Other Considerations

Car Storage

If you are on a wine tasting trip (visiting several wineries in one day), you will want to come prepared to transport your wine purchases back home. A large cooler packed with some ice can be most helpful on hot days—otherwise, as you travel from place to place, your wine may actually "cook" in the hot car and be bad by the time you get home. Come prepared with a way to keep your wines at a more stable temperature (preferably in the 55 degree range).

If you are visiting wineries on temperate days when you won't need a cooler, bring along a box that you can pick up from a package liquor store (or even a winery). These slotted boxes make perfect travel companions for your wine purchases. And, although you may transport the wines in the car in a vertical position, you can place them vertically on a wine rack or closet floor once you get them home.

Also, keep the wines out of the sunlight as much as possible when the bottles are in the car.

Cataloging & Labeling

Some people also enjoy cataloguing their wines—or making notations on the labels. You can record the date of your purchase, for example. This can help you to remember when you need to drink a wine—especially if you are purchasing younger wines, don't have any climate-controlled cellar, and will need to drink your wines with 1-3 years after purchase.

Along with your date on the label, you might also keep a small book that would detail your perceptions of each wine at the time of tasting. Your experiences then may help you to know which bottle of wine to open with a particular meal, for example, or which wines are dryer, sweeter, or fruitier. Keeping a wine record like this can be a fun experience and can also serve to jog your memory—especially if you have many wines or are not drinking some labels right away.

If you do have a wine cellar, or even a small wine rack, you can also purchase labels that you can place on the neck of the bottle for this identifying work (or you can make your own). These identifying notes are helpful to see at a glance and can save you time looking for a certain bottle among the many. If you have other memories of the wine that are important, record these as well. You might also include comparative notes or ideas about how a certain wine stacks up against another—on your own rating scale.

At Home

Finally, when serving your wines at home—don't forget that you can go through all of the previous steps in your wine tasting experience. In fact, once you are home and relaxed, you can usually have a much more enjoyable experience with a bottle, and your ability to visualize, smell, swirl and taste the wine will be heightened. Most of all—enjoy the wines you have purchased and see how they taste with some of your favorite meals or those new recipes.

If you don't have a great set of wine glasses, purchase the best you can afford, and try to obtain different styles of wine glasses for different varieties of wine. All of this can help you to continue your appreciation of your favorite wines—not only with family and friends, but when you are alone, too.

Who knows . . . in time, you may become a wine expert.

Glossary of Wine Terminology

Acid (acidity) — acid is naturally present in grapes and is what imparts the quality of a wine. However, if there is too much acid in a wine it will come across as sour. A low acidic volume, however, makes a wine taste flat and dull. Acid is one of the key elements that wine makers gauge when producing a top-flight wine.

Ageing — the process of maturing a wine in a steel container or barrel.

Alcohol — is produced by the action of yeast on sugar during fermentation. A wine's alcohol volume can be increased sometimes by ageing or distillation.

Alcohol content — as most wine drinkers will note, wines usually have an alcohol content (or strength) somewhere between 12% to 15%. Compare this to beer that is usually 4% to 8% and to a whiskey or bourbon — 40%, 50% or more.

Aroma — this is the smell of a wine. Many sommeliers (wine experts) can identify a wine's vintage and region by smell alone. Aroma is an important element in the wine appreciation experience and should be explored along with the taste. Sometimes aroma is call "nose". An important note here is that, as wine's age, they naturally lose some of their "nose", so younger wines tend to have those fruity aromas that are prized.

Barrel-aged — refers to the process of fermenting wine in oak barrels rather than in a tank. Some wines are aged in unused oak barrels while others may be fermented in previously used bourbon barrels, for example. Tastes will differ accordingly.

Body — a term commonly used to describe a wine's strength or fullness. In the glass, often called "legs".

Bottle — a standard wine bottle holds 75cl

Bouquet — the aroma of a wine, also a way that sommeliers (wine experts) identify characteristics of a wine by description ("floral", "citrus", "grassy" etc.).

Cellar — a place where wine is stored (usually below ground and in a darker, temperature controlled area).

Chateau — literally means "castle", but is a term used for wines of a particular vineyard, especially in France.

Claret — an English name for the red wines of Bordeaux. This is a French word that means "clear" or "bright".

Complexity — a term referring to a wine that possesses a balance of many aromas and flavors. A wine that is balanced.

Cork Fee — sometimes also referred to as "corkage", meaning a charge that restaurants issue for the opening of a bottle that the customer brings into the restaurant.

Cork — still used by many wineries to cap bottles, although many now are going to synthetic corks or screwtops.

Dry — another common term, meaning that the wine lacks sugar and usually has more tannins, making the experience on the tongue dry, or the sensation of dryness, when tasted.

Earthy — a term meaning that the wine smells of the soil or the vegetation in which the vines have grown.

Estate — a term used to describe wines that are produced from the grapes grown by the winery itself. To say that a wine is "estate grown" means that the grapes were grown by the winery (not shipped in from elsewhere, for example).

Filtered — a wine that has been strained to remove bacteria and other solids that are inherent in the wine itself. Not all wines are filtered — and if not, will likely have sediment. Sediment is typically not a bad thing, and there is difference of opinion among winemakers regarding the filtering process and what it removes from the taste and experience of a wine.

Fortified — a wine where additional alcohol has been added to increase the strength. Ports are the most common example of a fortified wine.

Fruity — a term meaning that a wine has reminiscent aromas and tastes of fruit (not always grapes). Some wines have "peachy" "apricot" or "blackberry" notes, for example.

Full-bodied — a term meaning that the wine has a higher alcohol content and experience as it sits on the palate.

Irrigation — water brought into the vineyard from an outside source (not rain).

Magnum — a bottle equal to two standard bottles of wine, and commonly sold in grocery stores.

Oenology — the science of winemaking.

Oenophile — a connoisseur of wine.

Off-dry — a term meaning that a wine is slightly-sweet but has some hint of dryness preserved, too.

Organic wines — wines produced from grapes that were not treated with pesticides, herbicides or chemical fertilizers.

Pruning — the removal of unwanted/unneeded parts of the vine in order to regulate the yield. A necessary part of the vine growing/grape production process.

Rich — a term signifying the full flavors of a wine.

Robust — a term meaning "full-flavored" and usually indicative of the taste of tannin.

Semi-dry — a term meaning "near-dry" or a wine that preserves some of both sweet and dry sensations on the tongue.

Semi-Sweet — a term similar to "Semi-dry" but meaning that the wine has more of a sweet sensation than dry as it sits on the tongue.

Sommelier — a wine expert. There are less than 250 Master Sommeliers in the world, and this status is one of the most difficult distinctions to achieve in the world of cuisine.

Tannin — the astringent acid from the stalks and skins inherent in red wines, often noted by the term "dry", but tannins also help to preserve wines and is the principal descriptor inherent in those wines that age well in the cellar. (Depending upon preference, some enjoy tannic wines and others not. This is a non-sweet wine.)

Vintage wine — wine made in a good year. Yes, every year for every vineyard is different and the same vines will produce various tastes from year to year. Many people collect certain vintages from certain wineries, and there are years that are superb as compared to others.

Acknowledgments

In the course of visiting the Indiana wineries and writing this book we have many people to thank. First, the owners and winemakers of the 70+ wineries in state. Thank you for your hospitality, for the conversations about winemaking, history, and business—and for frequently taking the time to show us your production facilities and for adding to our knowledge. We feel blessed by new friends and look forward to returning to your wineries in the years ahead.

A special thank you to some of the top wine producers in-state, and also some of the oldest. You enriched our understanding of the history of Indiana winemaking and vineyards while also demonstrating that leadership is not just knowledge, but sharing. Thank you for taking my phone calls and my emails and for providing answers to my questions. No doubt there are many other wineries which owe you a debt of gratitude for the wine community you have created in the Hoosier state. As you know, when one winery wins, you all win. You know who you are!

We also thank our friends and family for sharing in our wine experiences—whether as day or weekend trips, wine tastings in our home or in restaurants—we know the wine itself is not the ultimate enjoyment, but the love and conversation.

We owe other debts of gratitude to those who own and operate Bed & Breakfasts (which we frequented on our wine trips) and to helpful restaurant staff, many of whom offered us excellent tips on Indiana wines. Likewise, the various festivals and events in state who showcase the wines—we are grateful for these opportunities and hope to see more of them in the future.

On another front, we are grateful for those winemakers/owners in Napa Valley, Sonoma, Amador County, and the Clear Lake region of California as well as wineries in the Columbia River valley in Oregon and Washington state who provided, often, a personal attention and a backstage pass to learn about the winemaking art one-on-one. Amazingly, we often met folks in these areas who had Hoosier connections and/or provided information about the wineries back home.

Of course, no book can become a reality without a great publisher, and we thank Tom Doherty for seeing the promise in this title and for offering it to the public. We are blessed to be associated with Blue River Press and thank Tom for his expertise and insights. Thanks to Dave Reed for designing the layout of the book. Special thanks also to Ginger Bock and Andy Lee for their help, and to those who made the book better at every turn of editing, layout or visual.

Finally, we want to thank Chelsey and Michael and Logan for bearing with us through our absences at home.

Notes

Sample

Winery: Todd's Winery

Date Visited: 2-7-15

Wines Tasted	Description
Syrah	Pleasant nose, medium red, good balance of alcohol & fruit, spice
Cab	Neutral nose, deep color, seemed light for Cab, blackberry notes
Pinot Grigio	Fruity nose, peach color, grassy notes, hints of flower, rose, apple

Other: Selected three wines for purchase (Syrah, Zinfandel, Cherry)

NOTES

Winery:

Date Visited:

<u>Wines Tasted</u>   <u>Description</u>

1.

2.

3.

4.

5.

6.

7.

Other:

Indiana Wine Regions

Our travels throughout the state have provided a few basic insights about Indiana wineries and their locations. One should note, for example, that there are more wineries in the southern half of the state. Additionally, the various wine trails provide a basic cartography of the areas, and as such, we have divided the state into five regions for our purposes of identification and ease of travel. Here are the basic descriptions of these regions.

North

Includes all wineries north of the larger Indianapolis metropolitan area (including Lafayette, Kokomo, Anderson and Muncie and all points along the northern Illinois and Ohio borders). Most of the wineries in this northern region can be found along major interstates (I-69, I-65, and state highway 31).

Anderson's Vineyard and Winery	17
Briali Winery	31
Country Heritage	78
Fruit Hills Winery	102
Gateway Cellar Winery	105
Indian Trail Wines	126
McClure's Orchard and Winery	150
Oak Hill Winery	166
The People's Winery	178
Satek Winery	208
Shady Creek Winery	215
Stoney Creek Winery	223
Two EEs Winery	244
Whyte Horse Winery	248
Wildcat Creek Winery	253

Central

Wineries in this region include the greater Indianapolis metropolitan area along the 1-70 corridor (east to west through the center of the state).

Belgian Horse Winery	274
Buck Creek Winery	39
Chateau Thomas Winery	70
Coal Creek Cellars	75
Country Moon Winery	82
Daniel's Vineyard	85
Easley Winery	86
Harmony Winery	108
Hopwood Cellars Winery	114
J & J Winery	130
Madison County Winery	138
Mallow Run Winery	145
New Day Meadery	161
Tonne Winery	234
Trader's Point Winery	238
Wilson Wines	257
Windy Ridge Winery	265

Southeast

Includes wineries along, and east of, the 1-65 route south of Indianapolis—including wineries in the Columbus and Madison areas.

Chateau Pomije	67
Ertel Cellars Winery	91
Fiekert's Homestead Wines	95
Holtkamp Winery	111
Lanthier Winery	134
Madison Estate Winery	140
Power's Winery	185
The Ridge Winery	193

Rowland Winery	201
Simmons Winery	219
Stream Cliff Farm Winery	226
Thomas Family Winery	230

Southwest

This larger southern region would include wineries west of the 1-65 corridor and would encompass the Bloomington area all the way to the Vincennes locations along the Wabash river and the state line.

Brown Country Winery	35
Butler Winery	45
Cedar Creek Winery	57
Chateau De Pique	61
French Lick Winery	98
Huber's Winery	118
Oliver Winery	170
Owen Valley Winery	175
Salt Creek Winery	203
Windy Knoll Winery	261

South

The long narrow corridor along the Ohio river basin includes wineries located along (and south of) the I-69 interstate from New Albany to Evansville.

Indian Creek Winery	123
Monkey Hollow Winery	154
Mystique Winery	158
Pepper's Ridge	182
River City Winery	197
Scout Mountain Winery	212
Turtle Run Winery	240
Wine Shak Vineyard	267
Winzerwald Winery	270

About the Authors

Todd & Becky Outcalt have been married for 30 years and for the past decade have traveled extensively on wine-tasting adventures abroad (France and Italy) as well as in the U.S. (Napa Valley, Oregon, Washington State, Michigan). They have also visited most of the wineries in their native Hoosier state and frequently return to discuss wines and wine-making with these new and older friends. Becky enjoys photography while Todd is the author of thirty other books, including *Husband's Guide to Breast Cancer, Before You Say "I Do", The Best Things in Life Are Free, Candles in the Dark,* and *Common Ground.*

Two Links to two Key Maps

http://indianawineries.com/indiana_wineries/index.htm#map

http://www.indianawines.org/wineries/state-map